RETURN TO REGÍON

Twentieth-Century Continental Fiction

JUAN BENET

Return to Región

Translated from the Spanish by
GREGORY RABASSA

COLUMBIA UNIVERSITY PRESS
NEW YORK 1985

Columbia University Press wishes to acknowledge the assistance of
the Comité Conjunto Hispano-Norteamericano para Asuntos
Educativos y Culturales in the preparation of this translation.

Library of Congress Cataloging in Publication Data

Benet, Juan.
Return to Región.
(Twentieth-Century Continental fiction)
Translation of: Volverás a Región.
I. Title.
PQ6652.E5V613 1985   863'.64   84-27469
ISBN 0-231-05456-4 (alk. paper)

Spanish original: *Volverás a Región*
© 1967 Juan Benet and Ediciones Destino

Columbia University Press
New York   Guildford, Surrey

Clothbound editions of Columbia University Press books are Smyth-
sewn and printed on permanent and durable acid-free paper.

Book design by Ken Venezio.

AUTHOR'S NOTE

Even though the last page of this book contains a suggestion that it was written between 1962 and 1964, between Madrid and the Porma Dam in the province of León, its history and origins are far from being so simple and go back several years before that. The truth is that around 1951, and under the influence of reading *The Golden Bough,* I began to write a novel—which I would finish a couple of years later—in which I narrated some events in a single rural environment (which for lack of a precise geographical determination I baptized with the name of Región) dominated by the distant, nocturnal, and omnipresent figure of the guard of a country estate, a kind of vicar in our lands of the guardian of the sacred wood of Nemi. The novel was entitled *The Guard* and apart from the protagonist—who tormented all of its pages *in absentia* without ever appearing in them, without ever becoming anything but a conjecture—throughout it there was a parade of a goodly number of abnormal characters: a woman driven mad by the loss of her husband—bitten by curiosity to cross the boundaries of the accursed estate—two days after their wedding; an old aristocrat, a killer of dogs, gone over to the maquis out of spite; a young alcoholic, the last scion of a great family, determined to turn his house into a Cretan labyrinth from which he would never succeed in escaping and in whose most hidden part he would dig his grave; a tribe of gypsies who had become wealthy and were gradually taking over the whole region thanks to the distillation of a repugnant alcohol; and, finally, the venal lawyer who deceived himself with his own swindles. As can easily be understood, a whole showcase, a museum jam-packed with crude reproductions of Lee Goodwin, Sairey Gamp, Bertha Mason, Pechorin, and even Madrigal's pastry cook.

In spite of finding myself rather confident concerning its literary virtues, I was so convinced that it couldn't be published in Spain that I didn't even bother sending the original to any of the contests so much in vogue at the time. On the other hand, I arranged for it to reach a few publishing houses in South America and France where I had a certain entrée, and when I didn't get a single positive response, I allowed myself the privilege of mailing it directly to the publisher in Paris who seemed to me to be the most scrutinizing and demanding at that time, José Corti, on the Rue des Médicis. To my surprise, in a short time I received a brief personal letter that still warms my heart as a model of courtesy; not only did the publisher show thereby that he had read the manuscript, but without need for hackneyed words of praise he trotted out all manner of excuses for the impossibility of including such a book in his list. In those days I had finished my professional studies and was determined not only to follow my career outside of Madrid, but looked upon that literary adventure as the frustrated, worthless, and idle drive of a student who was restless and had time on his hands. But when all was said and done, when it was time to pack my bags, I carefully put in all my manuscripts—I had four of certain consequence—with the aim of reading them again when, having forgotten what they said, they might arouse some surprise.

I didn't look through them again until 1962, when I was working on the Porma Dam. But for eight years I had been going back and forth through a part of the northwest of the peninsula and in every region, every mountain range, in the remote and rotten boroughs and in the grumbling monasteries, I kept on getting a peek at the presence of that accursed guard, the founder of a lugubrious dynasty that kept so many out-of-the-way communities tied to their pauper land by their own haunting fear. A wandering experience like that led me to clarify a few ideas and—before opening the folders—to darken others that, by being too conclusive, seemed inexact to me. Then I reached the conclusion that rarely does truth illuminate, or, in other words, if it resembles anything, it is the shadows that close in after the flash of error.

In those surroundings I found the time and inclination not so much to return to the old text as to write another new one whose relationship with the first was limited to the personality of the guard, certain local toponymies and descriptions, and a few anecdotes of an ornamental character. So that between 1962 and 1964 I wrote a different novel that I entitled "Back to Región," based on a tripod (like the Church of Christ) with perfectly heterogeneous legs. To wit: the myth of the guard and the forbidden forest, the development and consequences of the civil war in a remote community, and the disorders caused by a frustrated pseudomarriage in the heart of the mountains. All in all, the text was becoming too extensive, prolix, and impertinent, even when a good number of insolences had been mitigated and made more palatable in order to make publication possible. And it enjoyed one peculiarity: it was a matter of continuous discourse, with very little dialogue, and with only a few—not many—periods.

Making use of the good offices of some friends, I sent it to a few publishing houses that in those days played the role of vanguard—if not literary, at least ideological. I have no report that it aroused any attention at all. In some cases I tried to make the submission easier by sending the publisher's reviewer a book of stories that I had published at my own expense in 1961 and which, in that aspect at least, proved to be that ambassador with terrible gifts that Talleyrand missed so much. The best I got were a couple of letters (quite different from Corti's) signed by young ladies who, not content with declaring the impossibility of publication, took pleasure in pointing out to me the vices into which I had fallen as a storyteller. "Your novel," one said, "lacks dialogue. Don't forget that almost all the public reads is dialogue, which is also the best exponent of a novelist's skill." I think that around the beginning of 1965 I sent the original to two friends, Dionisio Ridruejo and José Suárez Carreño, who, startled by several of its pages, insistently urged me to correct and unburden it. I remember that at first I was against that with all the vehemence of a person sure of his work, even though he has reached the end of his patience with it; not in vain, along with a few other things, had the text been written four times. And yet I decided to do it for the fifth and last time, good proof that my patience could still tolerate one more demand in the interest of an appetite for glory. In that last transcription the modifications were minimal; I eliminated one whole dubious passage (the story of a boy who, abandoned in a religious boarding school, created such a round of vice for his own entertainment that the whole community ended by being conquered or shucking their habits or falling into the arms of the abominable sins), I divided the whole into four chapters and—unable to forget the censure of that secretary who knew the duties of a writer so well—I eliminated all dialogues except one. I changed the title to one that was a little more dynamic. In a date book for the year 1965, in the entry corresponding to September 14, I noted: "Today I finished copying *Return to Región*. I hope it's the last time." Finding myself in Barcelona one day that summer, I personally delivered the manuscript to the receiving office of a well-known literary prize, where it was received and registered with the number 51. I waited three months for the decision, convinced that if it didn't win the prize, at least it would attract the jury's attention and I would attain the yearned-for publication. I didn't get the prize nor did the text succeed in being listed among the twenty most outstanding that had earned an advance selection and about which the jury would deliberate exclusively. I hadn't taken the precaution (because I was unaware of that trick) to introduce a barely perceptible hymen into its pages so that one could deduce later that it had been deflowered, but certain indications led me to suspect that no one had read it properly. From then on my disappointment was so supine that I decided not to bother anymore with that novel which seemed to be as accursed as the land it described and which no intervention would pull out of the apathy in which it had been engendered; so I began another new one.

One year later, in February 1967, and thanks to the insistence and persuasive abilities of Dionisio Ridruejo, Ediciones Destino decided to place *Return to Región* on the market in a very modest printing. The consequences, quite different in nature, of such a decision are neither here nor there; I shall only say that in order to make it possible I had to sacrifice the last obvious impertinences. Toward the end of 1968 the book caught the attention of two people—Pere Gimferrer and Rafael Conte—who reviewed it, each on his own. And there another tale begins.

For this second edition I have limited myself to correcting and repairing as far as possible a few errors of diction too elementary to be worthy of notice and to putting back in a few hiatuses that incomprehensibly were missed in 1967.

J.B.

February 1974

RETURN TO REGIÓN

I

It's true, the traveler leaving Región who wishes to reach its mountain range by following the old king's highway—because the modern one has ceased to be such—will find himself obliged to cross a small, high desert that seems endless. At one moment or another he will get to know the discouragement of feeling that every step forward is only bringing him a little farther away from those unknown mountains. And one day he will have to give up his intent and put off that remote decision to scale their highest summit, that limestone peak in the form of a death mask that imperturbably maintains its romantic legend and its blizzard crest. Or rather—calm, with no despair, invaded by a kind of indifference that leaves no room for reproach—he will let his last sunset pass, lying on the sand facing it, watching how in the naked sky the beautiful, strange, black birds that are to finish him off maneuver in high circles.

It takes almost a day by car to reach the desert from Región. The few roads that exist in the area are drovers' paths that follow the course of the rivers, with no transverse connections, so communication between two parallel valleys must be done, during the eight cold months of the year, along the streams to where they come together, and then back in the opposite direction. The desert is made up of a primary shield 4,500 feet in altitude, lying at its northern edge up against the youngest terrain of the range, which, in the shape of a violin belly gives birth to and divides the rivers Torce and Formigoso. Cut off on the west by the Dinant ridges, it gives way to those monstrous depressions in whose depths the Torce sings after having sawed through those elephant-colored cliffs that up until the last century formed a wall that was impregnable to any curiosity coming along the banks; quite the contrary, on the southern edge that looks eastward, the high plain turns into a series of irregular folds of unruly topography that transform the source into a labyrinth of small gullies, which only on reaching Ferrellan becomes a main valley of traditional cut, the Formigoso.

Almost all explorers of fifty years ago, driven more by curiosity than fondness for alpinism, chose the Formigoso route. Above the plain of Ferrellan the river, in a trough-like valley, divides up into a series of small branches and veins of water that run in all directions through swampy and barren terrain where, even today, it has been impossible to build a causeway. The road leaves the valley and, resting on a naked slope, climbs along up to the desert, crossing red hills covered with broom and heather; at the level of the inn of El Quintán, the vegetation becomes sparse and thin, low clumps of oaks and mounds of whitish soil in shapes tortured by the strong March gales, up to the place where for more than eight miles there is no other shade except that of an old masonry bridge under which—except on torrential days when a tumultuous, deafening, and red freshet passes— there runs a thread of water that almost all year long can be held back with a hand. As the road weaves and curls, the countryside changes: the low mountain is succeeded by those broad meadows (where it is said a wild breed of dwarf horses grazes) with a dangerous look, standing forth and crossed by the bluish and fetid crests of carboniferous limestone, similar to the spine of a Quaternary monster who passes his lethargy with his head sunken in the swamp; there, spaced and delicate in color, there rise up those mountain flowers with a complicated structure, colchicums and forget-me-nots, lavenders, tall azaleas, and tiny cattails, until a disordered and unexpected hedge of willows and myrtle seems to put an end to the journey with a log across the way forming a barrier and an anachronistic and almost indecipherable sign, nailed to a twisted pole:

NO TRESPASSING
PRIVATE PROPERTY

It's such a lonely place that no one—neither in Región nor in Bocentellas nor at Doña Cautiva Bridge nor even in the belfry of the church of El Salvador—talks about it, even when everybody knows that rare is the year when the mountain doesn't collect its human tribute: that eccentric foreigner who arrives in Región in a car loaded down with boxes and scientific equipment or the unfortunate and unaware hunter who, following a track or going after the cap carried off by the wind, comes across that grave newly opened by the aged guardian where the smell of aerated earth is still preserved and with a puddle of water in the bottom.

The journey, doubtless, cannot be more disheartening: a flatland without charm, a poor, dry mesa cut off to the north by the limestone outcropping—where a few eagles small as swifts nest—that can only be crowned with a rope; and on the east a desert of burning gypsum sprinkled with basalt rocks, broken down and sharp, that it would seem the Range has been grudgingly turning loose for amusement during its long and lonely days through centuries and hurricanes; mitigated only by the small pools of millennial water surrounded by unhealthy-looking reeds and Spanish broom and extensive flats covered mainly by underbrush, the bright and whistling rockrose and advent bush, woody, tenacious, and concentrated shapes, inhabited only by small reptiles, that

[3]

strange breed (a not desperate race that seems conscious of its approaching extinction) of beautiful, black, hungry, and silent birds that only trust in the phosphorescence for their maintenance, and a multitude of insects so colorful in cuirasses and prickly with arms that they always seem to be on their way to the Holy Land. When finally—in an unexpected smell, in the premonitory buzz of an insect, or in the whisper of the reeds (the melancholy song of its yearning virginity and the distant glory of El Monje, that peak in the shape of a death mask that from time to time sends down its disdainful and sterilizing breath)—one senses the proximity of the promised wood, the traveler suddenly comes upon a hawthorn hedge, a twisted pole, and a half-erased sign that warns him of the ancient prohibition. It is enough to think that the determined traveler is not about to return empty handed—after such an effort—because of the whim of an anachronistic warning, placed there over a hundred years ago, and which can be knocked down with a single kick without anyone's noticing. Yet, reality must be something quite different because even when people are told that a certain number have tried to go up there, nothing is known of anyone who came back. It's said that it's such a savage and deserted land that only one who is prepared for a risky adventure can hold hopes of reaching it because the impassible outcroppings, the high and interminable deserts where the spurge whistles, the canyons cut out by pickax where the mountain brooks sing under the mantle of a luxuriant and hostile vegetation (forests of giant ferns and uncrossable moats filled with holly, viburnum, and mint) are only the very smallest difficulties of the journey. In Región, Mantua is scarcely ever mentioned, nor is its strange guardian; he isn't spoken about in any of the towns on the plain, neither in Región nor in Bocentellas nor at Doña Cautiva Bridge nor even in the belfry of the abandoned church of El Salvador those few nights—three or four each decade—when a few survivors of the area (fewer than thirty inhabitants who don't speak to each other or greet each other and who with great difficulty remember each other, reunited by a common instinct of survival exaggerated by solitude, or by an old ritual whose meaning has been lost and in which the mysteries of their predestination are represented) congregate there to listen to the echo of some shots that, it isn't affirmed but it is believed, come from Mantua. What is certain is that no one dares deny the existence of the man, whom no one has seen but whom no one has managed to get to see either and whose image seems to preside over and protect the days of decadence of that abandoned and ruined area: an aged guard, astute and cruel, covered with raw sheepskin like a Tartar shepherd and wearing sandals, with the gift of ubiquity within the boundaries of the property he patrols day and night with his eyes closed.

The people in Región have opted to forget their own history: very few probably preserve a true idea of their parents, of their first steps, of a gilded and adolescent age that ended suddenly in a moment of stupor and abandonment. Perhaps the decadence begins one morning in the latter part of summer with a gathering of soldiers, horsemen, and trackers ready to scout the mountain in search of a wandering gambler, the foreign Don Juan who in one night at the casino absconded with their honor and their money; that's what the decadence is, the memory and the dust of that ride along the Torce road, the frenzy of a worn-out society disposed to believe it was going to recover its missing honor in a mountain gorge, a pile of mother-of-pearl chips, and a vengeance of blood. From that time on the dust cloud is transformed into past and past into honor: the memory of a shaky finger that a few years later will run along the frayed curtains of the dining room window to point out the proud silhouette, fearsome and distant, of El Monje, where it seems all the adolescent illusions that fled with the noise of the horses and carriages have gone to be lost and concentrated, revived in a sickly way with the sound of motors and the echo of the

[5]

shots, mixed with the whistling of the reeds just as on the last days of that age without reason it was joined to the sharp and evocative sound of triangles and xylophones. Because recognition disguises at the same time that memory glows, with the buzz of the motor, the whole past, the figures of an inert family and adolescence, mummified in a gesture of grief after the disappearance of the riders, is stirred up again with a mortuary tremor: a shutter creaks and a door hesitates, bringing in from the abandoned garden a breeze medicinal in smell that puffs up the frayed curtains once more, showing the abandonment of that house and the emptiness of this present in which, from time to time, the echo of the horses resounds. When the door was closed—in silence, without joining horror to fate or fear to resignation—the dust cloud had broken up; the sun had come out and the abandonment of Región became more patent: a warm breeze blew like the senile breath of that old and woolly Numa, armed with a carbine, who hereafter will guard the forest, keeping watch night and day over the whole extent of the estate, firing with ineffable aim every time footsteps in the leaves or the sighs of a weary soul disturb the tranquillity of the place.

A half hundred people at most: a couple of times each decade the ruined inhabitant of Región, Bocentellas, or El Salvador awakens from his nap and without waiting for the command of the echo opens the blinds or the frayed curtains with immutable indifference to observe the cloud of dust on the horizon of a road. With his eyes closed his hand opens a drawer filled with yellowing old photographs, silk tassels, and velvet arm bands of a vanished congregation, to extract from an old fruit box where he keeps remnants, a small piece of cord, shiny from use and knotted at various points like a rosary, on which, with a deft and rapid motion, he makes a new lump when the sound of the motor reaches his ears. Imperturbable, he continues his siesta, which he only interrupts two or three hours later to observe the maneuver that will be made at the narrow intersection in the town one afternoon with a bright sky, furrowed by clouds toward the east, by an old, ramshackle, and wheezing motor vehicle, loaded down with boxes covered with tarpaulins. In his look, through the curtain, there is neither curiosity nor surprise nor hope, but—when he leans his head once more against a chairback nibbled by rats, stroking the worn plush arm—he can't hide a glimmer of malice and a certain smile of relief when, at the end of the street and with a shifting of gears, the sound becomes located in an indefinable descent that seems to be a prelude to its early disappearance and an opening of the rhythm of silence before the tattoo of fate. Never, either in the abandoned town or in any place on the plain, has it been heard that a car has passed in the direction of the mountains; the fact doesn't go around nor is the rumor spread, but perhaps the presentiment is extended—that polar state of the air and that sudden smell of virgin gunpowder, saltpeter, and marine algae, that sudden vitrification of the silence one autumn morning prepared to receive the traveler, with bunting of auguries and grimaces and funereal whisperings—before and after the snort of a motor, tranquil, outside of time, indifferent, incapable of knowing that in its very panting its last death rattle is being gathered, was able to alter the tranquillity of the valley.

That same night the people who heard it pass hasten punctually to the solitary belfry of the church of El Salvador to await the moment of confirmation. It is cool at night and in the spring and fall the breath of the mountains arrives impregnated with the aroma of lemon balm and lavender in which mingle, revive, and flee once more the decomposed and abundant shadows of a tantalized yesterday: parents and carriages and dances and rivers and books with pages torn out, all the illusions and promises broken by the dust cloud of the horsemen that with time and distance will grow in size until changing into grandeur and honor what in its day was nothing but meanness and pride, poverty and fear. All they do is listen: the tower is so small that in the bell loft there is only room for half a dozen people, hanging over the emptiness: the rest find themselves obliged to wait on the stairs—and even in the yard on those occasions when certain unusual acts attract a larger gathering. They don't say a single word, intent only on the direction of the wind and the echo it is to carry from the forbidden lands. The wait is usually long, as long as the night, but no one becomes impatient: a few minutes before the first light of day breaks on the horizon—the moment when the captives congregated to undertake a common journey decide, after the first annoyance has passed, to get rid of their nervousness and give in to relaxation—the sound of the shot arrives, wrapped amidst waves of mint and vervain in the uncertainty of an act that by being necessary and undemonstrable can never be evident. The evidence comes later, with dawn, memory and hope at one, repeating the echo of that single shot that Numa must have needed; which their ears had waited for, as the sentence of the sphinx for sacrilege, and which, year after year, they accepted without explanations or perplexity.

Nothing was left over nor was there any explanation. Not even rumor floating through the burning dust of the valley of Región in autumn, postponing for another time the answer to the permanent challenge of its mountains; no one has come back nor has anything seemed to remain of those old limping vehicles that one day passed through the town and went off roaring through the white hills on their way to violate the barbed wire and the archaic barrier that no one has ever managed to see except from a legal position. All that remains is the continental silence of the mountain range, testimony to the shot that tore it one day, and the tracks of some worn tires that, a few feet beyond the log, are lost under a forest of giant ferns and blood-red bromelias.

On that occasion it wasn't a case of an old pickup truck loaded down with bundles and cords, but that of a black car, old but impressive. Not for that reason, nor from the fact that

[8]

it was driven by a woman did it awaken the curiosity of those who saw it pass at nightfall on a day that was gilded with September, sublimation, and the agony and the ecstasy of a thirsty summer and an urge for water; rather it came to augment a suspicion of strangers and a trust in their land, capable of attracting toward its end a breed of people never seen until then.

One day in that ancient summer a similar car had arrived at his house; at the time only his mother lived there, along with old Adela, and he, in short pants, dragging his solitude about in a garden retreat in the company of some clay marbles and beer-bottle caps with which there developed a battle between an uncertain, sluggish, and timid I and an open adversary, idealized and magnified, who made them run with precision and certainty. His mother called him from the balustrade, wearing her street dress, holding his lunch out to him in her hand. She didn't seem upset; he wasn't capable then of guessing her emotions under the rouge, the white city dress that gave off a certain smell of a chest and the high-heeled shoes, a getup he no longer remembered her in. She crouched down beside him, gave him his lunch, smoothed his hair, and brushed the dust off his pants and the mud off his knees. He didn't say a word; when he went to touch a locket she was wearing on her lapel it could be seen that her lips were quivering. She fixed his shirt collar again and kissed him several times; she told him she was going on a trip to get his brother and whispered in his ear, biting the lobe, a few maternal words—prayer, love and goodness, remembrances, reading, and cleanliness—while he played with the locket. It wasn't a moment of separation for him at that time as much as a promise: the best part of the afternoon had already passed and coming up was waiting in the kitchen, playing marbles on the bone-colored tiled tables with deep furrows filled with pumice dust.

"Tomorrow?" he asked her, looking at the locket.

"The day after tomorrow."

His mother knew that beyond tomorrow a notion of time didn't exist in the mind of the child and therefore it would be a tolerable separation, acute with nostalgia and fatigue for a couple of moments in the child's day. But the child has transformed his lack of knowledge into fear and is trying to keep the trinket in his hand, not to impede his mother's leaving, but to keep something of all that is going to be destroyed in an immediate future of uncertainty and solitude. Or perhaps for that very reason he can't retain it—or cry—because, obedient to his premonitions, he doesn't expect anything but to be free of that involuntary link in order to be able to fight the threat of fear and, in his duplicity, shorten the moment of separation so as to go back to his game, with which the solitude of the child—incapable of making comparisons, incapable of disguising it—closes over itself, protecting him and embracing him with a thousand silent ramifications joined to their trunk like a parasitic prop. After some months, lying on the ground in a corner of the garden playing marbles—while from the other side of the wall the radios give off news from the front and popular songs with war lyrics—the return of his mother is gradually transformed into the only symptom of his abandonment, a nocturnal emanation of fear and a filling of the emptiness produced by the withdrawal of the twin player during the mauve hours of the afternoon, by the sinister specter, the stigma of an ominous state. He didn't know how to pray and he barely wept; it's possible that his own perdition begins with the fact of not knowing anything else but seeing himself, distracted by the solitary combat with the twin player and intoxicated, through the chimerical transposition of his own image into a fictitious activity, by that accumulation of desires in the potential past where a kingdom is located—ruled by the "I was," "I did," and "I carried" that begins there where the realm of tears ends. But there are hours doubtless when solitude is everything, because memory, far removed from the game, can only bring forth images of boredom and the signs of that condition: the weak reflection of the street on damp windowpanes, the footsteps in the rain, the cars that pass without stopping, and the sound of the water that drips into the fount while Adela sews; without knowing it, he begins to yoke together all the symptoms of that state with hatred: the bed, the religious print that reflects the light from under the door, and the sound of the water, the sighs of old Adela, and the plate of fried rice, without even salt, that seems to rise up in the center of the bone-colored table, scrubbed with pumice, with the very light of its occult power, and the whole phantasmal order of the half-empty house that—like the temple abandoned, sacked, and sunken in shadows and re-duced to its laconic stones and enigmatic inscriptions—seemed to be imposing with greater severity its own discipline and its own ceremony than on its days of magnificence. In that critical moment the child is accustomed to his solitude in such a way that only in his bosom is he capable of being recon-ciled to a proper image of himself and he needs—in order to fortify and watch over a deformed growth—to despise the laws of the home: he won't hate the wartime plate of rice or lentils for their taste but because their presence on the table has put an end to the game and is the prelude to long hours in bed, just as the gambler in the garret of a casino hates the glow of morning on the windowpanes and those first and swollen echoes of street activity; the plate yes, and the sighs, and that invisible hand with a Samaritan gesture seems to come out of the same hidden tabernacle where the secrets of the domestic dogma are kept to deposit them in front of him with all the rigor of the rite and discipline of the peniten-tiary. But he doesn't know, he fears: his awareness still doesn't recognize as hate what a hoarding memory stores up in or-der to capitalize the little childish deposits for the day on which he would have use of his reason; no, it doesn't go along as part of it because even when reason delays or suspends that day, memory keeps the account open and hands over to the astonished soul the savings of a cruel age: a golden

locket and a hand with a plate of bitter rice and the reverberations of a dream in the marshes, the horror with which
they both saw pass, with the nose against the window and
attention fascinated by fear, the parades and demonstrations
of the civil war; in the glow of the night and the rattle of
arms, amidst the flashes of the battle in the mountains and
the whispering of old Adela through the frayed curtains of
the parlor, the end of the war barely appears, the sunny
morning with all the windows open for the first time in more
than two years and the shouts of the people crowded into
the square waving flags and handkerchiefs. It was only one
morning and memory refused to accept it, perhaps because
it didn't come guaranteed by the footsteps of his mother. Or
perhaps she came, disguised in a man's raincoat and with a
kerchief tied around her head, but she didn't want to see him.
First she closed the kitchen door, then the one to the hallway; she drew the curtain with faded colors in the parlor,
and closed all the windows, introducing the dusty stench of
the war into the house once more, the bitter aroma of old
upholstery, the uninhabited rooms and the halls in shadows.
It isn't the memory he hates; it's certainly what he believes,
what ten or twenty years later is pleased to present to a reason without memories a whole balance of afternoons in the
hallways, of frustrated hopes and useless inversions; it's more
than that, he doesn't even have to prove the balance of these
first and last energies that didn't hesitate to sacrifice his reason in order to maintain the integrity of a person babbling,
disoriented, and abandoned. The hand yes and her words too:
old Adela who cut his first long pants or took the stew off
the slow fire, slow so as to keep burning during the two years
the troops would need to enter the city, without doubt the
length of time she was to remain immobilized by the table
or the stove so that the boy's memory would fix her forever, imposing her in the film not of rancor but of the insatiable and frustrated appetite of hope. And the words that,
while she cooked with her back to him, came out with the

same irrepressible and gratuitous fluidity of the smoke, all the mishmash of Christian kings and bloodthirsty Moors, and standards that continued floating in the wind and in the most inaccessible crags of the mountains, all those cavalry battles that would end with a miraculous intervention, in anticipation of that vengeful ride of old lords routed by the guardian of the forest, who still receive the tears and lamentations of those old ladies who, for fear of confronting the ruins that surround them, hide their looks, hypnotized by the charcoal sheds of the abandoned mansions, as if they, fired by local history, watched over that slow and last combustion of an ember that one slight turn or weak puff will transform into an instantaneous burst of flames and by means of which, for lack of other stories, she tries to distract him during dinner or sing him into sleep in which the distant echoes of combat in the mountains kept him awake in bed, with his bright eyes fastened on the ceiling. That's the way they were on the night of his mother's departure and that's the way—it can be said—they continued being for two or three years after, waiting for her return. She said that she knew how to make out the sound of a carriage before even the dogs began to bark because for half a lifetime she had done nothing but accustom and train her ear for what might be coming; she never said to him: "Tonight," "Tomorrow," "Now I hear something coming, child"; nor did she say to him: "Sleep in peace, child, tomorrow will be a beautiful day" or "Your mother will be home soon"; maybe just "Madness, it's madness," "They're going to kill everybody," "Like good José, like your father, like everybody," "You'll soon see how they'll be back," "I told you already what shape they'll be in when they come back"; a grotesque hearse, given back by the mountains like the remains of a shipwreck by the tide, loaded with the mortal remains of all the forebears dazzled by their own ambition, led by a drunken postilion or a corpse or a team of maddened mules. If they knew anything it was how to hear—above the whispers of the night, the echo of combat, and the desolate barking of the dogs ("as if they themselves understood the futility of their act" *), or the menacing moan of the mountain—but instead the unmistakable signal returned by the wind to restore the peace of their consciences. The carts that approached, sunken down to the axles, loaded with lime instead of straw; in the deserted streets the wailing and the walled-in cries of abandoned grandmothers who in the dusty beds tried to regain the pangs of birth; the wavering image, phosphorescent and ashen, of the husband, wrapped in the aura of morning with a sinister rictus and a macabre smile as he shoved open the door and, with an expression of fright, tore open his shirt to show the terrible wounds and the black hole in the center of the lungs, who came back to visit her every year on the date of their anniversary, disappearing moments before the wind brought the evidence of his death in through the open door: a ball made up of pages from old newspapers that the wind unfolded on the threshold of the house so as to leave the wrinkled notice published by a provincial daily on the ground, a few days before he had left. Because if they had developed something, it was a certain sense of anticipation that allowed them to listen to the sound of the carriage before it crossed the border of the province, and the only one in the end in whom they could put so much trust, as much not to pay attention to the furious nocturnal calls of the inopportune visitor who might confuse the door of the abandoned house for that of a deceased midwife, as to wait for the shot, the sanction, the verdict pronounced by Numa to the demands of their anxiety. It was never a question of mirages: because the fugitive, the husband, the lover, or the father always had arrived afterward—like that tardy and uninteresting text written in a telegram passed on by telephone—with powdered face and an expression, not of grief or surprise or disappointment, but of aversion toward that past moment of uncon-

* Stephan Andres

sciousness that had led them to underestimate the sentence that the mountain had reserved for them. But for old age, all the more impatient and fearful as the wait became more prolonged, the only thing that matters is that testimony and that recognition of their fault which ultimately has come to justify and revaluate a mediocre youth and maturity, domestic virtues, economic difficulties, the horror of winter trips, and firmness with their children, consumed in the holocaust. Adela had had a son who, doubtless, in turn had had a father who, a few days before reaching that status, had abandoned his wife—not to flee into the mountains or take refuge in the mine or gamble away the remains of his estate in the casino—to set himself up in a country where he would try to prosper: for that reason nothing was known of him nor was he ever mentioned in the house, even in the confines of the kitchen. But since Adela had grown up in the neighborhood and company of good families, before becoming a mother she had acquired a very strict sense of honesty and the duties of the servant for which reason as soon as her son reached the age of understanding, she inoculated him with those residues of bourgeois upbringing that the humble classes are to receive like the used clothing of their masters: overcoats that must be turned into jackets and shirts from which one must make pajamas. Therefore her son must have understood from a very early age that if one day he had to abandon the hearth he must carry along some tragedy at least, because adding prosperity to abandonment was something that went beyond the limits of contagious morality. He abandoned the hearth in the opposite direction from his father: before fulfilling his military duty, he fled into the mountains and wasn't seen again, because of which Adela, in her solitude, saw herself partly recompensed with the possibility of waiting for the fugitive son, a privilege of good families, and of educated people. She would see him on some nights; when the lady of the house withdrew to rest, hidden in her room she would light a candle by the photograph of her son in uniform and, taking out a bottle of wine that had been hanging underneath her skirt all day, she would chat with him for hours on end. Sometimes she would also sing, in a very quiet, fluty, and trembling voice, adapting the three or four lyrics that she knew—"you, the cherubs" or "covered by the dust of tombs" or "just like metal"—to a long, slow, and primitive melody that seemed to conjure up the whisper of the wind, the murmur of the trees, and the nocturnal barking of the dogs and that, no doubt, Numa—and all his court of victims and cherubs—must have heard with ecstasy on a forbidden meadow of Mantua. Nothing had ever been said about him; suddenly he remained in a position of listening—a finger in the air, ear turned to the mountain, and a look toward him, without seeing him, mixing that supine and absorbed attention of a hunting dog with the idiotized and dreaming expression of the cook, who after several hours of cleaning lentils lifts her eyes to the ceiling to sigh. He, with his mouth open and his eyes together behind the thick lenses of his glasses, had learned to respect her attention: the few times that in the course of the war he had tried to get some information he had only received from Adela the reply of "be still, be still" or a sign with her finger, denying in the air or resting on her lips. He also wanted to listen— when Adela, alarmed by the lack of signs, left the stove to press her ear against the windowpane—but he didn't know to what. When she went back to the fire to stir the stew again or dry her hands on the towel, he would ask her: "Are they going to kill them? Have they killed them already?" because without her having said anything, he knew that it couldn't have to do with anything else. Since he hadn't learned how to listen—a faculty or a privilege exclusive to those who had a father, a son, or a lover buried in the mountain—and since Adela didn't know either what to say about what she heard, he had come to develop a science of interpretation of her expressions—as if it were a matter of the flight of birds or the language of intestines—from which he could translate the meaning that she hid so jealously. By the way in which she stopped her wooden spoon, took the pot off the fire, and untied her apron—then she dried her hands on the towel, told him to stay seated and silent and, leaving the apron over a chair back, she opened the window to peep into the night: some footsteps resounded on the pavement and someone knocked at the street door. She breathed deeply and fixed the bun of her hair: "Wait here, don't move." She turned on the hall lights and those to the stairs, lighting up corners of the house that had remained in darkness for two years, and an opal glow invaded the dining room covered with cloths and dust rags, like a small cemetery, and the steps were heard on the stairs again, heavy and hard—he understood that the war had ended but that his mother hadn't come back. There was a man in the kitchen—while Adela poured the soup into the cups—covered with dust, wearing a dark leather hunting jacket and a chauffeur's cap, who sat down on a stool across from him, breathing heavily. He took off the cap and from an inner pocket took out a package wrapped in transparent paper, stained with grease. He took out a piece of dry bread and put it in the soup, but it couldn't have softened it. He didn't say anything. While he was drinking his soup he was unwrapping the package and looking over a pile of letters and papers, wrinkled and dirty. He pushed the plate away and folded the last envelope several times. He got up, opened the lid of the stove, and, slowly, one by one, put all the papers into the fire without saying a word. Then he sat down on the stool again, taking off his jacket.

"What about his mother?"

"Quiet, quiet."

The child's eyes, enlarged by the lenses of his glasses, didn't blink. They weren't expressive and, enclosed behind the lenses and deformed by the enlargement, they seemed to incarnate that melancholy of the fishbowl where there is no nostalgia for the freedom and abundance of other waters, where the fish doesn't lament its loss of a state because it hasn't reached the level of nostalgia and the urge for freedom and who, consequently, only knows how to look with that mute, profound, and impenetrable seriousness in the depths from which a passionate glow, struggling to cross through a thousand afternoons of abandonment, is translated on the surface into an expression of surprise. Measured is the solitude that only the child—not interested in giving a name to everything and incapable of expressing his state of mind with his expression—can measure; there is the reply not to the accepted absence of two years before or the new moratorium, or even the orphanhood imposed by fate with the same lack of explanations and scruples with which nature imposed myopia on him and difficulties of speech, but the refusal of the urge for freedom and the desire to forget that urge with an aim, in the seclusion or abandonment, of building his own laws and his own code, and his own raison d'être even though they might only serve to make him roll a few marbles along a hallway in the dark. He hadn't moved, sitting in the chair with his arms on the table and his head on top of them staring at the intruder, trying perhaps to retreat into one of those somber afternoons of the war when, with the help of the language of signs, it was given him to wait and it was possible to go to sleep and wake up knowing that one day the fighting would be over and his mother would come back. Or maybe not, because the same afternoon that his mother had said good-bye, a cruel part of his memory had induced him to lose all hope of seeing her again (the part that wanted to keep on playing marbles, no doubt) and to make himself strong in that attitude of a man who— after having alienated his freedom in order to constitute his own code—despises the revocation of the decision imposed as a result of a judicial error because he has found in his own resources the sublimation of a freedom that not even his mother would be able to pawn. The man took off his boots and took out a black pistol; he extracted the clip and half a dozen cartridges that the child observed with the indifference and integrity with which a completely honest judge would have contemplated a pile of coins, and pushed them across the table. He picked up a couple, put them in the palm of his hand, and stuck them in front of his nose, but those two inexpressive eyes barely blinked, looking at him straight on, lacking fear or surprise.

"What do you think?"

He lifted up his chin.

"What do you think about all this?"

"Why don't you leave the boy alone?"

He gathered up the bullets and put the clip back in the pistol.

"I'm going to leave you alone, that's right."

"Let the boy be, is he to blame?"

He got up, picked up his jacket, and put the pistol into his pants pocket. From the other pocket he took out several bullets that he looked at slowly, as if he were counting a pile of change.

"Go down to the cellar," Adela said, "you can stay there. I'll be right down."

"Blame," he said at the same time as he put the bullets into his pocket, "always blame."

The boy didn't say a word or move a muscle, but he understood that the war was finished. They must have been finished by now—Adela had been ironing them—his first pair of long pants, made from others belonging to his brother; it could have been said that those two long years of war had not been anything for him except the interval of excitement brought on in back rooms by grown-ups for him to change his children's clothes for those of a man. That was what his mother had ordered the day she left. He left the marbles in the garden to give her a kiss and receive the usual instructions. Then he spent almost all his time squatting on the kitchen floor or in the shadowy hallway. He got up once in a while to follow Adela and stick his nose through the Venetian blinds, scrutinizing a demonstration by men and women dressed in overalls and wearing caps or berets, who, around some splotchy-painted cars some of them had climbed onto, shouting long live something or other or death to something or other, sang songs and waved handkerchiefs, rifles, and bayonets. He only saw the intruder one more time; emaciated and unshaven, sitting on the stool in the kitchen, he was holding up the edge of the blinds with his hand to peek into the street; he was breathing very hard and with every exhalation a ridiculous and monotonous whistle came from his throat. Until one day Adela came to wake him with a bag in her hand and a kerchief tied around her head. "Put these on," she said to him, leaving the long pants on the bed. "Let's go, don't fall asleep." A man in military uniform leaning against the door frame was looking at him and hurried steps resounded on the stairs. They took him to a house where they waited a long time, sitting on a bench holding hands. A man in uniform came for Adela and then he fell asleep on the bench, with his head resting on the bag. The next morning Adela came back to give him a kiss; she was accompanied by Dr. Sebastián. She told him he was to go to his house, where she would come to get him after a short trip. And, in fact, a few months later she appeared at the old clinic, with the kerchief tied around her head and her traveling bag. But only for a short time, because that same winter Adela died as the consequence of a pulmonary congestion.

The first engagements in the Sierra de Región took place during the beginning of autumn in the year 1936 as a consequence of the attacks undertaken against the villages on the eastern slopes of the mountains by a few insurrectionists from Macerta. The garrison at Macerta, a regiment of engineers, had joined the uprising during the first days, diligently stifling the proletarian revolution that a certain number of peasants tried to bring off in their own way. They took Macerta as a base of operations and, with Región as their primary objective, after requisitioning all the vehicles they found at hand, they initiated a mountain campaign, in which, by means of lightning raids, sudden ambushes, arrests, and security measures that lasted all through summer, they reduced by attrition all the villages on the opposite side with poor communications and too far away to be occupied by such a small military force. By the middle of September they had occupied all of the Macerta-Región highway up to Socéanos Pass, with the aim of carrying out in the months to come with the arrival of good weather and reinforcements of all kinds, a full-scale war against a Región that, with its scant resources and dying energies, had decided to remain faithful to the cause of the republican government. Even in those days when it was a question of an almost deserted town, summer played no small influence on that stand; no one important had remained and there was very little to defend: a name, an institution of secondary education, three mansions, and a few chicken farms. Certain intellectuals of Región—and the July revolution had made manifest the fact that there were still people left who not only attributed such a title to themselves but were proud to match the profession of ideas against that of arms and money—had made public during the summer a call upon the national conscience "to resolve all differences with words, the instruments of understanding," which soon became so out of date and invalid that it had to be replaced by "an energetic protest at that intolerable gesture of disdain for the civilian life of the nation, which, in its drive, had not even hesitated at the sacrifice of human life." At the time there lived in the town a tall man, along in years and gray-haired and with a look—exaggerated perhaps by the fact that accompanied by his wife he would go out strolling in the afternoon, wearing a frayed coat and a black beret and his face almost hidden behind a pair of dark glasses—of being in extremely poor health. Every sunny afternoon he would stroll along the bank of the river on the arm of that woman who scarcely came up to his shoulder and who, looking furiously all about, seemed possessed of that domesticated but irrepressible fierceness of a dog ready at any moment to throw himself upon passersby in order to guard the safety of a master whose head is in the clouds. He had settled in Región a couple of years before the war in a modest neighborhood boarding house in search of rest and recovery from an old pulmonary lesion that had begun acting up again. His name was Rumbal or Rombal or something like that—Aurelio Rumbal; there was no *don* before his name, he was known everywhere as Mr. Rumbal. He'd been in America but not because of money, rather from an urge to teach; he had returned poor but inflamed with a certain Jacobin ardor, endowed with the name of a fighter—if not a prophet—whom not even a pulmonary lesion was able to subdue. That was due in part to a leonine mane that had turned white prematurely and those dark glasses, behind which, it seemed, a ferocious gaze had its lair. He earned his living as a teacher, as an intellectual; he gave classes at the high school; he received a lot of printed matter, wrote letters to newspapers, sent out articles that it seemed were published in America, and maintained the last vestiges of an intellectual circle attended by a few young people who hoped, in time, to be able to call him master. His knowledge, by not being very deep, took in almost the whole field of culture: he knew what conditions would have to obtain in a society for a revolution to be possible, he knew avant-garde art well enough to define something as retrograde, and had in his possession the few rudiments of mathematics sufficient to teach high-school classes. Even when education had fallen into disuse in Región, since the second decade of the century, two primary schools and a secondary school had remained open; the courtyard, of course, had been converted into a carriage-house, the janitors had slowly been transforming all the outbuildings into stables, but classes were still given and on almost all the cracked blackboards in the classrooms, still sketched in chalk, more indelible than pyrography, were hyperbolas and ellipses, sentences in French, and chemical formulas from the days of the monarchy. In the morning some teacher still appeared, who, conserving his love for teaching, had lost his memory as to how to bring it about and tried—in the company of three or four students, aged, saddened, and driven to drink—to solve a problem in physics that (in the years of prosperity, during the first quarter of the century) would have served at best as a question on a trimester examination but which in those days was seen as the limit of science and the threshold of hope. It's not known if Mr. Rombal or Rembal got to solve it; maybe he didn't even notice it, because it wasn't necessary to enhance his prestige. Accompanied by his wife, he appeared in the door of the classroom, and after contemplating the scene of meditation with displeasure he crossed the stage with a firm step and, picking up the eraser, tried to wipe out the written formulas without the least bit of protest coming from the desks. It wasn't easy to erase them; not even his wife could do anything with them as she tried to make them disappear with soap and water the next day, but, dimmer, like the background of a gleaming blackboard that revealed its somber green color, the formulas remained there forever, a moment of pain, shame, and desolation in a worn-out and conquered land. But that didn't allow him a touch of hesitation: smoothly, with energetic and elegant writing, with great confidence and a certain disdain for what was written underneath, he filled the whole blackboard with an incontrovertible truth with which, bubbling with freshness and vigor (something like "In all gasses there exists a constant relationship between pressure, volume, and temperature"), he introduced a new spirit into the classroom that soon spread out into the street. From then on his lectures in that place became frequent; he didn't teach great things nor was he concerned in the least with the originality of his ideas, but he had the supreme skill—no doubt chastened by the disastrous effects of all teaching that confronts problems without first measuring its capacity for solving them—of limiting himself to obvious and incontrovertible truths, which for that audience—small but in a certain way select, clinging to old habits that had lived through the dispossession of their firmest beliefs and so in need of relief—constituted a priceless source of confidence and security after so many years of useless sacrifices, uncertainties, and uneasiness. And, besides, there was his wife, who always sat beside the speaker, facing the audience, hurling at the gathering furious looks in which were combined her love for discipline, satisfaction, and challenge, and with which she managed to abort—as the speeches became more enigmatic and hard to swallow, when (once confidence was reestablished) he passed from simple truths to complex ones, from mere exposition to exhortation—a certain tendency toward tears and drink that had begun to spread among the benches of the older people. One day in June he said some words of thanks and no one knew why, since the thanks should have come from the audience; then he said, ". . . we intellectuals have the duty" . . . creating a denomination and a link that, under the authoritarian look of Mrs. Rubal, was accepted by the surprise and ratified by the silence. Before the end of July they came to the classroom again—mistreated, cowardly, and hesitant, they tried to seek refuge among the back desks, to cover their tears and hide the wine—in order to listen, approve, and sign the manifesto drawn up by Mr. Rembal. When he finished they had all understood that the moment had arrived for them to pay the debt they had contracted with him a few days before. Then he left the document on the desk and, on a command from his wife, they lined up behind the table while the two of them, sitting in the first row, looked at the orographic maps and the anatomical figure of a man, one half showing the viscera and the other the muscles, with that involuntary and forced attention with which the moviegoer must watch the advertisement for a mattress during intermission. No one wanted to read it, however—it was too terrible; the most terrible part was, after so many years, finding once more a finality to acts and a motive for battle. The signatures were unrecognizable, the ink ran, the tears left it more soaked than if it had fallen into a puddle, but it was finally signed and sealed with a stamp that the lady had in her purse. Mr. Rubal read it again, in a low voice, raising his glasses to his forehead and going carefully over the lines until, with an air of fatigue, with one single energetic scrawl that went completely across the paper, he signed it too. And then his wife did, with vengeful ease, and gratuitously gave to all present—grouped and crowded together against the walls like a bunch of schoolboys out of which stones have been thrown and who try to defend their anonymity by crowding together—an artificial and bold smile with which she was giving them to understand—they knew it only too well—that from then on there existed a secret, an unbreakable link, a single will, and a common destiny. The formulas scarcely changed, even when politics came to replace physical sciences for almost the whole summer. Once again Mr. Robal knew how to make use of his skills to change the formula of interest, amortization, or the law that governs electrical conduction, by simply changing Capital into Committee, Revenue into Región, and Time into Trade Union, into mottoes that, born in the high school, invaded all the streets of Región in the form of large letters done in whitewash or tar that were to prevail during the whole course of the war: CRT, TIR, TDAP, UTE. For a certain time they were barely seen; shut up in their boardinghouse they gave up their evening walk and the noontime get-to-gether, perhaps because that accumulation of manifestos and slogans demanded such dedication from the two of them that it left no time for leisure. But in the beginning of September, when the situation was growing worse and the news from Macerta took on a disquieting cast, they appeared again; by that time already people left their houses as little as possible, the streets were deserted and peaceful, houses and

businesses closed, people in the town lived with that lack of
something to do that only happens during a civil war; they
appeared at the head of a group of people who walked
through almost the whole town at a very rapid pace, so rapid
that no one ever came to think it was a matter of a demonstration; at their head marched his wife, casting challenging
looks at the closed balconies and dragging Mr. Rumbás along
by the hand (forcing him to march at a pace too swift for
his health) and he seemed to be obeying the will of his wife
with the blind docility (not having forgotten his dark glasses)
of an elephant led by a midget dressed as a hussar in the grand
finale. They had to spend all day marching, both because they
had no finishing point and because a halt would have been
interpreted as a collapse: a town that for thirty years had desired nothing but to lack desires and had let the few it had
left be used up, which, as a better solution to the uncertainties of the future and the verdict of an unequivocal fate, had
chosen to disdain the present and forget the past; that had
closed its schools, torn up its railroad tracks, and chopped
down its telegraph poles in order to silence the laments and
the fearsome warnings of those who—abandoning their flat
on the Calle del Císter—went into the hills in search of a
gamble or to live a shepherd's life; and which, even more
painful and meaningful, one hot and dusty morning during
the last summer of the Dictatorship had seen the closing of
the last post and watched the last detachment of the civil
guard—a corporal and five privates, with their wives and
children, rifles, mattresses, and luggage in a pair of carts sent
to them for the purpose—go off down the road to Macerta
as a happy group anxious to leave a land that denied them
subsistence; that town—taking refuge in the stables and
charcoal sheds of the empty mansions, squeezed by the debts
of a bankrupt past, and bereft of all hope that destiny might
have cooked up as it saw fit to serve up as hopelessness—
had to be shaken up, moved in its most sensitive fibers, and
brought into action by marriage with the advanced ideas that

ran through the streets at a rapid clip, asking for the punishment of guilty people and power for the workers. But . . .
what guilty people? what power? what workers?

Mr. Rumbás had doubtless thought about it. His instinct
had told him that the moment for rising up with power had
arrived but—because of his formation—it was impossible for
him to forget the difference between a coup d'état and a revolution; first it was necessary to invent power—in an automatic way the working class would acquire an awareness of
it in order to demand its true place—in order to bring down
a first political revolution that would open the doors to the
social transformation of the state. And, furthermore, still
living in Región were the Asiáns and the Mazóns and the
Roberts, the last scions of liberal families, whom it would
doubtless not be difficult to convince that the country had
need of them now more than ever. Nothing was simpler,
according to Mr. Rubal's predictions, than to get them out
of that wine cellar in the Mazón house where ever since the
victory of the CEDA they seemed to have taken refuge to
play cards, drink castillaza, wait for autumn to listen for the
shots from Mantua, and teach Captain Asián's bird to sing.
So that—after a whole day of going through the streets—
they regrouped at the high school in one of the classrooms
where, with a certain solemnity and after sending off a courier
to invite some of the prominent youths of the town to join,
they set up the Región Defense Committee, which was to
be such a decisive influence in the destiny of the town during
the two years of war and who knows perhaps for the rest of
its days.

The first campaign undertaken by the republican forces of
Región—brought together and organized by the Defense
Committee—was launched in the area of the Socéanos Pass
during the first days of November in the year 1936. It was
a question of cutting off the advance of a column, made up
of Falangists for the most part, that had left Macerta by the

main highway with the intention of reaching the Torce valley. In truth, more than a battle between two armies, it was a fight between two caravans of antiquated cars and trucks (requisitioned automobiles, old buses, and milkmen's and woodcutters' trucks) that left the valleys of the Torce and the Formigoso respectively and tried to meet and confront each other in the *divortium aquarum*. But neither of the two showed itself capable of crowning the pass from either slope. The republican group was not a force but a sampling: of men, vehicles, shirts, songs, muskets. Commanded by Eugenio Mazón—in his capacity as the most expert and most generous driver (he was the first to put at the disposal of the Committee the old sedan that had been so important in local politics during the first years of the republic)—and guided by Luis I. Timoner (I. for incognito), as the one who knew the woods best, they didn't even make use of the lesson that unity of command is necessary. The battles—the cars were abandoned in the ditches with their tops gashed, their motors and radiators shot up, their gas tanks full of water, their batteries burst, and their wiring pulled out—were prolonged with the aid of their cavalry (and with a listlessness that was very understandable in people who saw themselves obliged to give up a sport and a luxury unknown until then) until the arrival of the first snow in the month of December, when both forces decided to withdraw, for all the rest of the winter, to their respective bases in Región and Macerta, keeping their swords uplifted and leaving the pass to the care of the woodcutters.

The Sierra de Región—8,060 feet high at the top of El Monje (according to geodesists who had never climbed it) and 5,411 at its crossing points, the passes of Socéanos and La Requerida—rises up like a last calcareous sigh of the Aquilan Mountains, a wave of farewell to its continental friends, before being lost and hiding among the Portuguese fingerings. The meeting of the Cantabrian range with the Galaico-Portuguese massif is produced in the manner of a collision that leads to the formation of those arches that had materialized in primary terrain, which, in contact with the solid hypogene, go off in a NNE-SSW direction with a curvature that increases as it descends toward the west, resting on the eruptive and crystalline formations that, in opposite direction and with convexity, lay down their folds toward the Atlantic. In that sector the range loses the linear continuity that, for a distance of six hundred miles, it has maintained from the Basque Pyrenees—even assimilating into its structure the secondary of San Vicente de la Barquera—to come out in a fan that opens up in three main directions: the original axis parallel to the highway of the sun that, made up by the folds of the Hercynian cycle, goes along advancing and concentrating opposite the Cantabrian foreground until it finds a point of maximum resistance in the eastern end of Asturias, at the height of the Picos de Europa, maintaining the watershed divide and narrowing to a minimum the coastal strip on the meridian of the Eo; the front of resistance resting on the Cantabrian foreground and introduced into the peninsula by the Galician extremity—in the direction of Estremadura—which will maintain itself by acting as a wedge during the whole Hercynian paroxysm; and finally the principal lines of rupture, produced by the conflict between the two previous dynamic axes and which come to coincide—like a demonstration on a tectonic scale of Poisson's effect—with the two families of bisectrices of the angles formed by the former, which defines the western borders of the tableland and which is repeated, in the reproduction of the conflict on a lesser scale, in the dominant directions of all the small formations, ranges, and valleys that cut through it. Therefore, the Hercynian efforts of the Westphalian period have taken shape (it would seem) in the Asturio-Leonese region along a geosyncline whose axis must have passed through some point in Galicia in order to break up into a family of arches of folds in an E-W direction, which, parallel among themselves in the west of Asturias, are closing up in contact with the resistant massif to show a recognized convexity in its Galician extremity. It is supposed, in short, that previous to the folding there existed and cohabited two massifs that functioned during the paroxysm as the ridges of the geosyncline: the first—which has come to be called the "Cantabrian foreground"—must have been a wedge formed for the most part by gneiss and which, located in the west of Asturias and in the center of Galicia, served as a pan for the eastern pushes; the second, located without precision, to the east of the Picos de Europa, could only be a powerful promontory with an accumulation of acid and gneissic rocks whose continuous leveling during the Paleozoic gives rise to those peripheral deposits of quite different power and nature, where the scope and influence of marine invasions is surmised. This hammer, introduced into the peninsula in the manner of a spearhead of the European platform and cut in the south by the sea of Tethys, is probably the executive agent of the eastern Hercyinian push and has molded, in its path in the same direction as that of the sun, the northern folds of Asturias. Yet, what happened to it? It's possible that the massif itself—a vehicle of the push—suffered a partial or total dissolution in its route in contact with peripheral sediments, but it's also possible that in its march toward the west it managed to cross the sea of Tethys so that—after an acceleration, which justifies the lack of residues—it was partially incorporated into the homologous massif of the foreground, creating a confused superimposition of terrains of similar nature but different origins and originating in the Leonese shield a whole system of folds that—from the Mampodre to Babia, from Rañeces to Láncara—presents a certain analogy with the wake of a ship that had cast off from Liébana to drop anchor on the slopes of the Eo. This multivaried system of folds would later be lifted and plated by the alpine pushes sent out energetically in a N-S direction, that is, in the direction of the maximum fragility of the post-Hercynian architecture whose linear

[30]

spines—coincident with the lines of the wave crest—would be fragmented like a keyboard, superimposed like tiles on a roof, displaced and scattered like a deck of cards, to give rise to that tectonic mixture of the Cantabrian, Leonese, Zamoran, Regionate, and Portuguese mountains. The Región range shows itself like an enigmatic witness, little known and disquieting, of all that disorder and those paroxysms: a base and some karst and permeable surroundings lead one to think of a delayed change, a trip into exile; its calcareous crown defines—just as the seashell left by the tide serves as testimony to the level reached—the southern limit of the Stephanian regression that, under the Hercynian influence, lifts the Dinant limestone to the highest summits in the region; the broad belt of quartzites, slates, and sandstone quartz speaks to us of those long, deep, and shadowy Silurian and Devonian immersions with which the lashed and broken body of the continent was introduced into the sterilizing balm of the sea to cover itself once more with a coating of calcium and salt. In shape the Sierra shows the form of the stomach of a violin, crossed by a bridge of detritic and carboniferous formations that link it to the arches of the folds that point toward the distant Eo, which on tightening—one might say because of a feminine bashfulness about the shape or because of a masculine impulse at emulation—takes on, with the Torres, the Monje, and the Acatón, the importance and bearing of a mountain range. Out of the strangulation comes the birth—and the divorce—of its two main rivers: toward the east the Torce, a leaping brook that with stumbling begins a brief and errant trajectory that only at its confluence with the Tarrentino brook (an impressive, somber, and blackish formation of quartzite in vertical planes and sawtooth edges) takes care to correct itself so as to render its waters where they are needed. And toward the west the Formigoso, which, in comparison to its twin, from its birth observes a straight, disciplined, and exemplary behavior so that, with no need for teachers, it will come of age accord-

ing to the model established by its parents and new induc-
tees. Such a difference in character and customs seems to in-
duce them to separate brusquely, interposing between their
mothers that primary shield of a tortured base on whose
eastern border the summits rose up—spiny, broken, tormented, and braced—the most impressive ones in the
mountains: the angular Torres, El Monje, Malterra, and the
bald mountain of San Pedro. Ahead toward the south, like
an outside tower of the Cantabrian wall, the range seems to
partake of the braggart and arrogant solitude of a bastion that
was avoided by the southern invaders in their route toward
the north and of the excellence that guards with the greatest
vigilance and zeal the mysteries and virginity of lands preserved without stain during the millenary siege. Curiosity
and civilization have always tried to reach them from the
south by using the course of both rivers as paths of penetration; but that advance had seen itself halted, throughout history, approximately at the 42° 45" parallel latitude N, at 2,500
feet altitude, north of which exploration has only been
brought off by a few sporadic, fruitless, and disastrous pen-
etrations. To the north of Región, above the Torce, and
Macerta, above the Formigoso—both located on the northern edge of cretaceous Miocene terrain characteristic of the
tableland—that advanced strip of first steps and complicated
topography unfolds, not even frequented when the ban is
lifted and which only wars, every fifty years, are capable of
freeing from its deserved oblivion. When the lower flatlands
and Quaternary valleys are left, the banks narrow, the first
closings rise up, pudding stone conglomerates, ocher in color
and with sparse vegetation. By a tectonic irony, the right
bank of the Torce, along those fifteen miles of the course
boxed into the Paleozoic, seems to coincide with the line of
greatest resistance of the whole formation, outlined by a
successive accumulation of almost all the primary floors superimposed in several sheets of landslides detained there not
by the antagonism of other younger and more resistant for-

mations but by the exhaustion of its advancing drive. In such a way that very soon, at the point of the Doña Cautiva Bridge, less than ten miles north of Región, the valley acquires its outline of a closed V, so characteristic of quartzites, and the presence of the range—so clear and neat from the terraces of Región—is suddenly hidden behind its own outcroppings. Hills become frequent, covered with a vegetation of small bushes with shallow roots and sparse branches, and the transverse valleys, small in depth, are closed off suddenly by a wall of mountain limestone; the road—it is impossible to cross the ditch the river has dug out for its own exclusive use—climbs up a small hill, and at the same time that it reappears—closer, unexpected and majestic—the silhouette of the summits (lined up like the units of a fleet in battle array) lay out before the traveler all the desolation of the wasteland: a sterile moor (to which the rigors of the climate even deny the vegetation of deserts and where only a few plants of primitive construction manage to take root, crucifers and equisetums, ferns and thistles that have endured since Paleozoic times, thanks in part to its infertility) fringed on its horizon by a changing, almost imaginary festoon of dwarf oaks. On that moor all roads are lost, divided, and subdivided into an endless number of hallucinatory tracks, each of which seems to be heading toward a splotch that glimmers on the horizon: ponds of dead and millenary waters, lacking drainage, that during certain periods of the year spread out and retreat with the same domineering and ephemeral drive as the flowering of bloody bromelias or fetid daneworts. Suddenly a gulley—the hermetic and impenetrable nature of the terrace is manifest, formed by schists, slate, and quartzites, feldspar clay the color of baked brick and placed in rowlocks, covered with a layer of quartz sand a hand thick—puts an end to many hours of traveling that will no longer be able to be recovered or prolonged. The Traveler then notices the reality of the desert where scarcely any traces of man remain: phantom roads and barren fields, piles of papers that run about driven by the surface breeze and which seem to have grouped themselves in a colony in order to seek the path of their migration jointly, observed with disdain and sadness by a newspaper page stained by the rain and toasted in the sun, tangled among the spiny branches that are born out of a sandbank; it has been some time since the last abandoned farmhouse ceased to be seen, four walls of bare stone—because the roof had been carried off by the wind one March—piles of bones, half-burned charcoal, and signs of the fires of shepherds and hoboes. Behind the fringe of oaks (the slope of the river is no longer remembered, nor is it known in which direction the waters will run) the soil changes: on top of an outcropping of limestone that has fallen off a vein forty yards thick, decorated with hanging vegetation, beeches glow and birds of slow and heavy flight croak around the natural dormers, tinted and stained by the course and fall of the waters. The steps follow each other, broken by cuts and parcels of quartzite, bumps of pudding stone, to be prolonged and entwined with abrupt slopes covered with the vegetation characteristic of foothills and siliceous rocks; heather and broom in a continuous tangle almost six feet high; narrow forests in the bottom of the valleys that at their base—seen from an airplane—are nothing but thin lines, scarcely more perceptible than the trickles of water that engender them and which only seem to define the complicated geometry and organization of the *thalwegs;* but it's really not possible to cross them and go through them lengthwise: all the vegetation that nature has denied the mountain and economized on the flats, it has made bountiful in the transverse valleys, where it stretches out and multiplies, is compressed, magnified and packed together, transforming those shallow and narrow cuts in inextricable forests where wild fruit trees grow—wild cherries, wild apple trees, wild pears, alder buckthorn, and hazelnut—among willows and myrtles, arborescent holly and whispering birches, oaks and centenary beeches, all mingled under the common embrace of varieties of mistletoe. And, nevertheless, those narrow and luxuriant valleys are also deserted, even more deserted than the moor because nobody has been strong enough to stay there. Because if the land is hard and the landscape is rough, it is because the climate is harsh: a tenacious winter that is prolonged for eight months each year and which only lifts its punishing hand in the first half of June not so much to give the victim a moment of relief as to make him understand the imminence of the next thrashing. In the first part of October the rains begin, until one sunny and cold morning—between Saint Bruno's and All Saints' Day—after some close days of rain and mist, the mountain range appears all covered with white. If the year is damp, the snowstorms are usually frequent after Christmas, with such regularity that rare is the snow that—between January and April—doesn't fall on the ice left by the one before. On the mountain and on the moor the signs of life are reduced during this period to the tracks of a fox, a chamois, or a wolf, the passage of a peasant—betrayed by the signs of a fire—who has been searching for many long weeks for the trace of a lost calf. But if the year is dry toward Saint Bruno's Day, the temperature begins to drop below freezing; there's no other thermometer than the thickness of the crust of ice, the depth of the freeze in the ground, in the roots and on the rocks, the expansive force of the intersticial water, which, as it congeals, fragments and cracks the smooth face of the quartzite; the whole flat is changed into an immense deep freeze, the corpses of dogs who die in December don't decompose until the month of May, when the first blooms come to coincide with a stench so extensive and unbearable that it no doubt had led popular imagination to relate the color of the bromelia and the poppy to the blood and guts of winter's decedents. On the slopes that look to the north, along many valleys—the most frequent—that run in a direction orthogonal to the path of the sun, its rays don't enter or touch the ground for forty or fifty days, and freezes

[35]

succeed each other and increase in strength the same as the snow up above. In general, January and February are the cruelest months, when—no matter how benignly it may arrive—it is difficult for a single pleasant day to dawn. Then the strong March winds arrive; nor are there any anemometers in the region. There are no other witnesses or registers of the force of the wind than that flora facing south, with naked and tortured shapes from the continuous lashing of the wind, those unbalanced and stripped oaks that serve as a perch for mistletoe, whose branches only grow on the part that faces south, opposite the dominant blow, and which seem hallucinated by their own condition; and the detrital dunes around the amphitheaters of the outcrops, broken by that atrocious climate. In years of snow the March wind is more fearsome than a tempest. When at sunset a slight Martian breeze rises up, barely able to shake the snow off the branches and cornices, the horizon seems to be hiding behind a pale mist that—on clear days—in less than an hour has covered the range with an apparent curtain of clouds; the peasant on the flatland or the herdsman on the moor knows then what to take care of: close all windows and bulkheads, bring in the cattle from the insecure sheds, gather all the grain and firewood that will fit inside, and, against the doors that face north, resting on the floor and the wall in the manner of props, place as many beams and logs as there are on hand so as to form a brace that will let a person go outside through a tunnel of ice when the wind dies down; with a windstorm—in contrast to a snowstorm—the temperature goes way down; time, sun, day, and night disappear under an opalescent whirlwind of powdered ice that spins and blows in all directions and knows no obstacle, altering and undoing, as is its whim, that superficial and egalitarian distribution of the snowfall. No one is capable of knowing where it will blow, what it will move, because it seems only to obey the destructive designs of an enemy Boreas who knows how to get in through the cracks, blow through a door, create a whirlwind and a void to sweep a threshing floor and place six feet of snow on top of a shed, burying animals, cars, and people, to concentrate its charge against one single side of a wall and sink it all for its whole length; or frontally, to accumulate in front of a door all the snow collected from ten leagues of moor, wiping out the dwelling under an avalanche that has the gift of opportunity to choose its moments of birth, the newly tiled roofs, the cattle acquired a week before the fair. The wind of March is the real designer of that rustic architecture of steep, smooth roofs, of sloping walls and small and tall hollows, like watch posts of rudimentary bastions that only know a truce during the thirsty months of summer. The impenetrable nature of the terrain, the violent topography, and the dryness and rigor of summer give way to a desiccation so rapid that in most years, between June and September, only in the beds of the Torce and the Formigoso is it possible to see running water, a spectacle that on the rest of the moor is always accompanied by damage and violence, by the final chord and catastrophic thunder of the storm's colophon. Because the measure of rain in spring and fall is harmful more than useless: the few plots and fields that have been susceptible to cultivation are soon wiped out under a few inches of blue Cambrian clay or red loam in which only a few famished Spanish brooms will grow; the rapid erosion of the thin vegetable covering is followed by the storm–borne invasion of loose subsoil, a mass of grayish groat that drags along chunks of quartz and rolling stones to advance uncontained through the *thalwegs* and canyons where a flow of melted snow and an alluvial sedimentation of clay will allow a beginning of cultivation, a mirage of meadow and a fraudulent hope for the initiation of a culture with which the shepherd always aspires to improve his condition by feeding a few head of cattle.

The three months of summer are generally rigorously dry. Only in the high regions of the mountains is there pasture: the whole plain in ten days of May or June sun becomes drier, hairier, and duller in color than an old rag forgotten on a windowsill. There are no hygrometers either, but the dryness of the air is such and the evaporation (when the haze makes the outline of the mountains tremble) so rapid that the dogs who die during those burning months (and sometimes they die hanged, suspended from trees, like sacks of grain, their visceral mass all gathered in their hindquarters) are mummified in a couple of nights and are preserved like dried fish over the whole dry spell to serve as food for the creatures that come down from the mountains with the first snow. Because in summer only insects fly there: those foothills, covered with heather, broom, and dwarf oaks that give no shade, hold and irradiate the heat to such a degree that the young and unaware eaglets and hooded crows who, abandoning their cool heights, come down to the flat in search of food (suffocating aromas, poison vapors, mysterious sparkles), often lose consciousness and fall, overcome to serve as instant nourishment for a swarm of buzzing flies, bluish and silvery, who can devour them in less than an hour with the frenzied clash and clatter of a rain of cations.

It's a land that through exclusion—not through resources—has found a certain cattle-raising compensation at the cost of so many agricultural disappointments. Resistant to the plow, allergic to fertilizers, and hostile to trees, it still seeks in the calm, green meadows and grasslands the richness that a promising and deceitful subsoil knew how to get out of it: the terrible vengeance of a region given over once more to ridiculous livestock raising and an archaic breeders association to cure and settle the wounds opened by wells, abandoned mine entrances, rotting towers, the gray and sterile trash heaps where only a few tenacious and sporadic nettles of unhealthy appearance grow. All the failed attempts at reform in the economy of that land of shepherds and rotten boroughs have only served in the end—from 1771 to 1836— to exaggerate the poor state of matters concerning property, the working force, and rural benefits: the common lands, snatched away from a few drowsy communities and put up for public auction, were acquired by the same distant and unknown potentates who arrived in time to acquire church properties at a tempting price. Then the well-known inversion was produced, the consequence of a law beclouded by the *idée fixe* of the colonization of uncultivated and amortized lands and the breaking up of large pasture lands, public or private. The lowlands, the property of the commune or the church, where in the eighteenth century the people affected worked and grazed their cattle close to their barns, were given to the highest bidder, an aristocrat from Castile, Catalonia, or Estremadura, while the upper pastures, good only for wool-bearing stock—which were the property of the great lords who controlled the tableland—were broken up and distributed among the expropriated neighbors, with a payment of the monies they had received in the previous transaction. After fifteen or twenty years of sterile efforts at feeding a few head of cattle among those brambles or cultivating some rickety rye, bitter, yellow, and gritty—responsible for malnutrition, the degeneration of the race, and the loss of vigor—the peasant, worn out and ruined, will not hesitate one day to take advantage of the annual visit of the administrator of the lowland farms to give him back his mountain property in exchange for being the emphyteuta of an insignificant part of his former property. So that the law only served—after several years—to convert the former rural smallholder into the tenant farmer of the great lords; and if it hadn't helped him progress before, what will it be now that he must share his income with a landowner, who, at the slightest delay in payment, rescinds the contract? Such is the physiognomy of the boroughs today, a sordid and grotesque translation of those proud rotten boroughs capable at least of feeding a scion whose voice resounded in Parliament: in the rear of the valley, twenty or thirty hovels of bare stone—which had reached the last stage of progress when straw roofs had been replaced by ones of slate or tile—around a huge church (and similar in their clustering and small size to that swarm of small barks, junks, and sampans of the small merchants that gathers about the side of an oceanliner that drops anchor in an exotic port in the Orient) and surrounded by a mosaic of insignificant lots separated one from the other by huge brick walls topped with barbed wire and pieces of broken bottles, all the instruments of defense and intimidation that the sharecropper can think of to protect a fig tree, two hay carts, and a pen with half a dozen birds from the voracity of his neighbor. Such is the borough, such is its peaceful togetherness: a gathering of tenants fearful of one another, all besieged by the hostility of the geography, the history, the geology, the climatology, and the breeders association, ready to resist the siege and maintain their status as much to defend a pauper's economy as to feed the fear inspired by any emigration and change in status and hearth. And up above on the black mountain range that surrounds the village, the isolated smoke clouds of those mysterious, unknown, and omnipresent enemies of the peasant—the shepherds—who, without doubt, take advantage of their strategic condition and peaceful appearance to spy night and day on the activities of the village and send to a distant capital a notice of eviction as soon as a peasant lifts his eyes from the furrow he is plowing. Because they are the secular arm of the Estremaduran or Castilian landowner; mounted on their small donkeys and on top of a pyramid of mattresses, bundles, and frying pans (and now they even carry radios), in the midst of an ill-smelling and dusty flock—flanked by those sheep dogs that before anything else seem to enforce the segregation of the sexes—they return every year at the beginning of May, with that supine, malignant, sleepy, tottering, and enigmatic look of a Tamerlane who, after having crossed and conquered all the steppes of Asia, scarcely opens his malice-laden eyes at the green countryside of European meadows. But since several years ago some of them no longer go off or return to their land even with the cold, even when—

in space and in time—the migratory laws of the breeders association persist; those who remain are usually very old, perhaps incapable of making the trip and their presence is only betrayed by the smoke; they have exchanged their traditional clothes of corduroy, their Béjar cape and their fustian blouse, for a kind of walking hut, which, like the St. Bernard in his hairy shell, they don't take off even in summer. Only fire makes them get rid of it. They're accustomed to living at an altitude of more than 5,000 feet, on the slopes facing the south, under piles of wool and leaves, which, seen from a distance, look like termite nests. It is said that of late, with the use of the radio, some of them have learned to sing, but no one is capable of backing up such an assertion; they didn't sing before, but they did intone some quite strange melodies—from the time of the religious wars or the Napoleonic campaigns—that (doubtless because of their simplicity, monotony, and sadness) could be heard several leagues away. In any case, they must be very old, so insatiable and cruel that when their proximity is noted in a village church, bells ring in a call to arms; and, nevertheless— in contrast to what happens with the wolf or wild beast— never, as a consequence of the call, does anyone come out to hunt the shepherd down. In general they die incinerated. Their dwelling is nothing but a woodpile, an immense heap with a central hollow—the minimum at first that grows larger with consumption—a chimney and the thickness necessary to nourish a small hearth dug in the soil for eight months; a pair of young goats, hanging from a winch by their hind legs (the two black heads like two enormous scabs, where all the blood in the animal is concentrating and drying, are the last, most tasty, and the strongest mouthful that the shepherd keeps in reserve for Christmas and Saint John's Eve) make up, with ten gallons of wine, their entire ration. And there is certainly no fire more inviting or more fearsome; there is no heat like the one reflected by a wall of dry oak roots, warmed by a nearby hearth where the wood is burning; there is nothing in the midst of the Región winter that invites sleep so much or demands the most vigilant watch, because with the slightest carelessness—a blister that sparks up, a surge in the chimney that raises up the draft in the hearth, a log that explodes into a hundred glowing coals—the whole rustic refuge, with shepherd, goats, and wine inside, can turn instantly into a bonfire, a glowworm nest that remains lighted all night long and which is received in the villages with joy and relief, with the explosion of fireworks and the ringing of bells.

That is why it is known that that race of shepherds—to which Numa, its fiercest and most stubborn son belongs—has been brought up in vigil and ambush; that they barely sleep and that—without leaving their refuge—they hear everything; they can see in the night and have, like all races accustomed to waiting, a sense of funereal anticipation of the future; is there any other anticipation of the future but a date with death more fitting to that land?

So, then, the traveler who leaves Macerta wishing to reach Región has a choice of two quite different routes: either going all the way down the Formigoso valley to its junction with the Torce and then following the latter's course up, or crossing the divide directly—through Socéanos Pass or the heights of La Requerida—keeping oneself in the same east-west latitude. The first route is difficult and labyrinthine, often impassable and during certain benign times of the year fatal. The traveler who attempts it without a previous knowledge of the terrain will risk many hours and leagues of useless walking through a maze of muddy roads used as water sluices during the irrigation season, which frequently come out into a pond, a swamp, or an extensive pool of mire. For of all the landscape of the surrounding region none seems more disorderly and whimsical than the irrigation ditches of the lower flats; alfalfa fields two hands high with water, that glimmer in the noonday sun, and where at sunset that furious, unison, and hallucinating croaking of frogs surges up, in whose spell sky, dusk, alfalfa, water, and horizon seem to blend in a sonorous and serene chaos that confuses the traveler (with the mud up to his knees, he probably swears that the sound comes from a cloud of insects that hides the stars and won't let a hint of light appear) and frightens animals. The junction of the two rivers creates a broad plain with luxuriant and carefree vegetation where the currents of water are divided and subdivided into countless arms and veins that run in opposite directions and where the traveler—lost among pastures, meadows, hedgerows of black poplars, and birches—will never be able to find the proper path or safe shelter to spend the night protected from the mosquitoes. Harassed by a swarm of them—who accompany him like a bridal veil—all his hopes at sunset are centered on that red strip, which, through the thickness, marks the Miocene hills that surround the plain and which he will try to reach—rather than going back—by cutting across the flooded fields to go and flop down between the robust roots of a cork oak that rises up over the still waters.

Although the second is the safer of the two routes, it is also the more difficult: from November until June, snow, blizzards, storms, avalanches, freshets, and March winds keep the pass closed, so that only with the beginning of the dry season do woodcutters and herdsmen dare open it on a seasonal basis for the passage of livestock and wagons. From time to time a lumber buyer—eventual grantee of a cutting that never managed to provide the slightest profit—would try, also in vain, to open it to vehicular traffic. But most frequently, before the improvement of the road—a few logs in order to cross culverts, some pick work to widen a footpath, some crushed stone to firm up soft spots—gets to the top of the pass, the contractor has gone bankrupt, or has disappeared without waiting for the rescission, with no one knowing why. With half the cutting done, the work is halted by the Civil Guard, and the logs of oak and yew, along with the tool chest, locked and sealed with a faded and illegible band, remain at the disposition of the Regional Court of Macerta, which has issued the embargo with an aim to preventing the possibility of any connection between the two towns—a connection that nobody, underneath it all, savors—during an insoluble judicial inquiry that can only leave out the military route during times of emergency.

This second was the road that Colonel Gamallo decided to follow in the spring of 1938—in frank opposition to the strategy dictated by the High Command of Army Group North—in the operation destined to liquidate the Región pocket, which up till that time, isolated from the rest of the Republic and reduced to its own resources ever since the end of 1937, had succeeded in holding out and even repulsing two successive attacks. After the vague attempts in 1936—and toward the beginning of summer in 1937—Headquarters put the direction of the operation in the hands of a Navarrese colonel, who, with three regiments of infantry and a battery of mountain artillery, tried to bring it off (paying heed to the previous failure of a motorized column) on muleback. When the division reached the pass—in whose climb the young Navarrese colonel displayed a notable show of energy and leadership spirit—with a view of the Torce valley, the only man who knew anything about the terrain tried to raise a series of objections to the advance that only got him into trouble with his superiors. Behind his back, among his young comrades, certain affirmations that were not too agreeable as concerned his person were bandied about—his lack of principles, his failures in family life, his limited sense of tactics, his bad manners, his tight-fistedness, his love of reading, and, in any case, his scant adaptability to life in the wilds and his manifest indifference toward domestic ideals—to which he must really have been quite accustomed already because his whole adult life, in short, had been dominated by his incapacity to get away from them. He hadn't reached the rank of captain and was already

[44]

an old man who bit his fingernails; his right hand was almost immobilized as the result of an old knife wound and
in order to bite his nails he would clutch it with the left and
bring it up to his mouth as if it were a morsel. He had never
stood out in his profession; he was neither methodical nor
energetic nor ambitious nor even sure of himself, but he was
stubborn and rancorous, endowed with that unalterable and
inexhaustible capacity for perseverance—almost independent of his successes or failures—of a man who knows only
one trade and lacks all possibility of change and who, with
the passage of fifty years, has been transformed into the
symbol of an essential professional security—paradoxically—in attaining victory in a struggle planned and begun
by younger, stronger, and more fanatical hands. He began
to feel an unwillingness when they reached the pass; perhaps
his useless hand trembled, shaken by one of those mysterious reflexes that make the heart of a man palpitate when on
the street he passes the woman he had loved thirty years before; when—before memory can notice it—the heart dis-
closes that through that entrance and up those stairs, thirty
years before, he had ascended to his first night of pleasure;
perhaps the heart is only reproducing the palpitations of that
time, conditioned by a reflex that it had acquired in one single night thirty years before. In accordance with ritual, a field
mass was celebrated before a backdrop of stark and tortured
mountains half hidden by a disorderly and graying formation of clouds on a clear August day. They didn't see a soul
at the pass, nor was there any trace of the slightest sign of
activity on the paths that lead down into the valley. He had
been assigned to the division in the post of adjutant to the
colonel, without any command, as a person who knew the
terrain and, in a certain way, in order to justify the promotion that he had won as much to rehabilitate him for so many
years of ostracism as to reward and certify his good will
during the early days of the uprising. Once there he suggested establishing a strong position at the pass—the key to

the whole operation by his lights and which should not be lost for any reason—with the possibility of supplying themselves on the Macerta side and initiating on the other—which all his instinct and his past led him to mistrust—a series of reconnaissance patrols before launching the final attack on Región. That presupposed a long-term campaign, however, which was the last thing the colonel wanted to hear about. He barely paid any attention to him and—worse yet—wouldn't permit him to enter into any tactical discussion that would only be settled by a series of reproaches and accusations from superior to inferior, which, because of decorum, was not very attractive to the colonel; so that—true to the military practice of assigning a function to the one who has misgivings about it—he decided to launch the attack without losing a single day and entrusted to him the organization of some small defensive positions, almost lacking in communication and information, to be set up at intervals in the rear on the western slope, while the column advanced toward the Torce. In the last days of August the column—in its descent—began to be harassed by republicans; the advance continued, however, into the middle of September with few casualties in spite of constant skirmishes—strong and unforeseen counterattacks launched with that unmistakable guerrilla style of Eugenio Mazón (by that time there were already three of them, he, Julián Fernández, and old Constantino), who at the same time that they showed courage and fiber, revealed the poverty of their means—by which they tried to lower the morale of the Navarrese troops, turn the tip of the lance toward the south, and contemporize until the rains and cold arrived. For the first time the colonel took the bait: when he reached the valley, instead of advancing toward the river, he turned his left flank south and entered Burgo Mediano on the day of the Virgin in August, in pursuit of Julián Fernández's brigade, which he took to be the main body of the enemy forces. On hearing news of it, old Gamallo quickly went—on muleback—to meet with his colonel, with the aim of having a talk and suggesting to him not to consolidate that position until he had taken or destroyed Doña Cautiva Bridge, but not on that occasion either did his superior officer—his spirit aroused by how easy it had been up to that moment and by a number of pigs, mules, barnyard animals, and holy pictures he had found in the village, standing now less than a dozen miles from Región and with no other natural obstacle between his column and the town but the River Torce at its lowest level of water—take the warning into consideration and he limited himself to sending him off with a few good words, because he had no desire either to modify his ideas or to oblige him, hierarchically, to keep his place and his distance. The memorable action of Burgo Mediano took place between August 26 and September 3; even as the Navarrese forces doubtless oriented their advance in the direction of Región, the republicans, as a provision against any change, split up into three groups: Eugenio Mazón's brigade on the right bank of the river, stationed by the Doña Cautiva Bridge and ready to cross it as soon as the Navarrese took up their march again and left Burgo; Constantino's people—he was the old miner, the old foreman—along the road from Bocentellas to La Requerida, on the slope of the mountain, dominating from up above and from a distance the Burgo plain; and, lastly, facing the enemy advance and posted along the highway from Región to the mountains that connects Bocentellas, Burgo, and the Bridge, Julián Fernández's battalion, reinforced by the few Germans left from the Theobald column. They had a heterogeneous armament: eight 15.5 pieces, a few 8.8s and howitzers; and, as for infantry, the formations seemed to have come out of an Epinal print, a museum showcase, or a parade of old and heady glories: peasants in sandals and turbans on their heads, armed with old Mannlichers from the first African war, alongside militiamen in blue caps and covered with cartridge belts, helmets atilt and unstrapped, Mausers or Brens on their shoulders, and in the rear a team of mules with the new Vickers, lacking coolers; and the withdrawn foreigners from the International Brigades in leather caps and jackets, pistols on their belts, on whose faces, after a year of combat, the smile of arrival had disappeared already to be replaced by the grimace of duty; and the squads of miners, wearing berets, marching with arrogance and swaying their waists that were loaded with clusters of grenades and homemade bombs of tin cans and black powder; and that last-minute—hastily formed and more than provisional—formation of officers and men, humble students who had acquired a tunic and braid in the hallways of union headquarters and marched off to war with a scarf: young men from furnished rooms and cheap boardinghouses who went forward alongside the battalion, walking in the ditches, with open shoes and flannel pants disguised by Italian leggings. Thrown against them at dawn on August 26 was the impulsive Navarrese colonel. The same night, between the 26th and the 27th, Eugenio Mazón's force crossed the river, turning immediately southward in the direction of Burgo after surprising and falling upon a small detachment with almost no defensive capacity that had been posted on watch in the vicinity of the bridge. Only a second lieutenant managed to escape to report to Headquarters the following day about the imminence of an attack on the rear guard. But Headquarters—in the belief that by such disciplinary measures one could guarantee a defense no matter what the nature of the attack—chose to have him shot that same afternoon and after a most cursory court martial for having abandoned his post. And the attack and the advance of the Navarrese went forward, to the degree that the enemy permitted them, in accordance with the plan previously established and put forward. For a division on foot with little artillery protection there is in all the valley of the Torce no front less propitious for attack than the flats of Burgo Mediano; a small village huddled around the church—all construction is of bare stone—and surrounded by broad and arid threshing grounds, without a tree, where a hiding place can scarcely be found and it is so difficult at that season of the year to find shade sufficient to shelter eight thousand men. That hinterland of sand, sun, and small fences, some three miles in diameter, is surrounded by the typical growth of the plain and a diadem of red hills, rustic lookouts, towers from which the slightest movement of the troops can be observed day and night. All through the night between the 25th and the 26th patrols explored the southern sector of the flats without observing any movements other than those of enemy pickets; during the first hours of dawn—before daybreak—the column advanced in a V-formation, at quick step in order to reach the plain by the light of dawn. But that was what the republicans were expecting, sheltered among the hedgerows, the stream beds, the unharvested fields of rye, the rows of poplars, distributed and organized in a mass of positions into whose grid the Navarrese would have to fall. Surrounded on almost all flanks and surprised in that labyrinth of fences they soon lost all sense of advance and limited themselves to a defense, right where they were, hoping in vain for a solution, a liberation, or a truce that wasn't granted them. By noontime there was only some firing around a half dozen groups clustered behind some mounds of boulders, who held out until that hour of the afternoon when, with mortar fire, they were crushed by the same rocks that had served them as a refuge. Almost a third of the column had gone down in less than ten hours; the rest managed to get back to Burgo and didn't leave it. But the colonel was not disheartened by the reverse; that same night Headquarters, irritated and spurred by the disaster but not fearful, held to the order to attack even though it was decided to change the direction in order to avoid the fatal plain, and to continue along the slopes of the hills where Constantino's unit was waiting—which, during the action on the previous day, had taken care not to give away its presence—with the 15.5 pieces. Such were the origins of the Battle of La Loma, the only real victory obtained by the republicans of Región in two years of war. In contrast with the previous day, the Navarrese column left the village en masse, with their commander in the lead. A few hours after the last soldier had left Burgo (because with the losses suffered it was no longer a question of leaving a rear guard garrison with scant resources for cover), the place was occupied, without a shot being fired, by Eugenio Mazón's people: the pincers of the republican plan had been closed, now all that was left was to see if they were capable of standing up to the enemy attack. At noon, on the hills of red clay, amidst the gulleys and small canyons, along the hollow roads, the battle had begun that would last for seven days with great bloodshed and intensity. Attacked on all sides, the Navarrese clung to the ground, tightening their lines, obliged to fight halfway up the slope; but, having learned from the lesson of the disaster on the plain, they preferred to push on in the direction of the mountain—which was less occupied—rather than tread the flatlands again. Not for that reason did they cease pressure on Constantino's people and in the last days of August they brought the inn of El Quintán under rifle fire, which would be the point of their maximum penetration. The others—doubtless surprised by such tenacity and such capacity for drive—decided to sacrifice their agreed upon strategy to reinforce old Constantino's brigade and try to halt the advance at that point. The Germans of the Theobald column were ordered to abandon their positions on the plain and to climb up to the inn—where the Strausse brothers themselves, forced to fire from the windows during three days of siege, set up their command post and quarters—and Eugenio Mazón's people, going beyond Burgo, went onto the plain to follow the enemy's advance closely at a lower level. But, most of all, they relied on the mobility of the 8.8s mounted on the trucks from Canada, with very high axles and which, moving along the Requerida highway—which the miners, stationed at the culverts, defended with grenades—lent quick and decisive support in

[50]

all sectors where the republican position became engaged. So that under such a strong attack the colonel had to adjust to the circumstances and saw himself obliged to halt the advance on the last day of August; thinking that he still held enough cards to bring off an orderly retreat along the same axis as the advance, he decided to double back against Burgo, which was reoccupied on the night between August 31st and September 1st. It was what the others had been expecting: knowing that he lacked the strength to get out of there, their only concern was to complete the encirclement; Mazón turned back toward the bridge again, a terrain he knew like the back of his hand; Constantino's force, after losing contact with those retreating (a disengagement that was caused and accelerated by skirmishes on the part of the Germans to the south of the stronghold) went on to occupy the Macerta highway, aiming to cut off the last avenue of escape and to bring about the final destruction of the whole division; they placed the field artillery on the lower slopes and went down to the plain with the pieces on trucks. Between September 1st and 3rd Burgo would change hands three times; but on the afternoon of the last day the republicans would barely take the trouble to occupy a pile of calcinated and smouldering stones, sprinkled with rags and corpses, which, at nightfall, would sink into the silence—altered only by the sputter of burning beams, the moans of the wounded, the sporadic and crazy rattle of burning cartridge belts—from which it would not emerge for the rest of its days. Old Gamallo got news of the disaster when the outcome was foregone; even so, he was able to muster all the coolheadedness, courage, and lack of prejudice necessary—in contradiction to his own feelings, put aside now—to regroup his scattered garrisons and to undertake an attack in support of the surrounded forces. At the head of some fifteen hundred men he only got there in time to watch, from a high point, the holocaust of the division; he waited for two days on that height, halfway between Burgo and Doña Cautiva Bridge, with his periscopes fixed on that pile of dust and smoke where everything, including the civil war, seemed to have been consummated. After witnessing, motionless and hidden, the movement of a republican column in the direction of the bridge and convinced that all of the enemy forces were withdrawing to their rear bases along the same lines where they had mounted the attack, he initiated a cautious infiltration in the direction of Región in search of survivors that the men of the Republic had left to their fate, aware that winter, freezing weather, and herdsmen would finish them off in a more economical and thorough way. He only managed to find a scant hundred worn-out and bearded men, their eyes hollow and their faces disfigured by blisters, who, after a week lying on rocks or with half their bodies in the water of a ditch were as incapable of noticing the arrival of their liberators as of removing the ants or mosquitoes from their mouths. For almost a week he roved through the theater of battle, using every means to pass unnoticed and ready to spend all the time necessary, saving as much as possible, to obtain as much information as he could and to discover the most practical and expeditious path to bring him back to the Macerta side of the mountain. That wandering about lasted almost a month, hiding on roads and byways, not returning the fire of enemy patrols, going over the same route time and again, following the lines of convergence of the republican positions and, finally, digging graves for his two hundred casualties. He didn't pass over through Socéanos or La Requerida, but over a much higher and more southerly pass, from which—if it had been a clear night—he would have made out the smoking horizon of Región and the flow of a few lights that were barely ever turned on in those times. He dedicated that winter in Macerta to the study and drawing up of an anachronistic report to the High Command in order to give a full account of the reasons for the defeat and its possible correction in a future attack. Perhaps the person to whom it was sent, having recovered from the emotions of Teruel with difficulty, paid scant attention to it and only commented about it to his superior with the merciful recognition of one who has seen himself in more difficult situations and has known how to get out of them successfully. But at some level of the High Command there must have been someone who saw in Gamallo's report—a premonition that would be worth the old man's colonelcy—a plan whose possibilities and implications were beyond the practical executors of the war, men at the front who think that the destruction of the enemy is the only aim in a civil war. In his report Gamallo backed an attack on Región in the grand manner, following in a general way the same route as the unfortunate colonel who had fallen in the Burgo Mediano action and based not only on his knowledge of the previous campaign, but also on many other reasons, obvious in a certain way for any man with an easy knowledge of that territory. In the first place because he had shown clearly and quite amply that the taking of Socéanos Pass, in stable weather, would not call for any sacrifice other than a large-scale mountain expedition; second because the occupation of the whole lower Torce valley—making progress in the direction opposite to the flow in order to be facing those narrows and points of resistance where a few men with a machine gun could halt the advance of a company—meant a campaign of at least four months and a prohibitive number of killed and wounded. Consequently, once the heights of Socéanos were taken, as they are two-thirds of the way along the valley, the forces of the Republic would have to choose a defense in Región and undergo encirclement or, as long as they faced an offensive capacity that forced them to give up the division of forces that had given them such good results in the previous campaign, to seek refuge in the upper valley and in the mountains. If they decided to defend Región and retreat downstream, all that was necessary was to pursue them in the direction favorable for the movement and wipe them out on the lower plains, sending out a force that would bot-

[53]

tle up the exit from the valley at the junction of the Torce and the Formigoso. Otherwise, if they chose to take refuge in the mountains, it was possible to assert that by merely laying on the operation in that way, Región would be taken along with the most desired and valuable part of the valley without need of firing a shot, reducing the pocket to a mountain sector of eight hamlets and fewer than a thousand inhabitants lacking the resources most essential to sustain organized warfare for more than a couple of months. The whole report, in fact, was nothing but a string of sophistries that the most inexpert officer on the High Command— knowing that the last thing the liquidation of the Región front called for in those days was an operation in the grand man-ner—could have torn apart with marginal comments. But in March of 1938, both at Army Group North and in Supreme Headquarters, a certain number of the highest ranking offi-cers—who with deep-seated suspicions were watching the political ins and outs of the organisms of the new State—couldn't escape their own fears concerning the progress of the Aragon offensive: their triumphal frenzy would change in mid-April of that year, with the spectacular capture of Vinaroz and the splitting of the republican map in two, into an appetite for speed first and into vertigo over the abyss later. Certain practical executors of the war understood in those days that up till then they had only sought victory, paying no attention to its consequences and inevitable de-velopment, leaving to men of the rear—who had never held a rifle or put on boots—the fruits of their triumph. All the offensives, if they can be called such, that would be under-taken in the spring and summer of 1938, would be trans-lated, through the express desire of the High Command, into battles of attrition, in frontal attacks which wear out cadres— field cadres often replaced by political officers—in long campaigns of useless attrition with the sole object of pro-longing to its bitter end a completed war with an establish-ment of victors who are too numerous and too restless. The

Italians of the CTV (at the moment when they could pull out their long thorns) and the Moroccan divisions—all politically inoffensive—are hurriedly and inexplicably withdrawn from the front lines to be replaced by fresh units coming from Valladolid, Galicia, Navarre, and the Maestrazgo, men who jubilantly occupied the trenches and who—before the manipulation of weapons—had learned to sing the triumphal airs with which they made ready for their entry into Madrid, Valencia, and Región. The Gamallo plan was consequently one of those last-minute ones and was studied severely and rigorously and was finally chosen as the most suitable for ending the campaign with the help of a couple of divisions of enthusiastic and pugnacious Navarrese, honorbound Vallisoletans, and phlegmatic and reticent Galicians, whose names were inscribed on a few crosses and marble slabs, the ornaments with which the new State decided to pay for the destruction it had brought to that region resistant to its credo. In a few weeks the author of the plan was elevated to a colonelcy and trucks—captured from the enemy on the eastern front—began arriving in Macerta crammed with soldiers and chaplains, all manner of supplies, and the most useless equipment for the prosecution of the offensive: field kitchens, autoclaves, signal equipment, flares . . . but not a bit of artillery. In any case, that campaign provided the opportunity for Colonel Gamallo—who had joined the launching after certain hesitations—after so many years of waiting, to consider it as an extravaganza in the realm of juvenile fantasies. It was no longer even a question of vengeance. Even rancor had disappeared to make way for the curiosity that had been reborn in his spirit and which—with the placet of his own daughter, held as a hostage in Región, which pushed him to the front in anguished personal contact that the exchange service arbitrated during the last stages of the battle—he was prepared to sacrifice at any price and which, when he was young, neither his pride had dared to anticipate as payment for the affronts, nor his honor as settlement of the gambling debts, nor his self-respect as vengeance on that provincial Don Juan who had cheated in the game and taken his wife away. In Macerta he had requisitioned a two-story house on the outskirts of town very similar to the one he had lived in with his aunts when he was a student. One of the rooms—which no one entered but he, locked in his absence—had been papered with all the 1:50,000 scale maps of the Torce valley (many of which were only blank spaces surrounded by altitude curves of doubtful accuracy), daubed with crosses, rhumb lines, tricky ellipses, and enigmatic inscriptions: "pile of files," "the dead donkey," "here the shepherdess," "we return." Every morning he was picked up by an olive drab staff car, with a chauffeur and two aides from his staff, to whom he rarely said a word; he barely returned their salute—a way of lifting his finger to his visor that was neither military nor civilian, a norm that, skipping over regulations, was being made into a way of making his disdain eloquent—when they opened the door for him and he got into the car after looking at the sky at the same time that he tightened his lower lip with an expression of permanent gloom. He didn't confide any of his plans to them and limited their work in common to matters of formalities. In secret—even when he didn't avoid any opportunity to show the personal character of all wars—he was wary of them and not so much because of their brilliant future (for it was about them, no doubt, that the newspapers spoke when referring to tomorrow), nor because of their technical haughtiness or their self-assurance and intransigence in matters of patriotism, but because they lacked a personal motive that brought them into the war and because they spoke about patriotism too much. Besides, he had to justify that unexpected promotion and conceal his cynical appetite for curiosity with a turn toward barracks taciturnity and—in some way—military lineage. He couldn't let his intentions show through and he imagined that a certain harshness, a certain repugnance for command and action were the best disguise for covering up a vengeance that no one now had any reason to remember in spite of its having taken place in the same territory, where an adulterous woman, a provincial Don Juan, and a gold coin on a gambling table destroyed his career and ruined his future. When, during the years of the Second Republic, his companions in arms who had repudiated him and obliged him to take off his uniform, found the same fate, they didn't hesitate to call him back to their side, with protestations of recognition and forgiveness, inviting him to join them in the conspiracy; he replied evasively, his eyes fixed on that mountain of heather where a rider with a bandaged hand tries in vain to transform his weakness of character into an appetite for vengeance and convinced once again that in that quest a change of esteem played no part but, rather, a need for help. But things changed in July of 1936 as a consequence of the advantage he could extract from the unrest that drove his colleagues. He knew that they would spare no effort to dismantle the government of the country at that time, which bothered them so much. Ready for anything, they seemed only to be waiting for the best moment to act—as is fitting in people who are accustomed by their profession to calculate the probabilities of success of an action as daring and as decisive as the one they proposed. In the first place, they counted on the rancor of the privileged classes, on the hesitation of an inexpert and timid government, and on the brutality of uncivilized and ingenuous masses, clumsy and bloodthirsty, less than satisfied with leaving the accounts of four centuries settled with the arson and murder of one anticlerical night. Apart from all that, he had never been a man with a future; the best opportunity in his life had come about when he was a child, when—as a consequence of ailments of the chest, of the sterility of his aunts—he became the only male heir of a family in which there had been an abundance of military men and which had a certain pride in its name. His mother—the only sister who had married and had had children—made an unfortunate match with a man without character who lived in a provincial capital, separated from his wife and his children, who were again sheltered by her father's hospitality, the only one capable of giving them the nourishment and education that they needed. Only once a year, during a brief period at Christmas vacation, did they go to visit him: he can barely remember an angular room with a foot-warmer table, a studio couch, and a fringed lamp; a single dresser holding two shirts for street wear, medicine, and the dessert platter, some mandarin oranges and a bit of nougat left over from Christmas. And a sad father, bitter and silent—without a word of reproach—sitting by the window next to the grimy curtain, reading the newspaper that he left on the rocking chair when they came in from the street to observe, standing, with furtive glances, the placement of the tablecloth and the plates on the foot-warmer table. He was a man with fine features, not too corpulent: he seemed to have no other gift than that of transforming light—even that of a Castilian summer noon—into that straw and purple coloration of a melancholy face. But his upbringing had taken place in Región with his aunts (every night they recited the rosary before a small oil or wine spirits lamp), who taught him to walk straight first of all. In the Región house there were two words that dominated all others: money and manhood, the first dominated through hypocrisy, the second through furor. The eldest of the aunts—she put her hair up in two balls over her ears, which gave her the look of a precursor of the telegraph or a test pilot—was the one who took upon herself the responsibility for making him understand what both of them meant. Alongside dignity there was the surname: every two or three months they would pay a visit to the cemetery, to a simple horizontal stone with so many male names that it was a memorial all by itself, before which they would kneel in Indian file, crossing themselves, pounding their breasts, and looking at the sky as they whispered the semi-Latin words of the Prayer for a Soldier. They only went

[58]

out to visit and to walk—two, three, four deep, with the child to one side—their chins held high, turning their heads in little jerks, just like a carnival procession of big-heads lacking a view of the ether, receiving—through shiny smooth balls of hair—coded messages about surname, decency, composure, and dignity. Every year, with the arrival of good weather, the matrimonial hopes of the youngest would be regenerated, as she was linked through an age-old engagement to a dreamy young man from a merchant family who only knew how to ride around on a bicycle. So that in the summer they often strolled with the bicycle man, who walked along the sidewalk, discreetly separated from his betrothed—who in those circumstances was assigned to lead the child by the hand—by the three older sisters, who always arrived home in a sweat. They would enter fatigued, burdened no doubt by a feeling of futility and stagnation brought on by the indecisiveness of the cyclist or by the accumulation of inhibitions that decency imposed, and, in the foyer in shadows bathed in the smell of the pavement and the aspidistras watered at noon, they fell without a puff into the old wicker chairs and focused on the child a joint look where all the wrath, the deferred hopes, and the uneasiness about a condition which the man could not decide to join for fear of losing his money were distilled; this is the flash that the child's mind will fix forever in a horrendous negative—a circle of mute and admonitory looks in the depths of a summer penumbra with the buzzing of fans and the agitated breathing of breasts in mourning—the indelible mark of his own formation: he will reveal it again years later in moments of combat; over the gaming table, pouncing upon the pile of mother-of-pearl chips, unaware, still unaware, of the gesture of a woman who retreats through the empty salons while the people run toward the table where his hand remained run through by the knife; on the back of a lazy mule, his mind (spurred by the vengeful and rancorous echo of the fans) concerned only with the weight of the coin he

[59]

never got to hold in his hand. Because all of that had been foreseen and decided as the consequence of an upbringing that rested on that implicit matter; such was duty—at the time his father had already gone down to the realm of shadows; he had never written him and only from time to time, while dozing, would there appear the melancholy of an expression wrapped in a cerulean light that barely lighted his taciturn cheekbones and forehead, in which there was no censure, rather a mitigated but impassable retraction born of a different concept of money—a correlative of the glory of the surname, a dogma with which to cloak the object of his urge with mistrust, a hereditary form of defense against the slander of the soul. Able to assume it had been the gentleman in a white jacket and striped shirt and straw hat who every Sunday morning leaned his bicycle against the fence, but he too was conquered, in spite of his pusillanimous spirit. And yet . . . he was also a different face—although more smiling—of the same corruption and the same avarice. During the winters, shut up in the attic on the top floor from where one could catch a glimpse of the mountains, they busied themselves sprucing up, with all the ornaments of silk and brocade that were left at the bottom of the trunks, an evening dress of indigo blue that one day finally she would use to put an end to the terrible battle between the two idols that fought in the house. They had mounted it on a tall dummy with an ample figure—which the woman would never be able to equal—which for many years now had presided over that sewing room converted into a temple and which seemed to fill the whole house with the enigmatic outpourings of a secret and forbidden cult. But he seemed to laugh at his own cult and sneer at his devotees. Sometimes, secretly, he would go up to see it; it stood out against the silhouette of the mountain range in the window, lighted by the moon, and might be said to be exchanging sibylline and threatening messages with it in a language of sparks that passed between the satin bodice and the limestone peaks. It was a plot from which the bicycle man was not removed either, and he had to flee—without saying good-bye or packing his bags, his vehicle found later in a grove of cork trees—perhaps the day after receiving the most meaningful warning in the sewing room: a rifle shot that cut off, like the explosion of a rocket, the trip through a lonely path in the mountains of a calash wrapped in a cloud of dust. Then came reclusion, the years of study and avarice. One clear afternoon in October the eldest of the aunts accompanied him to the crossroads where the coach to Macerta stopped, a highway flanked by golden poplars and sprinkled with dead oak leaves the color of dry blood. All the years at boarding school—corridors with bright tiles, nankeen aprons, and a farm smell that came out of the kitchen and seemed to impregnate all the hallways and classrooms, and the whispering steps of the violent brothers, and the rainy Sunday afternoons, contemplating the formation of pools and channels in the courtyard—passed in the hope of receiving money that never came; not only was he left out of all the extras, but when Christmas or Easter came he had to watch himself being left behind for lack of a ticket on the mail coach that beyond the wall of rebaked brick and cinders passed by every morning in the direction of Región, piercing the purple dawn with its fearsome sodium light. He spent eight years at the boarding school, not leaving it even for vacation periods, when the whole student body was reduced to four needy pupils who slept in a half-empty dormitory and ate in silence in the rear of the dimly lighted refectory, presided over by the one-eyed layman who took care of the garden, and separated by a curtain from the chattering and shouting brothers as, in the absence of discipline, they gathered at a single table to enjoy their leave at their ease. Then the letter came: it was a simple and brief formula, similar to the one a bank uses to inform its customer on the status of his account (and which, in the same way, seemed to demand his conformity with the figures), by means of which his aunt was pointing out to him that today's sacrifice and saving are nothing but tomorrow's well-being and manhood.

More or less as he had foreseen, during the first ten days of that month of September Colonel Gallano's forces raised their flag at La Requerida Pass again at the 5,380 foot mark, after a six-day march and no casualties other than the usual ill and injured, a couple of dead and six wounded from rifle fire, fallen in a night skirmish with unidentified republican elements. It was a Saturday. On Sunday morning—a clear day in which the north wind was blowing and the clouds coming from the Bay of Biscay were clustering on the horizon—a field mass was celebrated at the pass and special rations were distributed with canned meat from Mérida. The colonel wasn't to be seen all day; he wasn't at the mass or at the officers' mess, nor did he inspect the troops as announced for mid-afternoon and he limited himself to giving the order—through an aide—to fall out after four hours of useless formation. The higher-ranking officers tried, after retreat, to have a meeting with him so as to confirm and go over the instructions for the following day and which at no moment had he taken the trouble to draw up with the necessary detail. He kept them waiting for several hours while he drank a glass of raw milk and was lost in the contemplation—by the light of a carbide lamp—of a provincial postcard from before the Dictatorship. He didn't want to convince or argue; he didn't want any criticism, recommendations, or questions; he hadn't the slightest intention of letting them participate in a tactical plan based largely on the independence of sectors and on the fulfillment on the part of each unit of an assigned duty, regardless of the results of its neighbor. He knew that his plan, more than censurable, was inexplicable and not even he had any express desire to clarify it for himself; it was madness, the only adventure that a responsible leader would not have allowed himself no matter what he thought of his adversary's strength.

But the adversary scarcely mattered at that point; he was the last consideration to enter into calculations, and not because the experience of the previous campaign or more recent information might have led him to disdain him, but because such a factor, by not being decisive with respect to results of the campaign, might just be with respect to a definition of the motives that lay behind it. When one studies and campares the development of the two campaigns of 1937 and 1938 one can't understand too well how such similar executions could have led to such different results and how slow, old Gamallo was able to move along successfully where, a few months before, the Navarrese colonel had done nothing but stumble and fall. Without doubt the adversary was not the same, even though, technically and militarily, he had managed to keep his forces intact if not increased. But not politically; he was a sick body now, lacking any future, hounded by debts, broken by disillusionment, frightened by uncertainty, and given over to the progress of his own illness, "with no heat inside him other than that necessary to feed his fever." The whole course of the civil war in the Región sector begins to be seen clearly when one understands that, in more than one aspect, it is a paradigm on a lesser scale and with a slower rhythm than peninsular-wide events; its development is like the unfolding of dancing images in a film that, on being projected at a slower speed than is proper, loses intensity, color, and contrast. Because in Región there was no coincidence of dates; the republican aim of smothering a military uprising was not simultaneous with the proletarian revolution that pawned its resources to bring about the first. The effects of the July uprising that shook the country were noticed only in August, with the echo of some shooting in the mountains and the uproar of the horns of requisitioned autos mingled with the shouts of women; and the proletarian revolution that was to change the face of half of Spain during that bloody summer came to be repeated, through an effect of mimicry, with the soft and withered tones of autumn. Toward the end of 1936 a mentality more statist than revolutionary began to spread and prevail in the republican sector; in all spirits, their sights set on military victory—an indispensable condition for any other adventure—a certain conservative intention of going back to the *amalgame* began to make its way, in order, at the expense of party and class interests, to create an army ahead of a militia and to put the state ahead of labor unions. But that project, painfully built up and tragically broken to pieces in the countryside by the Jarama and the Tagus, in Brunete and Teruel, in a certain way prevailed in a Región surrounded by silent mountains and small settlements, inhabited by a collectivity that was homogeneous in poverty and lacking a proletariat, which had emigrated ten years before the last barracks-headquarters of the civil guard was closed, and where the most timid attempt at collectivization is considered madness, anticlericalism will never go beyond a few jokes, trade unionism is a pretension, and anarchy a respect for tradition. It was republican by negligence or omission, revolutionary by sound, and bellicose not out of any spirit of revenge for an age-old oppressive order, but out of the anger and candor born of a natural ominous and tedious condition. It prevailed for a year and a half, from the end of 1936 to the autumn of 1938, perhaps because the republican union, which did not have to pamper or indulge a revolution, was formed over a card table and was only concerned—not with socializing industries or collectivizing estates or burning churches or stimulating the political formation of the masses— with heading out to cut off those who were crossing the mountains to interrupt an evening gathering of friends around a deck of cards or a bottle of castillaza. The events of August and September that had not been born violently or spontaneously only served for the creation of that ridiculous Defense Committee, presided over by Mr. Rumbás, which— after helping to abort the August Falangist offensive—was put aside and replaced by a Popular Executive Committee, made up of almost all the men who had taken part in the ascent to La Requerida. On the Executive Committee not only all parties were represented, but also all passions and factions; there was no need to talk about delegates because nobody represented anyone except himself, since a party or a faction—in the Región area—was scarcely made up of more than six members at most, all of whom thought they had the right to attend the sessions. Therefore, more than an Executive Committee it was a parliament where whoever wanted to was seated and where it was possible—until a certain date—not only to air the differences among different groups without taking to the street (which, after all, wasn't interested in such things), but also to adopt large-scale strategic positions—the union of democratic forces, an antifascist line, a return to statism—with a certain tacit popular consensus. It's not that the people of Región had lost interest in politics; in reality they had thought very little about them and even the joyful outcry of April 14th was largely modified because in the whole town there wasn't a single flag to be dyed purple, nor did it enter anyone's head to climb up to the balcony of the town hall—which without doubt was in a state of ruin and would have collapsed, dying the day with mourning—to wave it. Politics—or rather the expression of republican joy and merrymaking—took place in a big old car that Eugenio Mazón had acquired, no one knew how. It couldn't have been with money—his mother didn't give him any and he didn't have any—even though he swore, a little evasively, that it was simply the reward of a lucky card. The car remained for a couple of years, its upholstery rotting among the thistles, cats huddling in its shade, its whole top covered with white excrement, in the garden of the house, where it only served as a hiding place for friends when it was a matter of drinking castillaza late at night. Because the house—silent, run-down, almost all its openings boarded up and the garden sprinkled with rubbish, broken toys and ragged clothing—continued being one of the most respectable in town in spite of the father's suicide and certain missteps by some of the brothers, thanks to the presence of their mother who lived there the year around, completely deaf and half loony, sitting in the shadows of a large wicker chair accompanied by an old serving maid, tirelessly knotting a hemp cord or a velvet ribbon. But in addition to that the car had begun to take on a certain iniquitous fame as a place for amorous trysts, up to the point where certain ladies turned their heads as they passed the garden and many women refused to get in it, even in the middle of the afternoon and in the company of their friends. It wasn't a question of reputation but of practicality that induced Eugenio Mazón to start it up; but only its evil reputation convinced them that, by getting new upholstery and a battery, they could use it to everyone's advantage and get some use from it that was impossible with immobility. Besides, it was a car which could hold eight or ten people all tight together who, in order to take a ride, had to come to a certain common intimacy and forget forever certain requirements of modesty and all the taboos upon which decency imposes the rigors of solitude. For that was precisely what they were trying to break, because in those years there was no other intent in a liberalization of customs than the abandonment of solitude, something that the young people of Región could only do united among themselves and in Eugenio Mazón's car. It also happened that one of those friends managed to sew up—no one knew by what means—his nomination as an independent candidate to the Cortes in the fall of 1933. That candidacy not only served as a pretext for many pleasure rides, but—as a consequence of the expansionist policies of the CEDA and its tactics of cornering forgotten election districts—constituted a bond of union and effort for all those young men who, in their enthusiasm, ordered dark suits from a tailor in Macerta. It was a brief but intense electoral campaign and even women grew accustomed to getting into the rear seat of the car so as, in a square in El Auge or Burgo

Mediano or El Salvador and to half a dozen farmhands who had left their domino game to listen to them in ecstasy, to give their well-known speech about the new sexual freedom that they supported. But even when a program like that would, of needs, generally be suggestive—coming from those lips (and except for a few enthusiasts who in the midst of great extremes and embraces tried to make the proposals effective and theirs without waiting for the vote), it was received with hostility and sarcasm when not with insults and stoning. In contrast to them, the opposition candidates showed that they were up to date: efficient, diligent, and aggressive, they didn't hesitate an instant to bring up short those unexpected amateurs whose program reflected in an obvious way the frivolity of their lives. In order to fight against the money of the CEDA, against socialist ideology, or against clubs of the radical party—and for lack of a political program attractive to the people—they decided to make use of a trained bird that Captain Asián had bought in Las Ramblas for a very good price. It was a large bird, clumsy and black and not very pleasant looking, which, with frantic flapping of wings, would fly for a short distance at six feet from the ground, to alight and, with those impertinent looks of heraldry eagles, give off a harsh croak that always sounded mocking. At first they would turn it loose in the street at the entrance to rallies to attract the public; little by little, the captain—who carried it in a cage hidden under a black cloak— became bold enough to let it out inside halls and even at those snack stands on the banks of the river, where the supporters of a determined candidate would gather, with platters of ham, some pitchers of wine, and a few watermelons, to celebrate the favorable reception of a speech of his. There was no event that could stand up to it, such was its fury and its croak; first they tried to catch it, attracted by its low flight and exposed feet, running after it through the streets, not noticing that only the captain was capable of getting it by blowing a special whistle that the Ramblas man had also sold him. Later on people ran away from it, because it seemed that as it flew it flung off excrement that burned clothing and produced pustules. And finally, when speakers repeated themselves and went on too long, it was called for, sought after, and received with relief and joy. In the end—and in large measure due to the bird and the feminine speeches—the people of Región, although they abstained from voting, couldn't help lamenting the loss of some politics that had given them such good times.

The offensive organized by Gamallo proposed not only the capture of Región, but also the occupation of the whole middle valley of the Torce by means of a series of simultaneous attacks: a first column, the strongest and placed under his direct command, supported by 12/125 pieces and a few Schneiders, would turn in a southerly direction from La Requerida, after crossing the passes where he had retreated the year before, to descend into the valley along a road located between Región and Burgo Mediano, cut the highway that links them, advance toward the river, and continue its march toward Región, on both banks, no matter what the enemy's disposition might be. The second column, green troops and rear guard militiamen who had never been under fire till then, grouped around a nucleus of veterans of the Civil Guard, with two batteries of howitzers mounted on muleback and four units equipped with those first Spandau machine guns—more impressive than effective—had a certain defensive character and were—in accordance with the plan—to establish, more or less at the point of Doña Cautiva Bridge, a strong dual position that would attract the enemy's attention and keep busy all of its forces located upstream from that point. If such forces did not exist, it would, after a prudent delay, back up the advance of the first, spreading out in echelon in space and time. The third column, some motorcycles and veteran volunteers, equipped with small arms and automatic weapons, grenades and mortars, was to head north, keeping at approximately the 2,850 level, to cross the river some twelve miles from the bridge and, depending on the enemy's opposition, stand firm there or take up the attack again downstream with the aim of joining up with the other formations. By that plan Gamallo hoped, in a matter of no more than ten days, not only to occupy all the middle valley—for some twenty miles—but also to damage the whole republican defense and reduce its strength to a couple of pockets cut off from the rest of the country, obliged to surrender or continue their resistance in the heart of the mountains. It seems obvious that his intentions were not dictated exclusively by the best strategy for the occupation of Región; if that had been his only aim, it would have been enough for him—in those days—either to launch a single frontal attack instead of spreading it out and breaking it up into three phases or to repeat the old techniques—tried and repeated so many times in the north, at Málaga, and at Madrid—of surrounding the city, cutting off its supplies, spreading panic, and leaving open one of its avenues of escape so an enemy with scant spirit for defending himself could evacuate by that way. In that campaign of 1938 there are several enigmas, many things that are not understood if they are analyzed solely through the prism of the economics of war; there persists, one might say, not only the desire for the final liquidation—and in as short a time as possible—of the enemy's resistance, but also—once the inevitable result that assures victory has been achieved, guaranteed already in spite of some local reverses—for the assurance of political stability in order to come to the end of hostilities with a minimum of threats and dangers and a maximum of internal security. The whole campaign of 1938 could have been resolved with greater economy and in a shorter time with a single attack launched against Región. He would have—inevitably—taken the place in a few days and—with a show of strength, energy, and resolve—placed all the republicans in a situation where they would have had to lay down their arms. Because, even if it seems paradoxical, a surrender en masse or the abandonment of all will to resist could have been brought about by the occupation of one single point, Región. On the contrary—the other face of the same axiom—stretching the fighting out over long months across an extensive and complicated sector of the valley only managed to encourage hope in the heart of the enemy, increase the will to resist, and prolong the campaign down to the consumption of all his energies among some sharp crags and inaccessible, rugged ground of that mountain he had longed for so much but had never managed to set foot on.

First contact was established at dawn on September 13th, along the Macerta-La Requerida highway, some four miles from the bridge. An advance by volunteers, coming off the slopes and going onto the flats, came within sight of it at noon on the 12th, bringing it under mortar fire for that whole afternoon. In the early morning they saw themselves under sporadic shooting, coming from the Macerta side, which—to their own surprise—was pushing them toward the river. Since they suspected an ambush, they decided against crossing it. For five days an uncertain and not too energetic battle went on, with shooting across the river and without any combatant's getting closer than five hundred yards from his adversary. When reconnaissance informed them of the size of the nationalist column, all the republicans in the sector decided to regroup on the right bank and wait for the attack, moving and maintaining artillery control of the highway. Until the 22nd they were able, with the concentration of Mazón's whole column in a limited sector facing the abutment of the bridge—digging trenches on the sides and hiding their mortars in the heather—to hold off the enemy attack, which managed to advance along the esplanade opposite only sporadically and for a few hours: the last Moors—bluish stockings and broad capes, a white kerchief and an occasional red cap that peeped from among the hedges—who, roused up by cheap cognac, tried for seven days and nights to assault the old flagstone towers (and as descendants of the same tribesmen, the same necklaces of bone, jade, or malachite strung together with esparto cord, the same beads and the same canvas bags loaded with dried fruit from the Rif, the same Maghrib dust that twelve centuries before had forded the same river with the same Hagarene shouts to cut up a hundred knights erect under their standards, whose moans and clank of armor amidst the splashing of the horses in the water seem to evoke and interpret the commemoration of a date again every year, the days of the freshet), to lay under the smiling and timeless gaze of the Bourbon lion resting on his escutcheon a few corpses that in the light of the moon on the esplanade gleamed like sheaves on a threshing floor, their capes moved by the morning zephyr while the new light of day aroused the shrieks of the wounded, maddened by thirst, who dragged their viscera across the sand and called to their comrades in arms hidden among the thorns. On the night of the 24th Julián Fernández's brigade—much larger—joined Mazón's group in expectation that the enemy attack would be launched in that sector with its best forces and energy. But doubtless the enemy, after that first and eventual reverse, decided to reorganize and reconsider the situation for three days of relative calm; action ceased on both sides and reconnoitering increased, trenches were dug, positions were consolidated and reinforced, machine-gun nests were placed in high points. During the last days of September the cancer that was threatening the republican organism showed some symptoms that demonstrated the extent of the illness and the inevitable end of that sick body, which only yesterday had a look of health and the reserves necessary to overcome the crisis. But the body that in 1937 had learned—by making an abstraction of its own discords—to forget about its constitutional ills in order to fight the exogenous illness, had already abandoned itself to the process of the illness, shaken by rebel cannon fire, the fighting among groups, and personal differences, and was dismembered into a number of factions that no longer worried about the health of the whole. It was an organism—that Defense Committee transformed into a Popular Executive Committee and transformed back into a Junta of Defense—that wasn't hierarchical, a kind of parliament without any government that found itself very far from being able to cut off personal discords and decisions; for that reason, a few hours after a political leader left the meeting room in anger—in the town hall of Región or in the neighboring building that the Committee had requisitioned, or in the Sebastián clinic, or in the hotel of ill repute on the highway to the mountains—people in the lines would abandon their positions to retire to a private domain and continue the campaign as franc-tireurs, when they weren't shooting at their former comrades in arms. Since after ten days of the offensive the Junta was unable to make a decision—not even that of abandoning Región—the defense was maintained and continued at all points with no other plan except what each one, on his front, was able to work out under the dictates of his own judgment. The group made up of Asián, Mazón, and old Constantino, in favor of abandoning Región and arranging as far as possible a negotiated surrender, managed, to a certain degree, to preserve the discipline of friendship and maintain during the whole campaign a line of conduct that was unanimous, economical, and logical, even though dictated by certain defeatist feelings. Negotiation became impossible—and all their efforts and sacrifices useless—because of the intransigence of other groups who, deceived by their strength and their beliefs, raised the insignia of resistance to the death without stopping to think about their famous invincibility. Even in those last days of the year the greatest obstacle to abandoning Región was not the insurgents' bridgeheads or their irregular and unpredictable bombardments, or the air attacks that with only two appearances to machine-gun a highway crammed with evacuees spread panic, but was the forces of Julián Fernández, who, stationed at all exits and crossroads, seemed more disposed to watch over the observance of orders from their leaders than to defend themselves against the common aggression.

On the night of the 27th, obeying instructions sent by messenger from Región, the three hundred men of the Mazón column—under the protection of the bombardment—abandoned their positions on the esplanade and, splitting up into small groups and following different paths, began their march toward the mountains to regroup some fifteen miles upstream from the bridge, with the object of opening and securing a route into the mountains that would be ready for the political fugitives from Región. The latter, surrounded as they were by the hostility of all the elements of the 42nd, could only count on the protection of a small personal guard lodged in the same building as the Committee and the more than doubtful support of the people of Asián who, with the help of the Germans, was defending in the Bocentellas sector direct access to Región along the left bank, facing the main body of Gamallo's forces, in such apparent lack of haste and aggressiveness. The action at Porticelle, Nueva Elvira, and Bocentellas came to define the lines of action of a direct strategy whose object was not difficult to surmise; toward the end of October, Gamallo was entering Bocentellas, a burned-out village among whose ruins lay the annihilated remains of the old Theobald column, three dozen Germans, Central Europeans, and Jews who, lacking ammunition, preferred leaping into the flaming barns rather than surrendering to the insurrectionists. Then, in all of its extension, the price that the command of the 42nd would have to pay for its indecisiveness of the previous two weeks became evident. Because, as the attack on the bridge progressed, by securing the position on the right bank and cutting the Región highway for the distance of a mile, the problem of where and how and why to set up a defense flourished with the greatest demanding and unavoidable urgency every time that, in those days, after two months of struggle, it was easy to imagine where surrender led. Only old Constantino—the first among the defeatists to renounce a peaceful solution—understood that with the main body of Gamallo's forces camped on the Nueva Elvira plain, the only viable way out was to abandon the defense of Región so that, by grouping their forces, they could try to wipe out that bridgehead and recover possession of the highway. During the course of that last and dramatic week in October, Región was left deserted; deserted it will always be, eaten by the leprosy of the bullet marks, roofs full of holes, and sewers open, the wind that swirls and whispers through the openings, the torn drapes, the doors that squeak on their hinges and beat against their frames, incapable of being closed on an age of shame and stupor; sunken in dust and surrounded—like the Nineveh of Jonah—by fire, ash, and flintstone, the woebegotten emblem of that fratricidal will. It also remained in the dark, except for one instant at the tail end of the battle, isolated in that somber hinterland between two armies ready to fire the fatal shot and—it might be said—slowly sinking into the shadows of history, surrounded by the fleeting flash of cannon fire and the blinking of the bivouacs, like the lights of small fishing boats that have abandoned their tasks to run to the place where the colossus is sinking. Gamallo's advance was halted, with the news of the break in the line of the 42nd, when his advance troops reached the first houses on the left bank; but they didn't decide to enter or even to cross the river, while on the *épave* surrounded suddenly by shadows, smoke, and mist, the echoes of the street fighting rang out, the crisp and regular sound of the Moroccan snipers and the languid reply of the bursts, growing in its furor to the unlikely pitch of the final display of a fireworks festival, ending with a few furtive flares, sparkling remains, and pink pinwheels. Old Constantino had no doubt guessed his thoughts and tried to anticipate them as far as his forces went; he evacuated almost all the forces from the town, surrounded it with a cordon of sentries, and through reciprocal

[74]

efforts tried to bring about the linkage between the 42nd and what was left of the 17th in order to bottle up the enemy garrison at the bridge, having decided to come back against the main front once he got rid of the threat to his left flank. But in that relief operation the battles at the bridge would be prolonged over twenty days more in which (along with an endless string of switches in fortune) that Spanish *Landsturm* miscellany composed of peasants, very few workers, old anarchists and ideologues, communists of the new stamp, three or four career military men faithful to the republican ideal, and some musters of young men whom only conscription was capable of drawing out of their rustic atony demonstrated once more the same vices and virtues as in the days of Hannibal and Sertorius: insecure and violent, as undisciplined in moments of victorious ardor as they were uncontrollable in moments of dismay. It was nothing else but an aggressive force sent off after its prey—disdainful of all forewarning, indifferent to plans, and lacking in resistant fiber to such a degree that it was never able to consolidate its sporadic triumphs—scarcely ready or prepared to bear up under the rigors of a *guerre à outrance* and, as soon as its aggressive desire was satisfied, its appetite seemed to be free of all warlike intent and its only urge was to find a place where it could withdraw to the side and hide, fleeing the consequences of its previous conduct; it was like an animal in heat who, after consummating the sexual act, seeks, restless and panting—its eyes rolling and its hair standing up— a hidden and safe refuge where it can shelter its exhaustion—even when the republican forces managed on two occasions to attain their local objectives, they stayed out of combat. The points of the push managed to join, crossing the Región highway again, and forcing the enemy to go back across the river; they were cut once more as a consequence of the reinforcements that Gamallo dispatched—peacefully sitting opposite the shambles of Región—and the battle was limited to and centered about the possession of that crossing. The following effort—the most aggressive and bloody drive, the only one that the 42nd fought inch by inch, aware, perhaps, that it was a matter of the last one—developed in the opposite direction; after abandoning the whole sector between the bridgehead and Región, the forces of the Republic, before the final flight into the mountains, attacked in a north-south direction and came into possession of all the flat land by the bridge—it was the middle of November and the first snow had fallen—which in the last days of their combat would be the scene of their end: their objective, their trap, and their tomb. On getting news of that final action, the old fox decided to shake off his drowsiness and abandon his camp opposite the village plain and—crossing it without need to occupy it—go on to deliver the final blow to that unfortunate force which, dazzled by the conquest of the bridge, had refused to perceive that it no longer had any reserves left to defend it with. Then the occasion he had dreamed of ever since he had planned the operation presented itself: to go upstream along the valley, in a northerly direction and with a division under his command, which was considerable and unified, in pursuit of the remains of a combat group that would try to seek refuge in the mountains by all means. He withdrew the recruits and the Moors, gave leave to the cadres who had shown outstanding and gallant deportment, and, placing the Navarrese in the point of the advance, began that slow and sure march that would end in the ancient domain of his elders. A month later, on a day he was to visit his advance forces and a little after he had left the small headquarters he had set up in Dr. Sebastián's clinic, at a bend in the highway his car was fired upon by a guerrilla group and there, in a ditch and in midmorning, along with his driver—only an aide escaped with some head wounds—died the man who, by mobilizing a whole army, had attempted, with the pretext of an old affront, to violate the inaccessibility of that mountain and bring to light the secret that its backwardness holds. A few days later the High

Command ordered the mopping-up operation suspended *sine die* and the war came to an end in the mountains of Región, leaving things (as far as tradition is concerned) not only just the same as they had been in the year 1936, but aggravated by the hidden and undenied presence of a few men of the resistance who sought shelter in the forbidden terrain.

Years later it will be asserted that it's a matter of a ghost army (with clothes, flesh, and hair besmeared), hidden among the broom patches, that floats foglike over the unhealthy fens and which rises up from amidst the heather in the early morning as the night mist withdraws. A new spectral regiment that has come to join the fierce Carlist volunteers who sank their lances and planted their streamers in the valley of the Tarrentino; the monastic and blond and armored knights who awaken with the coming of October to stroll with their hauteur and disdain along the banks of the murderous river; the rancorous guards and gamekeepers of the old estates, carbines on their shoulders, tunics in rags, and beards entangled with the same parasitic gossamerlike threads of cotton that grows on wild rosebushes and briers; the old and hostile herdsmen with small, lively eyes who live on the heights and hide under their piles of wood. In reality there is no single exact piece of information regarding those fugitives who—one very cold January morning in 1939—abandoned the last corral, climbing among the brier-strewn slopes with difficulty to be lost in the mists on a day so lowering that even the limestone outcroppings were hidden from sight. It is said that hours later a series of shots caught the attention of a Navarrese advance party that had climbed up to the refuge of Muerte and had come out into the open during the whole afternoon, returning to the same place soaked with water and dew, unable to have found the slightest trace. Nor is there any agreement regarding the identity and number of the fugitives: perhaps there were only ten or fifteen—according to common belief—and among them Eugenio Mazón, old Constantino carried on a stretcher, wounded in the foot and with an eye bandaged, the godson of Dr. Sebastián accompanied by that mature and enigmatic man who had not left his side during the whole war, three or four soldiers and— bringing up the rear—the elder of those German brothers, who kept looking back (he had straw-colored eyes, an unchanging look, not expressive but emotional) not so much to keep watch as to say good-bye to that valley of the Torce where all of his men had lost their lives.

2

It certainly was a similar car, the same black color as the one his mother had gone off in at the beginning of the war. But if the memory of his mother had been erased—a myriad of small changes by means of which the touch of a cheek is changed into the taste of an apple—that of the car had remained isolated in his recollection, unassailable by sorrow. All afternoon it stood locked up on the highway, under the shade of a live-oak tree, a ways off. All afternoon he watched it, from a distance, behind a stone wall, his eyes fastened on its two headlights, incapable of curing with recollection what memory had sealed with sorrow, until a tall woman suddenly appeared beside it. A purse hung from her shoulder; she was wearing dark glasses that she took off as she opened the car door; she lighted a cigarette and got into the car, after looking at the sky.

Then he began to run, through the fields of newly cut rye, leaping over stone walls; all morning he had been cleaning the irrigation ditch with a long-handled hoe, his feet in the water; when he sat down to eat he spotted the cloud of dust on the Región highway for the first time, but he wasn't startled. Recognition that queries the will in vain about something that had been registered and entombed by solitude, by a thousand sunny afternoons of abandonment, is transformed into upset and unrest; he could barely chew the rye bread and was gradually losing his appetite as he contemplated the cloud of dust that was slowly coming toward him. When he got to the house he was out of breath and his shirt was tied around his waist; he leaped over the gate, ran to the stable, climbed up to the loft, and, dragging himself across the straw, went over to the small window to see the reddish cloud that was momentarily hiding the swirl on the highway. Rarely had he dared enter that room and least of all during the time when the doctor—in later years he scarcely left that bedroom—was accustomed to sleep his siesta in an old black leather armchair. He opened the door quickly, the doctor raised his head and saw him trembling in the shadows; a corpulent and clumsy figure, his back half naked, his head outsize, a pair of large glasses, a mat of prematurely gray hair, and those features lacking energy and character, denoting a person who has matured in apathy and ignorance.

"There it comes," he said.

The doctor, reclining in the chair with his feet on the stool, scarcely moved.

"What are you saying? What are you doing there?"

Consciousness and reality mutually penetrate each other: they are not isolated, neither are they the same, even when both are only habits. Rarely does a nonhabitual event manage to make an impression on the consciousness of an adult, doubtless because his consciousness has covered it with a protective film formed of acquired images which not only lubricates the daily brush with reality but also serves to use a familiar set of sample emotions as a point of reference. But occasionally something passes through that delicate gelatin that memory spreads all over—even though it doesn't know its name—to appear in all its crudeness and wound a defenseless consciousness, sensitive and afraid that only through the wound will it be able to segregate the new humor that will protect it; and then it is converted into a reflex habit, a fictitious recognition, into dissimulation because, really, fear, pity, or love never come to be recognized. There is a word for each of those instants that, although understanding recognizes it, memory never recalls; they aren't transmitted in time or even reproduced because something—habit, instinct, perhaps—will take pains to silence them and relegate them to a time of fiction. Only when that instant comes about does another memory—not complacent and, in a certain way, involuntary, one that feeds on fear and extracts its resources from an instinct the opposite of that of survival, and from a will contrary to the drive to dominate—awaken and light up a time—clocks and calendars don't mark it, as if its own density casts a spell with the pendulums and gears in its bosom—that lacks hours and years, has no past or future, has no name because memory has been obliged not to legitimize it; it only relies on a scarred yesterday in whose very insensibility the magnitude of the wound is measured. The black car doesn't belong to time but to that atemporal yesterday, transformed by futurition into an unpregnant and abortive present. The doctor understands it and looks at him: "All right, all right," because he knows that a person who has undergone depression, horror, or pity is too disabled to know what they are or to seek their proper cure; he knows that the morning at the inn by the crossroads is not part of time either, the morning that degenerated into afternoon while he waited, with his bag on the ground, sitting on the wall by the crossroads, for the arrival of María Timoner. Precisely there is the fear, the depression, the loss of justification of oneself, and from then on he will have to mistrust, reject all hope, yearn for an end. Later, when he opens the door, he will have to say: "Sleep, yes, sleep, it's so obvious! Love, too, is obvious, once it's gone there's no room for pretexts or justification; nothing is worth anything only for itself.

Treatment? The treatment of others? What's that?" Confidence doesn't exist and therefore he no longer has any need to keep track of time; nor do those steps in the empty parlor after the stabbing belong to him; a group of armed men—and their whispering voices, the creaking of the step—who climb up the half dozen steps in the purple hour of dusk, they don't belong to anything because if they are present it's because they were and no longer will be: they return almost every night (whistling, bearded, and barely visible, their steps heavy from the weight of the arms and the fatigue of the hike, the dust of the wasteland) to disappear with the slam of a door at dawn; there also exists, hanging from the rack, a heavy woolen coat that still preserves, after a postwar period of not being used, the dampness of a night of search; all that exists is a long and spasmodic instant haloed by the light of a juvenile excitement converted into desolation, lacking in meaning, in past, in pain, and in hope. And dusk beside a windowpane that catches the light to reveal the half-shadow of the room, a long and somber porch of pale and naked walls and a ceramic floor with uneven slabs and a border of tiles in two bloody colors; it was an old and run-down house, lacking in taste; almost all the rooms were without furniture, the little that was left was grouped in the corners, the walls betrayed the shadows of the mirrors, the pictures, and the diplomas that one day had decorated them, preserving the original color. Only the doctor's office kept the greater part of its old furnishings: a disordered bookshelf stuffed with old newspapers, books, and unbound magazines, an empty bottle or two, and a desk in the same condition, a lamp with a shade and the old easy chair done in black leather with arms and back worn to the stuffing, where the springs peep through and where a man—identified with the furniture—already on in years, contemplates the sunset on the windowpane, that fortuitous and illusory coloration (the garden in abandonment since that hour yesterday—this side and that side of climes, seasons, years, and vigils—which

[82]

reduces it to one single feeling in duration, scarcely altered by the flutter of a flag, the shot of a hunter, or the flight of an eaglet) revived on the first nights of autumn and with the first shadows of the shrubs—always the fiction of an aborted movement, a clump of branches that grew too much and which leans over the ground to bring back to the memory that hunched-over gait—around a moment in suspension in the bosom of a faded yesterday, saturated with a could have been that never reached precipitation. The bells had not yet tolled, the whisper of the poplars had quieted down, the shouting of the troops, the echo of the shots, the clamor of the war songs repeated with an indefatigable and guttural tone by the victorious radios, giving way to the passage of the hours under whose imperceptible wave the might have been that follows and destroys itself is submerged. "Oh, it's not the time," he will say later when he opens the door, "not even fear, the only apparatus for measurement that consciousness has; it's the lack of something else that makes it be something. It's the lack of something else . . ." He had lost all color; his eyes lacked color, nor was his suit black or his shirt white; as if his own colors—and words, of course—had been made from a cloth that had ceased being what it was. He got up slowly, went over to the other window that was shut, opened the blinds, and discreetly watched the length of the highway. Then, his pulse agitated, he closed the blinds again and, from across the table, contemplated the young man—framed in the doorway—with evident upset and pain. "All right," he said to him, "all right." From a drawer in the desk he took out a key and some rope. His eyes, behind the glasses, seemed flooded with tears and his lower lip, with his mouth half open, was trembling intensely. "All right, all right," he repeated going along the hall and up the stairs. In the upper room there was nothing but an iron cot, a wash basin on the floor, and some sandals, a few piles of scattered dirty clothing, sprinkled with mud and straw. The window was protected by a thick and double screen whose exterior

[83]

panel was sprinkled with dead moths and insects. He turned his head toward the window and put his feet together; then, without need for much effort, the young man seemed so accustomed to it, he tied his elbows behind him, leaving his hands free. When he had finished, he softly pushed him along to the edge of the cot and made him lie down on his side with his face to the wall. He said a few words in his ear and, at the same time that he brushed some bits of straw from his pants, a few thorns caught in them, he gave him a few pats on the shoulder and withdrew from the room, double-locking the door.

The automobile stopped a very short distance from the garden gate of the former clinic. Hidden behind the blinds he watched the woman open the door and get out of the car—looking hard at the house—without taking the trouble to close the car door. In a while the bell rang, but the doctor didn't dare open it. He closed the blinds, checked the whole downstairs to see that the doors and windows were locked and went back up to the young man's room, on the second floor, at the back of the stairs, to listen to his breathing through the door: it was deep and rhythmic breathing that at regular intervals produced a weak, metallic squeak, just like an electric clock. He remained that way, sitting by the bottom of the closed door for a long time as computed by the rhythm of the breathing, scarcely bothered by the ringing of the bell downstairs, after spaced and patient periods of silence. He went back down—fidgety, in a state of uneasiness and anxiety—and set about looking for something in his study without knowing clearly what it was. In his bedroom on the old unused dresser there was a pile of papers and articles from under which he withdrew a bottle where a little bit of yellowish liqueur was left. He carried it into the study, half-opened the blinds again to check once more the presence of the automobile (with the doors closed, it was still in the same spot and was receiving the last rays of the afternoon sun on its windows) and took a long drink of liquor. Then he began to cough and shake his head; he seemed unused to the taste of the drink. Some female footsteps could be heard on the cobbled walk, cracked and hollow; he dropped into the chair again, clutching the bottle by the neck, put his feet on a stool, and stuck a finger in his mouth to try to bring on sleep. He wasn't awakened by the bell but by a long, sharp cry from the upper floor that seemed to slice the silence of the house in two; the steps were heard again, a hand pounded on the outer blind and the cry was repeated, followed by some violent thumping by the body that was bouncing on the mattress and trying to get free of its bonds. He peeked at the garden through a crack in the shutter and only managed to see a shadow that was scarcely moving; he went upstairs once more saying, "All right, all right" on each step. On the landing he heard his sobs, he knocked softly at the door. "All right, all right," he said. He hesitated for an instant and finally seemed to make the decision that he had resisted so long; he went to a bathroom and from a small, white, faded cabinet took out a syringe and the hypodermic needles that he cleaned with alcohol, no need to boil them. While—with a trembling wrist but with a skill that indicated long practice—he was filling the syringe with one hand, holding up the ampoule with two fingers, the bell rang again with unusual insistence and the cry was repeated in the room upstairs. With the syringe held high, he uncorked the bottle, took another swig, went up the stairs, and rapped on the door again. "All right, all right, how are you feeling? Lie on your stomach." He listened with his ear to the door, turned the key with his right hand, and opened the door wide with his shoulder. Without giving him time to turn his head, he sat down beside him, ran his free hand under his waist, loosened his belt, lowered his pants a bit, stuck the needle into a buttock with skill and trembling. When he was finished he took a deep breath and ran his hand, with the empty syringe, over his sweat-spotted brow. The young man was lying with his head to one side on the sheetless

[85]

mattress, his mouth half open and panting and his hair in disarray; his glasses had fallen down his nose and his eye, fixed on the wall, seemed to adjust to their freedom of vision with a slow and rhythmic blinking, like the breathing of a freshly caught fish tossed onto the bank of a stream. A lock of hair had got into his mouth; nose, lips, and chin were wet with tears.

On the threshold appeared the mournful figure of the doctor, surrounded by shadows, and while he held the knob he looked at her without surprise, curiosity, or reproach—shy and withdrawn, he was trying in vain to recover the fetid penumbra that came before the gesture that seemed to demand a justification. He hadn't tried one because the longer the wait, the more suddenly the solution comes; it seemed that—looking at the woman and the sky alternately—he was searching for some reasons that he hadn't forgotten but which he couldn't remember: "Oh, yes, I've opened up, of course I've opened up. What difference does it make to whom? What difference does it make when, sooner or later this moment would have to come, something I already knew when I decided on seclusion. You've come, although a little late. You also might not have come and it would have been the same, a prolongation of the delay. You know what I'm referring to, there's no need going into details, *che senza speme vivemo in disio*. Has there ever been a time when it was different? What a question! No, no, it's not pride; there's a seclusion and a denial and an abandonment of everything except peace with oneself that aren't dictated by cowardice but by pride. But what has pride to do with this, I wonder? You should know that in the first years of my profession I covered these lands with nothing but a cart, a mule, a kerosene stove, a slate, and a bell; and that I would announce myself with shouts on village squares, to extract molars, assist at births, and cure dropsy. So it's not a matter of pride; if you'd said logic to me, well that's something else again. And that's the sad part of it, because we've been given a logic in order to think about the future and a past on which to test the results. And, in conclusion, I'll tell you that I haven't been worried at any moment, not even when I was waiting there inside. I'll tell you other things too, things that aren't good for anything—not even to sharpen the understanding—for someone who, like you, has something left to do. I've been watching you carefully ever since you arrived and I've come to the conclusion that you've got too much confidence; it's strange how a person who is said to lack hope can come to trust so much. I don't know in what, and yet that's how it is; no, I'm not referring to a few predictions that don't even exist: the wheel we might have consulted no longer exists. It doesn't matter, I have and I keep a certain security about the kind of end that awaits us and that's why I think sometimes that the only positive note there is in my character has its roots in my lack of resolve. I'm sure too that—out of fear, cowardice, reluctance—this situation has been too prolonged. Everything ends when desire runs out, not when hope clouds over; but the desire that seeks an explanation and tries to justify itself contradicts itself; so that the age of reason and enlightenment is nothing but a survival—and perhaps immortal, as people believe, because it's the only thing transmissible. And if that's not it, what else matters to you about me? Therefore what reason did I have in denying you entry or if you don't want to come in, in keeping the door closed?" He'd scarcely opened it in two years. The house was a rural residence of two stories, of that ever so civil and solemn taste that the nineteenth century implanted everywhere without making any distinction between a city house and a country house, built sixty years before by a returnee from America who didn't live to see it finished; it was completely surrounded by a small garden in a wild state—nettles and shoots had destroyed the former outline, had invaded the walls, and weakened the trees, had buckled the columns of the porch, and had conquered the balcony—fenced in by lance-tipped grillwork, almost all of which had lost its points

[87]

or had fallen down; the entrance lamp had been lost—all that was left was the hook that had held it—and the door had been blinded with sheets of tin, from which the bell hung. A short time before there had been a brief cloudburst and all the gutters were dripping at the seams. The sun was beginning to go down over the hill of elms and live oaks, lighting up with orange tones the edges of a head of hair that still hadn't lost its color or its softness; she was a woman on in years, but in that dim light it was difficult to guess her age; her face wasn't pale or thin but her smile was one of weariness, instantaneous and involuntary sublimation of an art of dissimulation that desires—but doesn't want—to leave translated the true state of her soul in a country sunset; she was wrapped in a light vanilla-colored coat, tight-waisted, wearing low-heeled shoes, and with her hair gathered under a silk kerchief whose knot fell over her back with indifferent and macabre relaxation. She didn't seem impatient, she had rung unhurriedly and without excitement and now she was smiling in a confused light—while the gleaming tufts of hair on her forehead were moved by the evening breeze—with the same serene, cruel, and pedantic delight with which the collection agent calls at a house in financial trouble; a house truly in trouble, a clinic where only the incurable were received and where nothing was known of anything else (doctor, doorman, patient, or whatever he was) but predestination.

"Wait," the doctor said. While she went back to the car he again observed the sky while he left the door ajar. Above the horizon a silent explosion of orange and pale clouds was taking place and from time to time the breeze stopped blowing and the leaves were silent, so that, to the dictates of a wild rhythm, the murmur of the insects and the small ditches that ran under the bushes could be heard. She took from her purse a small leather wallet and took out a card— an ancient yellowed card, wrinkled and with its edges eaten

[88]

away and dirty (or was it a photograph perhaps?) that she handed to the doctor.

"Tell me, do you know if . . . ?"

"I? What makes you think I know something?"

Because he scarcely took the time to look at it. It might be said that he had no need to read it or that—after a quick and sagacious glance out of the corner of his eye—preferred to have recourse to a pretext in order to justify his lack of disposition.

"I haven't got my glasses, I'm sorry."

But she didn't take it back, looking straight at him and moving her head with a gesture in which there was a mixture of disdain and pity and an invitation not to let it go with his refusal. He observed her again and understood that in her attitude—above all in an expression that was no longer smiling and in a look that, serenely, was making no effort to avoid blinking—there was more firmness (and perhaps less hope, more weariness) than what he had presumed. She had also brought a small traveling case which, with the purse, she held in both hands with patient tranquility, as if instead of a resolution from the doctor, she was waiting for the arrival of a train. But he lowered his eyes, stuck his body halfway out, leaned on the door frame, and looking toward the Región highway, said: "It's a very bad road." She nodded without answering a word. "And even though you've picked the best time. Two or three weeks later and you wouldn't have been able to get here. First the rains, then the snow, and afterward the mud; everything leads to discouragement. So that for four months you can only come up by horse. And what for? Because after a short time here someone who has managed to make it becomes so accustomed to peace and isolation that he soon has to give up the return trip. That's the beginning of the illness. Who is capable of recovering old illusions, then?" He looked at her again with admonitory intent: "So before you go any further I want you to understand the risk you're running. It's easy to come but . . ."

"Do you know what it's all about? Why do you think I'm looking for isolation?"

"No; I don't know anything and I don't think anything, believe me. And I don't want to know either because I don't care about the root of the sickness. And as for the cure . . . it's beyond my reach."

"Do you consider the case so desperate?"

He put the card away from his eyes as far as his arm could reach in order to read it without need of his glasses. After turning it over several times and examining it like an expert who suspects a counterfeit, he held it away again:

"Of course, completely. Beyond all doubt. A lost case." He didn't have the slightest hesitation. "In a little while the sun will set. But the least is knowing the reason for its hiding behind so much rubble. I've never seen its cunning but let's not talk about that now" (he remembered then the rhythm of the tranquil and peremptory ringing of the bell) "the important thing is knowing up to what point it will be capable of facilitating means equivalent to those that it consumes. The trip is madness, of course. There's no cure, if that's what you want to know." He seemed decided not to speak anymore and to cover his presence by turning his look to beyond the trees, with an indifferent and slightly disdainful expression, like that of the doorman of a club who tries to ignore the presence of an inopportune drunkard. He stopped himself, he didn't want to let it be seen that he was tightening his mouth and looking away because in an instant—passing but recurrent—he understood the pain that his own convictions produced in him, no matter how much he wanted—in a different age, with a different pain—it to remain in others, not so foreseen as less reasonable. He breathed through his nose and closed the lapels of his jacket to let it be understood that a chill was approaching; he looked straight at her again, softly nodding his head, with an expression in which were combined reprimand, sarcasm, and compassion.

"Maybe you're right." She was holding the suitcase in both hands. "I thought about it for many years but I could never decide to do it. Not because it was madness, as you say, but because I was afraid of ruining the only thing really sane and clean that I had in me. So it's the uncertainty that has changed into madness, all the rest is cure, extirpation perhaps. It's not that I understand it, but that I confirm it, by my presence here; I've always known and feared that the sane part will end up winning; that is, what you people call the sane part, just the opposite of what I understand by it. But I couldn't permit it without attempting, as a last resort, the final test that I resisted for such a long time, bringing off so as not to fall into the desperation of saneness, of good sense, and of resignation. You're doubtless right, Doctor"—she had opened her purse to take out a handkerchief and bring it to her nose, but she wasn't weeping or sniffling; it was rather a gesture of struggle, the way someone will bring out money in order to force a transaction that the seller is resisting. "What you don't know is up to what point it is; the least part is that it looks like it to a person who is reasonable and enjoys good sense; the terrible thing is that it represents a madness for someone who has never been able to get out of the . . ."

"Out of the . . . ?" the doctor asked.

"I was given to understand that this house was just the place for curing . . . such doubts." The doctor showed no change; he leaned—resting on the door frame—to adjust a slipper on his left foot. "You're not asking for that," he said at the same time as he straightened up. "I haven't asked for anything yet." She closed her purse, aware that it might be the last gesture of the conversation and that there was nothing left for her to do but put away her money. "The road to the mountains; not far from here some time ago there used to be an inn with a not very good reputation. How many miles is it?" "Oh," the doctor answered. The purse snapped;

[91]

she was impatient but not restless; there was something in her that wasn't enthusiasm but which exuded determination—even in her steps. "It closed many years ago. It's in ruins. Only some gypsies camp there once in a while, and people hunting chamois." He looked at the sky with mistrust, as if he were expecting the storm to start up again. "I don't understand what you could have lost there. It's like a legendary thing." There was—and it could be perceived— an intimate contradiction in his words; it could be said that they were coming from his soul very much against his will, as if he were repeating a lesson in whose recitation the effort with which it had to be learned is translated. "You forgot this," he told her as he handed her the card.

"That?" she asked. "It was a calling card. What do I need it for now?"

"Oh," he waved it in the air, like a fan. "I don't understand your interest, I repeat. I don't even understand your attitude. They're things that belong to the past. What's the use of all this? Aren't they well off where they are? They're things that belong to the past, that don't count anymore; the only thing that counts is this peace. Do you know that tomorrow might be a very beautiful day? I think it will be cool and clear, a very beautiful day."

"That's what I want; for you to tell me that they don't count. That's precisely what I need; for me to be told that by the only person for whom it does count."

"You're going to catch cold if you stay there. These nights are quite treacherous." He took a few steps forward, crossed in front of her—without looking at her—and closed the door that had been ajar. "I've stopped receiving visitors for some time now." A slight gust of wind blew open the door of the house and for the first time—as he came back—he brought the paper to his eyes with the intention of deciphering what was on it. "Please wait a moment; it seems that bad weather is upon us. Summer doesn't last long here, not long at all. Summer really doesn't last very long"—he was trying to read

[92]

the card on both sides—"not very long." In the vestibule
some old tubular chairs of the kind that are common in hos-
pitals could be glimpsed in the shadows and newspapers were
spread over the floor. An intense smell of closed rooms that
hadn't been aired out for several weeks emanated from inside. A pharmaceutical calendar hung on the wall and still
held some pages of a year long gone by; the chairs—and a
small reception desk—were covered by those embroidered
wool mats and coverlets of faded colors that were the best
exponent of that ingenuous castaway art, having been born
and died in that house: a donkey with saddlebags and a
peasant with an umbrella, a sunset among palm trees, the
belfry of a church, and a bridge over a river, conceived amidst
sighs and desolate looks out the window, sketched with
wanton, patient, and useless prolixity, as only with waiting,
a lack of anything else to do—but not recreation—can a
puerile pastime be prolonged and developed. They were
without doubt the work of that woman she had heard spoken of during the war; she had kept weaving all the time she
was married, spreading her ingenuous embroidery everywhere to fill the hours her husband left her alone, busy
searching the woods for the object of his drive, sitting in a
chair and hiding under the cushion (for fear the doctor might
come in and surprise her at such reading) a book on sexual
hygiene for Christian youth that she never got to finish and
which she always read secretly, amidst alarmed and watchful looks, deep sighs, and impatient twisting. Because during the years her immaculate marriage lasted, not even the
embroidery gave her a moment of peace. It might be said
that the astonishment that the doctor brought her when he
presented himself in her parents' house to contract the marriage was to last until she was on her deathbed. At least he
didn't bring her any more; after three days he had disappeared, wrapped in his brown coat and wearing his city hat.
The first time, after a few months, he had sent a postcard
from a remote city she didn't know (it showed a downtown

street full of people, streetcars, and automobiles) which said, "Don't forget to take care of the plants. If the bathroom drain gets clogged, tell Feliciano at the inn. Yours, Daniel," and which she kept among the pages of that forbidden book. She couldn't help looking at it every day, absorbed, far off, illusory and stupefied, put off by that word "yours," to which she would return time and again to confirm that possession to which the sexual hygiene book was doubtless referring; perhaps those looks and those readings were made of the same substance that would make her yield, thanks to which—and to the art of embroidery—she was capable of feeding and resisting her desire without the necessity of thinking about love. Perhaps she had refused him, a single disappointment would have been enough for her to seek refuge in the chair, the book hidden in the crack behind the cushion, and the postcard held in its pages. At the end of the first year—with the arrival of spring and the cultivation of the plants he had left—she understood how happy she was, the good fortune that her marriage had lavished on her. Her mother-in-law—attacked by rheumatism—dozed and languished in a bedroom on the second floor until, disillusioned, tired of waiting for a hot dinner and a brace to support her back before sleeping, she went off to live with a married daughter who had to tolerate her for only two years more. From then on there was nothing to distract her from her thoughts; she must have felt herself so intimately and constantly joined to the doctor that she began to fear the arrival of the intruder. He would arrive one night without making a sound; her hands would be weaving tirelessly while her look rested on the postcard and the open book in her lap, when the door would open and he would say: "Good evening." Wrapped in his tobacco-colored coat, wearing his city hat, all he did was put his suitcase on a chair; he closed the door again and went to the bathroom to see if the drain was working. When he came back the book and postcard had disappeared and she, with her back to him, her head hidden in the back of the chair, was weeping intensely. With the greatest care—and walking on tiptoes—he picked up the suitcase again, crossed the room, and opened the cupboard where he kept his instruments, medicines, and reference books. He took some items and empty bottles out of the suitcase and replaced them with others from the cupboard until it was filled. All that was heard was the snap of the lock, the muffled sobs on the back of the chair. Passing by her—walking on tiptoes, he observed then, with a certain surprise, that disordered flowering of embroidered pillows and mats with infantile sketches—he stopped for a moment, from the crack in the chair took out the book, whose title he read, and after putting it back in the same place and saying "Good night," he closed the door with the same stealth with which he had entered. He hadn't taken off his coat or his hat, but from that visit on his letters and postcards became more frequent, two or three a year. In one of them, which showed a military parade, he had tried to reassure her with a phrase of which she only understood the last three words: "There are no sins but those of thoughts, but when there is only thought, all is virtue. Yours always. Daniel," which was followed months later by that other one with a view of the Tibidabo, which said, "Virtue, in order to be such, can never expect its recompense. See you later, Daniel." She died a virgin, without ever having learned anything about the man to whom she had been married for twenty years, and probably without having been able to come out of the astonishment (to which her parents were also not alien) with which her nuptials had been brought about—she was startled one rainy afternoon (her father was a crossing guard on the Macerta railroad that never went into service) by that doctor, always wrapped in a well-fitting and long overcoat and wearing a felt hat, whose name she learned for the first time in an outlying parish of Región, and transported in that car that was the delight of her parents, to a rest home that she took possession of after first being ushered into the presence of an old, fat lady in mourning whose

[95]

disdain couldn't be shown, flooded by the wrath that surged from her breast when the doctor told her from the threshold: "May I present Mrs. Sebastián. That is my mother," with the tone and brevity of a person addressing an employee who had been found wanting to introduce his desk— not his person—to the replacement who is waiting in the rear*—and without having given the world any other fruits but those engendered by tedium, surprise, and ignorance, a few labors of hook and needle that still hung from the walls and covered the chairs in the waiting room. But it wasn't a matter of deception, or abandonment, or—least of all—vengeance; the first because, it seems, he confessed his plan to her openly the afternoon of his proposal, leaning on the barrier at the grade crossing, while the bride's parents, all busy and excited with the trousseau trunk, were going in and out of the small house, running and shouting, fascinated by the rented car that was waiting by the door. And she agreed, knowing what awaited her and confident that her wifely virtues, her perseverance, and abnegation would succeed in modifying such an abnormal decision; so that she too sinned of egoism. As for abandonment, it is never such when a man leaves his house—and his mother—to contract marriage. As for being vengeance, against whom? "It's not a question of that," the doctor's godson confessed to her during the period of the war. "It's much simpler; if somebody leaves home some evening, tired and bored up to here, and heads for a café or the movies . . . what the hell, he's not going to go back home just because the café is closed or the movie theater is full. I imagine that he'll look for another one, that's what I think; you mustn't give too much importance to things and, least of all, to marriage. You're saying it's for a whole lifetime? Everything's for a whole lifetime and that isn't se-

---

*His mother, sitting like a queen, openmouthed with surprise, drew in so much breath that she rose out of the chair like a balloon and with her moorings loosened, slipped majestically and without saying a word to the room on the second floor which she never came out of except to leave the house for good.

rious either, if true. This town and this house are also for a whole lifetime and do we give them any importance because of it? Look at this house, he didn't buy it because he liked it but because it was available and at a good price. And he bought it fully aware that death would overtake him in it. So what? If the woman he loved wasn't available, didn't he have to go looking for one who was? And in line with that he was intelligent enough to seek out and choose the most innocuous one, the cheapest and the most expeditious; what I mean is one who would cost him the least affection, one with whom he wouldn't feel (she either, don't forget that) the slightest need for love. You probably think it's prudent to join up with a woman who follows that other one that has to be given up in affection. Well, then, if the first one is given up, affection is given up too, and that's all there is to it, that's what seems to be the most sensible thing. On the contrary, if out of weakness the slightest touch of affection is introduced into the new contract, he's signed a pact with the devil, who will not only make him conform to a painful and unsatisfactory solution, but will make him, for enjoying a little warmth, stir up the fire that will burn him. Where's the sense to that? So that just as soon as he brought you here he went on a trip. What was he going to do? It's certain that she wasn't just a pretext; I'm talking about my mother; and just as well that she didn't keep the date. He was waiting for her all afternoon, with all his savings in his pocket, ready for anything. What she'd intended doing with him she did with my father, that's all. He'd also made preparations for a long trip; a man so faithful to his thought could conform too with a taxi ride to the crossing guard's house. So he went away and if he didn't come back it was less because of her than because of my mother, who decided to have me in Mantua and raise me there; she wrote to the doctor then and told him what was going on and he not only helped her with the birth—without looking at her face, covered with a horrible veil—but from that moment on, every year more or

[97]

less, he took a trip to oversee the rearing and the steps of his godson, taking advantage of it to greet his wife: and see that everything at home—including the bathroom drain—was still functioning normally." Independent of all that, when he went away he had no intention of returning, distant from his mother, who did nothing but eat cabbage soup. The whole house—and she too, in particular, because she'd grown quite fat, thanks to those dishes of cabbage, potatoes, and chopped meat that annoyed the doctor's father—smelled of fermented cabbage. The humblest patients had abandoned it. Then he understood—the same afternoon that he had waited so long—that with the direction events were taking it wasn't just a matter of going away but of trying to see that in that house—which, after all, was his and his alone—no more cabbage would be cooked. So before agreeing upon the ceremony, but after making her privy to his plans for traveling, he asked her if she liked cabbage. "Cabbage, what kind of cabbage?" "Cabbage. I didn't know there was more than one kind." "Oh, yes, cabbage. We don't like it at home; my mother never serves it." "Let's go then. Tell your parents to hurry up, that the car is waiting." So it wasn't vengeance but a solution of fate that had happened to him, around nightfall now, when he was convinced that María Timoner wasn't going to appear, sitting on the wall by the cross-roads, wrapped in his overcoat and with his feet resting on the suitcase. He remembered her then; the first one to notice her had been María herself, one day when she lifted the bar-rier for them (which, since the railroad wasn't functioning, was always closed) when they took the road to go to the casino. "See how funny she looks. The poor girl, having to spend half her life there. What can she think of us except that we belong to a different world." Later he remembered her with tenderness on a couple of occasions. Consequently, it was a case of a transfer of feelings—those that he had for María and which, as a consequence of her nonappearance, were placed in the name of the person for whom she had shown a certain interest at one point and on various occasions—to bring about, with all the strength of the law, the depreciation of a form that, with just a change of names, dates perhaps, crosses the frontier of guarantees. But she was tenacious, she never awoke from her dream to lament it. If she had opened her eyes she wouldn't have been able to lament anything other than the failure of her patient, sleepless, and phlegmatic throbbing—that credulous and proud blood that, obeying a strange moral imposition, tries in vain to adapt to the code of society, that obstinate pulse that awakens every morning, like a child who can only remember a punishment and a prohibition, panting and tearful, who during the supplication, at the same time that he forces his lips into a seraphic and brainless smile, makes the valves of his heart pump as it pounds furiously on its walls to demand an attention that is denied him, that useless and sterile maternal urge silenced by the tinkling of the metallic needles whose offspring she hates and pities in secret.

"You must understand," the doctor said. "There are many things to which one can't or shouldn't return, only because that's what our health demands. It's better to leave them as they are: it's the least we can thank age for: having pulled us out of that mire of the twenties or the thirties. Because that, like summer in this country, is nothing but a legend. It isn't that it doesn't last long, but that it's a matter of a mirage that's rather repetitious, as if to strengthen and reiterate the deception." He didn't seem to be addressing her; he'd left the door open after having invited her in and was talking alone, distracted and absent, at the same time that he was putting his glasses on to read the piece of paper. Then he put it down—dejected but not upset—with that clinical expression of a man for whom the reading of an analysis only serves as the confirmation of a previous diagnosis but not telling him anything new—a new mass of heavy clouds advanced beyond the farthest planted fields. A weak gust of wind and a squeak of the door made him turn his head toward the visitor.

"Excuse me."

"There's nothing to be excused for. Tell me, do you recognize it?"

"Yes, I already knew. It couldn't have been anything but that; that or something like it."

"Now you will have to realize, at least, that I had and still have good reasons for having made the trip." She had scarcely moved from the threshold.

"I don't know."

"What don't you know?"

"I don't know if they're good or not. Or I don't know if they're good for not doing it. I don't know anything, that's all."

"Why do you say that? Do you think that's what I need?"

"I don't know what you need either. Maybe what you need is for me to tell you: that man died in the year 1939, or around that time, as the consequence of wounds produced by a rifle bullet. Will you believe it? If you believe it, why are you here? And if you don't believe it I can do very little to get you out of your doubts. The business of believing and not believing is always a personal thing; if it weren't for that we'd have to believe only in harmful things."

"My name is . . ."

"Oh, let's not talk about that now," he'd gone down the steps again, passing by the suitcase. Leaning on the door jamb, he scrutinized the sky again. "Understand, it's been a long time since I've had any visitors. The afternoon is getting cold, I don't know but that it's going to rain tonight. A long, long time." A smell of dampness and decomposition enwrapped the vestibule—the other inside door was hanging on its hinges, it was opening and slamming by itself from the effects of the breeze—sunken in that sudden explosion of aged and fetid dust in which, at nightfall—at the incantation of his words, those instants before the rain so propitious to the photochemical process—the last coloration of an unstable fluid loses its diurnal structure to break up into a thousand fragments of a gaseous and chaotic time, in each of which is lodged—like the germ in a grain of pollen—words, bits of memory, indications of aborted and false recollections and deceptive echoes that night and day will erase with the reestablishment of the balance of the hours. And it's an instant in which—in the presence of a catalyst of memory, a room that was lived in years ago, a card with an illegible name—a fissure is produced in the apparent outer layer of time through which it can be seen that memory has not kept what happened, that the will doesn't know what will come, that only desire knows how to equate them, but that—like an apparition conjured up by the light—it disappears as soon as the soul restores the hateful order of time. "Understand," she'd put her hands in her pockets and the doctor perceived that she gave a long shudder. He finally closed the door and the vestibule was left almost in darkness. "I'm not going to ask you to tell me what I've told myself so many times and wouldn't have had to tell myself if I'd known one single moment of repose. I wasn't aspiring to anything else because of all the rest, including fidelity, I thought myself cured. But a body that grows old without having received the confirmation of juvenile glory looks with apprehension and hesitation at a future surrounded by sterility, a spirit of decadence that doesn't even dare recognize with honesty and affliction the sum of its ills, only because a disobedient and impudent memory likes to have fun with another tricky age. It would have been better to silence it, reduce it to what it is; because memory—I can see very clearly now—is almost always the vengeance for what it was not—what was is engraved on the body in a substance that our lights never reach. I might be wrong, but it seems so obvious to me now . . . except that what couldn't be is kept on the level of memory—and in indelible registers—to constitute that column of what should be along with what the soul wishes, to counterweigh the possession of the body. So that memory never brings me recollections; it's rather quite the contrary, the computable violence of what is forgotten. I have no intention of telling you up to what point my breakdowns go, or when the source of fidelity dried up, or in what bed, between what sheets my embraces and drives ended up, what kind of illusions put an end to my hopes— because a fortune always ends with an IOU or a promissory note, alas, not in the release of a good-bye. I don't know whether I've returned or come for the first time to test the nature of a fiction, but in such a case, what cure can I expect if my vanity stops me from taking on its own beliefs, if my self-esteem—in accordance with confession—rules over my will? Then I say to myself: look inside yourself, what are you keeping in the depths of your innermost redoubt? It isn't love and it isn't hope and it isn't—even—disillusionment. But if you put your ear to it carefully, you will observe that in the depths of your soul a slight and restless buzzing can be heard—made of the same nature as silence——and the fact is that it's asking for a justification, it's conformed to what it is now and only demands that you explain to it now why is it like that. And then I tell myself: 'Go back there, Marré; go back there for what you love most, go back once and for all.' How many times had I tried—how many afternoons, with any pretext whatever, will I abandon this room decorated with all the care that the secret captive hates, faithful to the faith that she nursed on in infancy, and how many mornings does a soul who is seeking the real reason for its appetite or a faith, broken up by so many failed propositions, try to prevail in the renunciation (it's not a question of a satisfaction in search of a desire) of a few love affairs that deceive and distract it—to find myself disturbed and disoriented in the end, sitting on a bench on a deserted railroad platform in the middle of the barrens, eyes fixed on the somber horizon of the mountains, an instant before breaking into tears? How many times will I retreat, not invaded by fear but—with eyes fixed on the mountains or on the timetable, facing that announcement of the arrival at the Macerta station written in chalk and a hurried hand and in which the will resists believing because it can't conceive the steps that would have to be taken, once the train would have stopped—by that feeling of saving that the soul sets apart when, hesitant, it feels the necessity of preserving the only thing it has left, after the fire motivated by its urges to the dictates of a reason that, lacking in tears, imposes itself on a desperate and pitiful flesh that drums on the ticket window or bites the tip of a glove. Until one day, on the threshold of an age not defined by years but by the fading out of the last desire, a reason at the limits of its resistance consents to satisfy that whim of the fickle flesh. Only in order to hold back the weeping and the kicking and aware that all her so-phistry will be given the lie as soon as the ticket window opens, as soon as she is handed the ticket to Macerta, as soon as she boards the local to Región to head for the house that she hasn't been able to get out of her mind ever since the war was over. Nor does hope exist either because it's not legitimate, because an instinct of survival that doesn't be-lieve in it tries to ridicule it so as not to fall into its same dementia, into an age without enchantments. Who can be-lieve, consequently, that I came here in search of a cure? Isn't it rather an abandonment to the forces of the illness, against which in vain and for so much time the single body has fought together until it was out of breath? Isn't it probably a consolation of the last moment because—just like the fish who draws the food that he can't find outside out of his most vital intestines—it now only seeks to distract its appetite (a vice-ridden, disdained, resented, and loss-leading soul) with the somber words of affection, understanding, and justifi-cation that it will no longer ever be able to hear if it's not from its own voice?"

It had started to rain. The first drops, more than water,

seemed to have been formed from a fragile alloy, founded and transubstantiated on contact with the sand, covered with a swarm of filings. Soon the water began to filter through the porch and the doctor, opening the door once more, stood in the frame catching the wind and getting his pants wet. The dust swirled about his feet.

"I lived in this house during the war. A very short time, one or two weeks."

The doctor didn't answer; in a few instants the sky had covered over completely and the whole garden—and the neighboring field—changed coloration, fleetingly shining with a covering of varnish; a horizon of heather and brambles, sprinkled with sage and hawthorn, that beneath the armor-plated sky seemed possessed by that malicious sense of saving that allowed it to retain and magnify the last light of afternoon in order to dramatize the instant of its disappearance. He only asked, by way of a reply, and he closed the door behind him and threw the bar: "Do you think summer is on its way?"

"Lights?"

"Ah, yes, the lights. Do you know I scarcely ever use them? But there ought to be a switch here." He tried a couple of them, neither of which lighted; on the third attempt a pale and trembling bulb blinked in the center of the hallway, going out at once and coming on again with renewed intensity, as if it were trying to overcome its own stupor with an excess of zeal. She didn't remember when she had picked up the suitcase that a pale and hairy hand had left on a chair in the entrance way; a door—perhaps that to the office—was beating against its frame too, as if protesting against the invasion of electric light into that noble dwelling of darkness. Then it opened, to the rhythm of his step, as if activated by an automatic mechanism: a cane armchair with no bottom or legs, a pile of newspapers, papers and cans and bottles, an old wheelbarrow, some broom handles, a pair of worn-out sandals, an enameled receptacle—that held a bit of sand—seemed to mill about and huddle in a bunch, like a group of weary travelers disturbed by the intrusion of the customs inspector. The walls had been—some years before—whitewashed or painted with tempera, but the leaks and dampness had reappeared, impregnating all the corners with a rotten smell. The paint had peeled, some window-panes were broken, and almost all the furniture had disappeared after having left its mark on the wall; all along that bankrupt hallway, along the mosaic floor, ran a stream of lime stains, the track of a wounded ghost who had probably fled through the large window in the rear. The same damp-ness that had destroyed the paint, rotted the wood, and raised the floor, seemed to have affected the tone of the doctor's voice.

"Yes, it fits. I'd be lying to you if I said it hasn't been opened for a good many years. I say years so that you'll know what obtains with respect to this house. Only by that unit can you measure the number of times a light has been turned on, a door has been opened, or a bed has been used. And that doorbell, which since the end of the war has been heard fewer times than the echo of the shots in the brambles or the laments of the suicides." He opened the first door and put the suitcase in; the room gave off an intense and unhealthy aroma of a medicinal plant that had dried out in its darkness; there was a big bed of the kind that had its four corners dec-orated with inverted pinnacles, that kind which at one time must have held a canopy that time had devoured; the head-board was adorned with interlaced initials on marquetry, drawn in *fin de siècle* letters with broad and grandiloquent strokes. All the furniture—no doubt the last items of value that were left in the house—was of the same tone: a cup-board of majestic and funereal bearing, a console with a marble top, with a china washbasin and jug—the same com-bination of initials burned in—on which there was a little dry earth, a dry insect, and a dishcloth that told the age of the century, along with a hog-bristle brush and a sewing basket inside of which were accumulated long cuts of yellow cloth, some velvet samples, and a few old patterns cut from newspaper pages with the society news and events of thirty years ago; a few fragments spoke of ocean voyages, without any definite date and coloration, in whose delicate style, a rather dithyrambic and ornate prose—more lacking in meaning than in interest—there seemed to be portrayed the state of limbo that the paper—and the whole room, in short—had attained with the loss of actuality, like the house of a hero, which, converted into a museum and protected by a silk cord, is preserved in the same state in which he left it when he had to leave—unable to finish a letter—to wage war overseas. A portrait of his still hung on the wall; one of those tinted photographs, fierce and oval-shaped, that the camera manages to catch only when it senses that the personage is placed before its lens for the last time. In his look he had concentrated all the fire and fury necessary to overwhelm six later generations. The cheeks and mouth were hidden by a large, hairy, and violet-colored mustache, like a hedgehog hanging by its nose; he had puffed out his chest and raised his chin to the point of giving the photograph a feeling of convexity that would hypostatically transubstantiate the person shown—and who may never have existed—into the symbol of another or of the glory and link to the past of a family in need of a certain respectability.

"Because the house"—the doctor was to tell her as he observed the rain through the office window with his hands behind his back; she had finally dropped the suitcase and had thrown the coat over her shoulders, throat held high. The intensity of the storm had lessened; a sparrow perched on the windowsill was shaking raindrops off its wings and with quick head movements was studying the trees across the highway in order to choose one where it could spend the night; in the upper part of those poplars the timid chirping of his comrades was beginning to be heard, hidden in the foliage and announcing the end of the rain. He ran his finger across the window frame and looked at the trace of dust left on the tip—"was one of those last-minute purchases that cost five or ten thousand times more than the money given the former owner if every expense starting from the moment in which the title and keys are turned over could be measured in money. If there had been some arithmetical doctrine or some table that might say: your mother is worth so much and your brothers and sisters so much, your wife and the children you couldn't have so much; and the future that you pawned in exchange for these four walls of rubbish and the illusions that you fed when you were a student so much and the profession you believed in at one time and in which you never managed to do anything so much and finally the payment in rancor, resentment, annoyance, and solitude bought along with the title of landowner in a hostile region so much. Such is the trap into which *nouveau riche* families are accustomed to fall, deprived of vision, having gobbled up their existence with a knife poised over the budget and a fork stuck in their savings. When the moment comes to invest their savings, they make mistakes, they will always make mistakes, not in vain have they always refused to learn the science of spending. I don't know—I'll never know—if it's true that money attracts money; but what I can assert is that savings attract ruin. And in the face of such an axiom one can understand that there is a state of false well-being based on saving that is much more pernicious and harmful than Ruin itself, which, as old Themistocles said, always keeps us from a worse one. This whole state of things—and I don't know whether or not money per se is the demon, the only thing which man in this century is ready to be bewitched and ruined by—comes from a moment of ambition—and tragic enthusiasm—on my mother's part. My family didn't come from this region. We must have arrived here some time before 1910 when my father, a clerk in the Postal and Telegraph Service, was transferred to the central office of Región at his own request. In spite of his being a civil servant—and at that level—he must have been a sweet and dreamy man, not too much given to facing up to reality and with a manifest aversion to bad manners. But all of his delicate pessimism was slowly changing under the daily blows that only a spirited wife and family know how to provide with the tenacity of a forge, into a tendency toward fatalism, withdrawal, skepticism, and witchcraft. Toward the end of his life he no longer loved anybody; I—who as my mother said had inherited his same lack of character (which means that I had been born to be a well-mannered and modest person, affable and sincere)—served him many times as a crying towel in his last years. Because even the wheel had begun to deceive him, to play tasteless jokes on him. How soon he left me and how much I wept for him, because a father is the best help in bearing up under the obligations of being the firstborn in a family spurred on by a drive for respectability. One day I will tell you about his knowledge of the wheel; I think it was the only thing he loved in the world. And I think too—in secret—already fed up with a woman who was sufficient unto herself in everything—even for her fertilization—he had married for the second time that silent, discreet, and resigned companion with whom he carried on very long, very sad, and low-keyed conversations every night in a small room next to the public office. It was the only place my mother didn't enter because everything else—from the conscience of her children to the public safe that my father had to answer for—was unquestionably her property. I have understood that in the hands of my father the wheel must have given her such displeasure that it took away from her the desire ever to see it again. She consulted it, possessed by her pride, convinced that its very fictions had been changed into undeniable truths; but it would seem that not even her surname contained as much honor as she wanted, nor had her mother known how to maintain the necessary absences from a husband who worked in the mines. Only the wheel, with its sibilant, sibylline whistles and its unalterable spiritual presence, dared to make it manifest and in writing. I don't know what motives influenced my father's spirit so decisively as to come here; a certain beginning of prosperity, an obsolete influx of good families—the ones who invented summer vacations—a highland climate and, as always, the quality of the milk. But with the help of the wheel my father must have foreseen what was approaching and therefore always refused—in spite of his wife's interests—to become a landowner. In his last years he no longer cared about the strongbox; messages from other parts of the peninsula were scarcely ever received, coming rather from the witches' sabbaths, cemeteries, and hidden grottoes in the heart of the mountains where that diabolical mechanism captured its strange and sibilant messages, which my father listened to in ecstasy for hours on end, shut up in the small room with a bottle of clear castillaza. He scarcely ate dinner; in those days all of us children sat at the table but we weren't many. They were sad and frugal meals, presided over by a mother who was withdrawn, dense, and dominating, like an oriental idol, who served us in turn a little barley soup while she, with a thousand pretexts, gobbled up a beautiful plateful of carrots, potatoes, and chopped meat. My father would enter then, almost at dessert time (my mother's dessert, that is), with an absent and fatigued air and a face stained by tobacco. I think that every day he was expecting a change and when he found the same state of affairs that he had left at the last meal, he was filled with a terrible lack of appetite and only to cover appearances did he nibble a piece of bread while standing, contemplating the scene with distress, feeling incapable of improving the nutrition of his children. Because the few times when, possessed by his former *joie de vivre,* he tried to put a spoonful of that cereal soup into his mouth—perhaps at the same time that he stroked his daughter's curls—he found himself obliged to abandon the dining room in a hurry in order to spare all of us a lamentable spectacle. And when he disappeared, my mother—with her mouth full—never missed muttering an insult, with the deepest look of disdain I have ever seen on a face. By that time already his only passion was the wheel, his only food tobacco, a horrible tobacco—much to the taste of civil servants—that he bought in pound packages and which filled the house with a thick aroma of burned leaves on the nights that my father consulted the wheel; he himself maintained it, oiled it, and made any minor repairs because he wouldn't let anyone, not even the government electrician, lay hands on it. After the presumptive dinner he would go down to the little room to be alone with it until the light of dawn. He knew how to look through its spokes in order to calculate its velocity and predict the letter at the very moment that the wheel began its deceleration. He tried to pass that knowledge on to me when I had scarcely reached the age of reason. I didn't know very well what he was doing; I suppose that he limited himself to listening to and transcribing messages that a demented echo in a demented country, some dead, some desperate survivors, a buzzing ether, and a bit of maddened acceleration had tried to make reach the unbelieving witnesses of a catastrophic war. And perhaps, too, the terrible words of those herdsmen's songs, songs that always make reference to dust and destruction. Because very rarely did he consult the future, that scarcely interested him; then he would release the coupling, make it turn by pedal and ask: 'Let's see if the wheel can say where my days will end' and the wheel, after four quick accelerations, jotted down on the paper a word that left no room for doubts: 'Jaén.' My father died during the Dictatorship; he had scarcely come up in four days either to sleep or to eat and my mother sent me to look for him not because dinner was served but because 'It is his duty to set a proper example for his children.' I found him reclining in his chair, with one hand resting languidly on his companion in conjectures and confidences, a week's beard, a serene, indolent, downcast, and, in a certain way, smiling expression. He didn't say anything to me, simply handed me the paper perforated with one of the last messages to be received in that house and in which he was being told that because of the needs of the service he was being notified to transfer temporarily—I think to Linares—to help in the establishment of a new station. The two of us had kept the secret of the old prediction so that—to each other—we deceived each other into thinking we had forgotten it. He scarcely said good-bye one dusty afternoon toward the end of summer, his face smiling and a small bundle of clothes under his arm. For two weeks I waited eagerly for news of him, standing guard and vigil by the small shrine and spying night and day on the slightest movements of that parricide mechanism. Then came the period of doubts—during all that time my mother scarcely noticed his absence——I began to suspect the fraud—first of the wheel, which so many times had shown its whimsical liking for the spread of mournful news and jokes of macabre taste and then . . . of my own father, so much in need of a change in climate and so lacking in the courage to make a decision of that nature without an unshakable alibi—until one night the unmistakable buzzing of the wheel woke me up out of a heavy sleep to tell me that my father had died in an inn at Linares, shortly after his arrival, of a heart attack. But after a few months the same seed of suspicion, hidden by affliction and mourning, began to germinate again during a burning month of April and to grow and develop without my being capable of uprooting its progeny or trimming its ramifications. From then on I will never know for certain the true outcome; on occasion, when I tried to reconstruct the mocking buzz of the wheel and the grimace of sarcasm in the reflection of its spokes, I thought I guessed all the details of my father's feint (which at other times I had seen when he played cards with old friends, absenting himself for an instant with a nostalgic look, to think about me) that would appear to me at night, enveloped in the smoke of his tobacco and surrounded by unintelligible sounds, the victim of a civilization dominated by a mechanism and some women who, born in slavery, had subverted the order of their masters in order to impose a set of incomprehensible laws. I remember that one afternoon when my father was feeling playful he consulted the wheel concerning my fate and it answered him that my days would end in Región in a rather violent way, in the decade of the sixties and in the arms of a woman; and that's one reason—and not the least important—that has induced me to withdraw here to wait for the consummation of my fate, which I neither oppose nor evade. That death always puzzled me, with my head in a woman's lap all the more so because since the end of the war nobody in skirts has been seen around here. Once an expedition of Belgian alpinists came, with the aim of climbing El Monje; the poor devils . . . they all died, maddened by envy and thirst. They were dressed in khaki. There were three or four of them and—along with a lot of equipment—they brought a woman whom they made love to in turn. Well, if you can call anything that woman did love. At first I was alarmed, thinking she might correspond to the one in the prediction, but then I understood that, by wearing pants, even though she was still a woman, it couldn't be said—properly speaking—that she had a lap. So you're the first person to combine all the foreseen circumstances. And as for the violence I'll tell you that even when it doesn't seem to exist, it's always there in these lands; it's a latent state—and very understandable—but which can pass into eruption at any moment. You'll soon see that you'll understand." He had grabbed the dirty bottle, half filled with a yellowish-colored liqueur, by the neck, which he lifted to his lips as he turned a provocative and biting look toward her, giving her to understand that maybe it was necessary to understand his words beyond their mere meaning.

"Are you joking?"

"Oh, no, I'm not joking. In no way. You must know that;

you'll know it soon, isn't that why you're here? Why don't you sit down. I told you before that there's an accumulation of things against which it's useless to turn. We're incapable of thinking about death, not even on a limited scale. There exists a faith in survival in our soul, an unlimited confidence in that what happened once can never happen again. And yet, that's not how it is, reality doesn't confirm it. There doubtless exists a certain defensive valve in our body, thanks to which reason can refuse to accept the inevitable, the perishable; because it must be quite difficult to exist if being loses the conviction that while life lasts its possibilities are inexhaustible and almost infinite. Only underneath our convictions a bastard memory flows that never lets itself be known (it awakened with the age of justifications, at the end of the age of the obvious, we'll speak about that later) because it stores up a supply of disenchantments that, as soon as a failure is produced in the system of our hypocritical and defensive illusions, goes on to occupy the terrain marked out by vanity so as to rob us materially of an antiquated motive for living. But why don't you sit down?" Standing, with the back of her neck resting on the door frame, she had been listening in silence until she lowered her eyes toward the floor: "All right . . . you're the doctor. Maybe you're right; maybe my cure (if you want to call it that) depends on making myself susceptible to blandishments again. I don't know."

"Nor do I, I must confess; besides, you can't say that I'm a doctor anymore. But there are still illnesses that only former patients who have gone through them can cure. That's why I say it."

"It's starting to rain again. I think I was quite lucky in my choice of days. It will start getting cold up above soon. What a long trip! Long, Doctor, long! A rainy afternoon, a deserted and devastated landscape, horrible roads, an inn at the crossroads of purgatory and an innkeeper who seems to be waiting for the arrival of a troop of rain-soaked souls, and, you know? the same places, the same walls from the war, impossible to recognize, impossible to remember. Can it be so long because it's given me back to the other world?"

"Who knows? I won't say it hasn't."

"But, do you know what I'm talking about, Doctor?"

"I think I do and you're making a lot of sense. Another world, it's quite true, and, of course, much more ominous and silent than the one you left."

"That's the least of it. Tell me, why do you enjoy your own tears?"

"I don't enjoy anything. I haven't known tears. I've never wept for anything or yearned for the past. That's for those who live in society, for those who know how to conform to melancholy. Those of us who live in this land need a stronger dish, a more brutal diversion."

"More brutal?"

"I'm referring to fatalism, a more substantial dish. Because my family wasn't good; people of humble extraction, that is, but, at least without principles. My father only had half an education and a few lessons in peninsular geography. My mother's family was also humble but it had more airs; it was the humblest branch of a provincial trunk on whose crest a few peaceful garrison soldiers had flourished—the kind that liked zarzuelas better than command—and a few belli-cose lawyers of the kind called dry wells, local paperhangers who only seemed to preserve and nourish a rancor against Providence because they weren't consulted during the days of Genesis. My mother always spoke highly of them, as un-attainable examples, the origins and models for all conduct, and, as an ark of the covenant, she brought to the conjugal bedroom the photograph of a character that from the wed-ding night on doubtless cut off and frustrated any intent on my father's part of going up the ladder. You still have it by the head of the bed so you won't forget how vain the glo-ries of this world are. And she wouldn't pardon anyone, I can assure you. I was halfway through my studies when my father died, who knows whether victim of his curiosity or his drive for freedom. What I can assert is that the same morning that the message arrived—the accomplice wheel brought it with a precision that led one to believe that it had spent a great deal of time preparing the news—I swore silently to hate and fear that curiosity, keep my hands free to the limit of my strength, resist the encirclement of society and women, avoid that game of duties and rights, favors and wrongs, offers and disappointments into which the will of a people who refused to present their demands to a fate that had taken over their fields had fallen. Neither my brother nor my sister had yet reached the age of reason, something that if they were on the point of attaining at any moment, my mother was careful to snatch away. So that beginning with a certain day—and my father's body still fresh in an Andalusian graveyard or in some hideaway tavern near a station—I saw myself changed into the figurehead of a family who, trusting in my capacity, had put everything in me in such a way that in order to pay for my profession in Salamanca they had to make any number of sacrifices, the enumeration of which took up a good part of my mother's time every day. So that when I got up every day, when I took the trip to Salamanca, when I went back to the boarding-house every afternoon, my first obligation wasn't to study—which, after all, was only one form of payment like any other that I might have undertaken and which my mother would have accepted—but to the recognition of the debt. What a tragic tradition—that of such families who only aspire to a presumed well-being, who don't stimulate any other desire but that of avarice, and who don't instill any other recognition than that of debt; who don't hesitate to restrict the freedom of their children, instilling them from childhood with the sense of a sterile responsibility. What dark contradictions, what a lack of generosity, that of so many people who pass through this world not to enjoy its good things but to run after an atrocious deception and arrive at the end of their breath without having known a moment of repose and de-light . . . vicissitudes of misery, alas, arcane mysteries of the will. Were you telling me something? I thought . . .

"Foolishness. You've spent very little time here to have become superstitious. Foolishness, accommodations of the imagination. I won't tell you what my student years were like; quite squalid, quite lacking in everything. Only at a given moment did I have to draw strength from weakness in or-der to deny myself the simultaneity of my studies and some examinations for my father's unit. It too was an idea of my mother's, who, not content with living in a dwelling to which she no longer had any right (but whose return was never demanded of her, I don't know whether because the office was no longer used or because the administration was afraid of her), every time she entered that deserted office and saw the motionless wheel and the endless spirals of perforated paper that had invaded the floor and the desk (a kind of post-mortem solitary segregation of my father's spirit), and which must have been considered an intolerable waste, she com-plained about my ingratitude, crossed herself over my lack of will and repeated—until she went to bed—the long series of sacrifices that she had undertaken in order to give a profession to a forgetful person. But I was afraid of the wheel; even at the age of twenty I would run past its door and awake in a fright with its whistle buzzing in my ears; during the few moments when I had to find myself alone with it and saw it half-hidden in its corner, three-quarters of its circum-ference peeping out from among a pile of disquieting pa-pers—proud and enigmatic and smiling like a silent sphinx that has been put in a corner for having accurately predicted the disasters of its worshipers, possessed and conscious of its occult power—then my whole youth began to tremble and fear, to suffer insomnia and diarrhea. And if, indeed, I never tried avoiding payment, I decided that I would do it in in-stallments at least and in the form that best suited me. If you come from a family that has lived by being tightfisted, you must know up to what point that whole consequence of details that seem so secondary in the beginning form a whole entanglement of links and resentments, rights and duties in homes where everything is scarcity. I think that I got my degree without any brilliance, but at a relatively early age; I managed shortly afterward an internship at the Santa Mónica Hospital for the incurable, which a few months later I saw myself obliged to exchange for a bedroll and sailed for Africa in the 1920 campaign. I was in Iberguren with the Medical Corps, and from there I ran away, I don't know how, crossing the mountains in a state of delirious anguish that wouldn't let me distinguish between the plains and gulleys of the Rif and the depths of the strait, which I crossed I don't know whether swimming, or on foot, or flying. When I got back home, with empty hands, a pair of boots, an illness in the ureter, and half of my wages in my pocket, my mother presented for collection the IOU that I had signed when I was fifteen as a concept of filial duties; it was a room on the upper floor of Dr. Sardú's clinic, with a hundred pesetas a month pay, room, and board. My family didn't live far away and my mother—who was already beginning to suffer from chronic arthritis that was giving her unspeakable pain—doubtless decided on that placement because the nearness of the clinic allowed her to exercise an implacable control over my activities and because her instinct told her that at that point—defended by ill people, the unhinged, the pregnant—the attack on the fortress of respectability must begin. The clinic was on the outskirts of town and had a garden that opened onto the terraces of the Torce; for most of the year it was open as a health or rest home—as they used to say—where the nervous depressions, the cases of fatigue and loneliness of the members of those good families who—under the blows of the casino and the floods in the river—were slowly submerging into decadence were treated. Sardú was very much appreciated at that time for his competence, liberality, and discretion, and his establishment was

[117]

being converted into an obligatory place for people—from Región and elsewhere—in need of a long and anonymous withdrawal. I mean that also treated with care and dissimulation were a few inconvenient births and the doctor himself had acquired a name thanks to his suave manners and to his abortion technique. Halfway through the decade of the twenties—following the general exodus—Sardú disappeared in the woods one Sunday morning before the prohibition was on; one of his executors, two weeks later, came to tell me the decision of the deceased to hand over the direction of the establishment (which at that time was only a shadow of what it had been) to me, including the management and the tri-monthly accounting to a family council, with a salary which, if it could have been collected for any month, would have been quite tasty for those times. But times had changed, the country even had a great scarcity of illicit pregnancies. My mother—who wasn't sensitive to the change in the times—dazzled by that opportunity, thought that the moment, so yearned for, of the attainment of respectability had arrived with the filling of a position that had been abandoned. Nothing easier in those days than to acquire a house at a very low price, buy a dozen beds, and fill the gap left by the Sardú clinic.

"The house, as you can see: a squat edifice that with difficulty has lasted the half-life of a person, with a peculiar smell, walls that are falling down, an instinct, an urge toward destruction and ruin. Maybe it's what it always was—less secret than what is thought—an impulse and an effort that only lead toward the consummation of its own usury because the sinful proposal that raised it is only associated—tacitly and paradoxically—with an urge toward innocence that is always translated into a premature death; not only the denial of, but the most bold-faced mockery of the aspirations of a birdlike family (did it exist at any moment? was it anything more than the fleeting and hateful decoy of a virtuous and ingenuous appetite, destroyed and derailed by a mar-

riage bed?) that is only capable of conquering family titles—
the same as checks that bounce—when they have been
transformed into symbols of insolvency, falsehood, ruin, and
abjection. In those days a house was much more than a simple shelter, a roof over the head of a family, the indivisible
calcareous carapace of the many-celled organism; that is,
house and family couldn't exist one without the other and
outside that symbiosis there could only be corruption. In fact,
all the disorders of the century were born—one might say—
in the bosom of a few families who lacked a house or took
out naturalization papers under public roofs that didn't shelter real families. I think that you will see, with things like
that, what it meant for my mother's pride around 1920 to
hear about her, 'The Sebastiáns? Aren't those the people who
live in the telegraph office?' Because in my youth the family
was deprived; there was nothing—not even a criminal will,
a fraudulent act—that didn't obey family determination. A
man couldn't do anything—think, exercise his profession, or
(less still) abandon his family—if not driven by family conscience and will. I see my father, consequently, while we were
beginning our painful rise toward the age of puberty, hunched
over his wheel—weepy and withdrawn—like one of those
old and ragged guitar players who find themselves obliged
to earn their living on corners with what in their youth had
only been a hobby. Later on, in fact, he has a small recon-
ciliation, an insignificant recompense that in his eyes is a lot—
it's not translated, even into a few more coins, but into a
certain esoteric smile—that's the fruit of the value of his renunciation and the measure of his own failure and—all the
more—goes on to prove the honesty of certain feelings that
very few people believe in and which don't matter to anyone. Every home is a struggle for stability and in any one
of its vicissitudes there will always appear the germ of its
future decomposition. And they (homes) not only die before people, but, in comparison with them, consume their
lives struggling to live, affected by a terrible, chronic, in-

curable, and lethal illness. I would say that behind those walls and those ceilings and that plaster are hidden ruinous intentions that don't prescribe and, just as one day they frustrated the dreams of the returnee who built them to shelter his illicit loves, in the same way later on they reserved their potential to transform the refuge into a trap for a group of the defeated or to create the fiction of a home for a woman—not deceived as they must have made you think, but voluntarily disposed to sacrifice—who had always lacked one, bequeathed to us—that family reduced to the Christian gelatinous invalidity of the snail, whose shell has fallen to pieces—the fraud of its roofs. You mustn't be surprised at the manifest reserve I have become accustomed to cloak all expressions of the family cult in; nor should you be surprised, in the end, at the lack of enthusiasm with which, when the moment has arrived, I will participate in my own adventure. I mean: the small enthusiasm with which I shall attend a play whose denouement I already knew beforehand. The little that remained of that enthusiasm—the deserter spirit that abandoned a semi-corpse stretched out on a reddish hill in the Rif, the one that accompanied my father on his trip through the lands of Jaén, refreshed by wines at inns, absent from the memory of his wife—remained at that crossroad on the way to Mantua, I can assure you; until that moment I was sincere, ingenuous and sincere, simply because I didn't need to explain to myself (and less to justify to myself) what I wanted; I just wanted it, and that was enough. The last fraction is consumed in a poorly developed calculation of possibilities, a trip in a taxi, a birth in the heart of the mountains, and a last disappointment—the least painful—with the crowing of the cock in the background; but before saying that my mother was right, I considered it my duty to try to contradict and silence a way of thinking that, on taking advantage of a mistake of mine, made itself pass for correct in order to subsume my freedom. Because the first thing a mother says is: 'That's crazy,' without knowing that—un-

[120]

fortunately—half the time she's right. I could have abandoned her just like that and got far away forever from that Philistine mentality that in its pride can only think about its investitures; but I preferred to assume my role precisely in a direction opposite to the one foreseen by my mother; not to grasp the family tiller, but to board that same ghost ship and return it to its authentic state, *l'épave*. The governing tiller, what do you think that baneful visitor was called? María . . . wait a minute . . . Gubernaël, that's it, Gubernaël. No doubt that night she was completely disoriented, not only in names, but in the rooms. We still hadn't bought the house, but it was during the last days of Sardú's clinic. I understood very much later and then I induced her to leave there because the visitor, apart from her confusions, left no room for doubt with respect to the fact that she had it noted on her list. When I saw her after two years, covered by the veil, I couldn't help associating her with that visitor who had got hold of me under the elms by the highway, who, in order to speak covered her mouth with a handkerchief perfumed with cheap cologne, but even so it wasn't enough to cover up the stench of a very hot breath. When I got into the car that morning, while the cocks were crowing, the only enthusiasm left to me was to affirm that none of it was left to me anymore, with all my capacity for vehemence and reiteration, during the trip to the mountain. It wasn't a long trip, but it was significant and conclusive: a squad of cavalry and a poor village doctor were searching, each in its way, for the victim who would redeem them for their mistakes, the loan shark who could pay his debts or the vehicle of their vengeance . . . call it what you will . . . We came out with our thing, what doubt can there be? but . . . what was our result?"

He had the feeling that she was barely listening to him. On several occasions he had inserted, like the mistakes and suppressions that are covered up in a sketch in order to give rise to a game of riddles, certain insinuations and veiled comments with which he hoped to awaken her interest and

[121]

stimulate her curiosity. She asked him nothing: surrounded by shadows her face—and her silhouette—seemed to have blended with the wall that in the darkness still kept a certain purple coloration of the last light of afternoon, of the same tonality as the withered leaves of the poplars that covered the windowsill. He had invited her repeatedly to sit down, but until then she had remained standing, motionless and attentive. The doctor didn't know what she was waiting for; she still hadn't told him—although he imagined that in the end it would be a question of that—that she intended to continue her trip into the mountains and even though he was sure that in such a case he should dissuade her, he didn't know very well why. He tried to see if her face was known to him, but he couldn't manage it without obliging himself—in a recurrent way—to insist in his memory at the moment in which he had opened the door to her, to ascertain whether some kind of recognition had been produced.

"Sometimes I've come to think that the family is an organism with its own entity, which transcends the sum of the creatures who make it up. It's the true trap of reason: a rapacious animal who lives on a different level from man's and who, made up of a myriad of fractionary impulses, microbeings with no other form than an incipient will, a voracious appetite, and an automatic instinct to combine its forces about the sacrifice of a man, prevails thanks to his condescension, to a desire for tranquillity that—even though he may deny it—he is harnessed to with his lack of gifts for the struggle; one of those colonies of pelagic animals (like a school of herring who gather around a cetacean who feeds them with his excrement and whom—acting as pilots—they end up leading to zones of plankton, which they don't eat), deprived of a reason for being until the day when they manage to group themselves around the individual, lacking in predatory instinct and manacled, enslaved, and subjugated by a reason that can no longer evolve; still, it was considered a good theory in my youth—who knows whether

[122]

or not born of the horror for all forms of social respect—
that in the liquidation of the family saw the emancipation of
an ankylose instinct gagged by an astute reason that always
asks itself about the object of its enthusiasm (and in that I
judge its difference from passion) and that only on very few
occasions dares utilize its knowledge, ignoring its propositions and intents. I'm not sure but what it's another fraud,
a new absurdity, a new decoy set up by society to distract
the individual from his original drive, passion. Whatever that
precarious instinct might be like—which isn't conjoined so
easily with the suicidal urge revealed by its satisfaction—it
too turns out to be false, because inconclusive in facing the
decoy, its aim was off: that's why sometimes I see a reason
for myself as the trap into which man has come to fall, pur-
sued by a whole swarm of unstable passions, each one of
which has required an amputation. Put into better words,
this world isn't a trap but a hiding place (in a certain way
gratuitous and frivolous, very proper for the dilettante who
lacks energy and motives to undertake a serious activity)
which that man has fabricated in order to hide his own demon. Even humor proceeds from there, from the attitude of
one who, quiet and hidden, sees how the others run franti-
cally after the hole he occupies. Except that existence in the
hiding place of reason . . . comes to fatigue one, soon people yearn for those mad runs, that not having as much need
for lucidity as for legs, breath, fear, yes, fear. The nostalgia
of fear! Even his very reason is debilitated in the dampness
of that hole: one day while he languishes, the prisoner of his
own protection, in order to overcome his affliction he lets
himself be dragged into the terrain of confessions. He's already lost; then, with the pretext of affection, of compre-
hension, of company he begins to be devoured by a certain
number of creatures who consider him something that belongs to them. He will no longer be an individual, a man
who is master of his acts as well as of an instant, a redoubt
of freedom. Not only will they demand total surrender of

him, the primacy of his duties to them, but they will consider that gesture outrageous, bothersome, and punishable—the most futile and innocent—the one by means of which
he tries to reserve a piece of life for himself. That never! What
I don't understand is how up till now he hasn't been capable
of drawing up a code that will be in accord with his desires,
that would take care to defend his most intimate nature. In
contrast he never wearies of drawing up laws for the protection of his most bitter enemy, family, society. And no
doubt because codes are drawn up by reason, an apparatus
that is scarcely interested in what man is and wants. I ask
myself: if man besides having reason could count on a calcareous carapace, with four pairs of articulated legs and a capacity for reproduction of sixty eggs per laying, perhaps the
code couldn't help being the same, a series of principles of
form elaborated with the abstraction of nature; not a rule of
convenience but a stimulation to sociability, to alienate and
make atrophy that inexhaustible urge for solitude and emancipation and freedom that makes up the trunk of his species.
Because man isn't a monument to love, but disdain for the
other person, one who wants to forget what is confused. In
my father's generation they were already talking about the
human community and even about the 'great family.' How
well we're paying for it, how dearly it's going to cost us! A
great family, yes, poor in resources but loaded with principles; everyone owing everyone else and no one relying on
himself. The few men who were born in this land and tried
to fight against that current—because they were too ingenuous to renounce their self-interest or because, too uncouth,
they saw with disdain or compassion how a doctrine of love
sought nothing more than the degradation of the flock—were
hunted down, penned in, and wiped out like dangerous
beasts."

Settled into the old black leather armchair, so worn out
that the springs peeped through the holes and a second tobacco-colored covering, he looked a little restless. The pre-

vious spring, with the longer days and the starch smell of the chestnut trees in bloom, with the shrilling of the swifts, who, drunk with speed, spun about the chimneys of the house and the elms across the highway, he had perceived again certain symptoms that sought a deep and permanent ill feeling in him. He couldn't say for certain what it was about, some evening voices, a nocturnal and morning buzzing that only noontime silenced, some sporadic lights on the somber silhouette of the mountains, flocks of birds who didn't wait for October to head south, and several piles of paper carried up the road in clumps: pages from newspapers rolled up into a large bundle and which, when they reached his door, opened up insinuatingly, and which he never approached but which over the whole summer tried to get into the house by every means, beating against the windowpanes, swirling across the balconies and plugging up the chimneys (every afternoon he watched them while behind the window he repressed a shudder) to end up faded, with holes from the rain, torn by the wind, hanging from the branches of the underbrush and brambles. And also—and not any less serious because it was the most usual—the echo of a motor—or several motors—of small power that, accelerating and worn-out at the same time, for several months had tried in vain to climb up a distant grade that was virtually close by thanks to the resonance with which a malignant topography had gathered it in, magnified and repeated, after a glimmering August afternoon. None of that had passed unnoticed by the doctor even when his awareness—his desire for peace, his renunciation into inconformity—refused to accept the proximity of new facts and possible wonders. He had lived and known many unfortunate cases and many mad adventures and few times the premonitions had come to affect the peace in which he lived. At no time had the Traveler stopped at his house (with the exception of the day when the Belgians knocked on his door to ask for some potable water); a couple of days afterward the echo was repeated and transferred to an octave that the ear couldn't tolerate, the buzzing of the motor, and a few hours before the wind brought the calling card to his door he had seen the cloud of dust, after leaving the pass behind, climbing the rocky road to Mantua. And yet he had opened; he repeated to himself that perhaps it was fate that had put that test to him and not in order to return, restore, or regenerate confidence in himself, but, quite the contrary, to strengthen a kind of abstract indifference and radical distrust that had never been contrasted, at least since the civil war had ended, with a reality—no less unpleasant, of course—that was going to sanction the same source of his reserves in the end. Sitting in the twin armchair in the office she turned to the doctor from time to time with that meaningful, rude, and lively look that is kept for the prosecutor accused by the merry delinquent who in the midst of the stupor and surprise of the courtroom shows himself incapable of understanding the magnitude of his crime. But the possibility that his guest, in order to avoid all justification, was taking refuge in a kind of artful indifference with which to silence fear of failure even at the cost of making evident a hypocritical intent had not passed unnoticed by the doctor. On the other hand he didn't have the slightest doubt that, by making use of his penetration in order to verify the reasons for the trip, even with prudent means and only with deterrent ends, he could not help revealing a series of opinions whose real origin and strength was far from wanting—or being able—to confess; so that he was contemplating that situation in which—voluntarily or involuntarily, anecdotic in the end—he had become involved with that mixture of pleasure and intrigue that is provided the viewer of those paintings with mythological, biblical, or religious themes and whose subject matter he doesn't know fully (like the "Landscape with the Veil of Thisbe" or the "Voyage of Saint Gennaro") in which the whole nature of the plot is centered in a fleeting and distant figure in the background of an exuberant scene; and in the same way as in such paintings ignorance deems capricious certain happenings that take place on other planes that in a different way are joined to that enigmatic figure by a link that can only be deciphered by a missing erudition or the key to an esoteric language that the artist used to make manifest a forbidden belief, thus tried to understand the reasons for that visit and the relationship it might have with the auguries of the mountains and the intolerable calm that seemed to emanate from the range since two springs before—after so many years of disasters and resignation that even the few surviving peach trees had become accustomed to producing dried fruit—and which he, as an old man surrounded and protected by astute disillusionments, sensed that was foretelling the beginning of a new revulsion. He couldn't believe in the omens and yet he couldn't put aside—without making use of all the local prejudices—the relationship between two or more series of events that no science could summarize: every year that the hyacinths flowered there was a violent death in Mantua. He had only managed to feel restful—and at peace with his country—on days—which were very rare—when the bad weather had cleared up, even if it was only for a few hours, for an environment as peaceful as it was disquieting. And in spite of the fact that his inner law repeated—without convincing itself—that a renewed coincidence could only give way to a fiction, a mirage, or some form of superstition (because he no longer believed either in time or in the health of the body; he knew that the future didn't exist nor snowfalls nor freshets), in reality he only had faith in chest colds and storms to get out of his spirit a yearning for omens and events that was translated into a permanent ill humor. He had understood that he was living in hesitation when he perceived that—after many years of having held in oblivion, or, rather, sequestered in a level of the memory where independent of good sense certain ridiculous registries are hidden to cure them of too stiff and unpleasant a taste and transform them into that conceptual gelatin on which serene temperaments feed—since the previous spring at almost every noontime he wondered about the state of the sky. At that moment he was ready to believe—such was his impatience—that that malicious look knew quite well what was being plotted in the upper atmosphere; sometimes he was silent, suddenly turning toward her to catch a movement, an expression or a twist by means of which to unmask her intentions; sometimes he seemed sunken in the chair, with his finger by his mouth and his breathing tranquil and a wandering, indolent look wrapped in a halo of damp flashes provoked by anachronistic sketches and tardy plans. Nevertheless, he did a very good job at avoiding mention of his fears; at first he thought that when the moment arrived he could allow himself certain questions without abandoning his attitude of discretion, but he quickly rectified that; all his strength rested once more in his capacity to contemporize and to wait without getting ahead of his guest's questions with an interest that with difficulty he was able to show without making visible the symptoms of his helplessness; that was precisely the last thing he would have confessed and the first thing he would try to avoid, consumed and mortified from a long time before—and in his most intimate fibers—by an incurable feeling of failure (and consequently by certain residues of enthusiasm—no longer passion—with respect to certain things before which he considered himself disaffected and through which could be glimpsed the contradictions of his supposed passivity, the survival of perished hopes) that the most skeptical attitudes and the most delusive remedies had been incapable of mitigating. And it was not so much a last residue of modesty or a clinging to the land or its customs, nor yet the horror that could be produced in him by the opinion of a stranger and one who was so ignorant of some circumstances that dominated any interpretation, but rather a form of disturbance and stupor (that is as often translated into disdain as into upset) that since his return to Región had shut him up in that

[128]

house, had aborted all decisions, had condemned him to that run-down easy chair beside a window on which dust was accumulating and facing a desolate landscape while in a lucid head there still bubbled the old rancors, the fire of disrespect, and the smoke of adolescent impetus, and that openmouthed look, expectant and suspended, of a man who is awaiting a frustrated sneeze, detained at nose level with a singular itching. He had come to think that his father was still living, having taken refuge in Mantua under the tutelage of old Numa; that he was awaiting his return, that from time to time he would send a message that—from fear, lack of skill, cowardice—he had never learned to grasp. But he had never come to believe it either: it was too much time and, above all, too much idleness. On the other hand, his mother . . . perhaps she was the one who was shooting; it wasn't a vengeance, but the renewal of the time cycle, the Saturnal celebration of an archaic mind that demanded the *regressus ad uterum* in order to erase the mistakes and deviations of the present age and prepare for the birth of a new race. When she knocked on the door he found himself facing the disjuncture of giving entry to the visitor or—on refusing to accept the stubborn bell-ringing—putting aside forever the difficult balance he had managed to keep between the sign of the times and his own upset. He had not wished to make—with respect to her conduct—a decision because he had neither an urgency in dissuading her nor enough reasons to convince her of the inanity of her hopes and because, definitely, it was not in the traditions of the country—tolerant to the point of indifference with regard to the most unexpected behavior—to take on a mission that only events would know how to place in its proper framework. Certainly the whole country was suffering from a chronic illness and an epidemic because (apart from the fact that nobody could feel attracted by the ministry of an augur) in popular consciousness the slightest warning about the dangers that the attractions of the mountain enclose had come to be considered punishable, insensate, and imprudent; it was that point of hypocrisy that conceded the value of a rite to the annual trip, the mystery of a faith, and the feeling of a confirmation. Doubtless the repetition of the case had led to the formation of a link in popular awareness—from which willy-nilly the doctor was unable to withdraw—between that confirmation and the preservation of the secret by the inhabitants of the flatlands; some archaic races—and that's what it was, or is—have arrived at astuteness through a periphrasis—a long, complicated, and redundant period into which premonitions, customs, superstition, and myth are inserted—perhaps to avoid a causal scheme that is too brief and expeditious, too simple, and in which there is no entry or possible justification for the contradiction of a species that can't learn to live in peace. He knew only too well that the moment was ill fated; he only left the house for a while, before eating and after nightfall at the time when (just like dawn for a person condemned to death) the darkness over the mountain imposed one more date in that disquieting truce; he would go out to lock the outer gate and take a stroll through the garden, which the doctor took advantage of to urinate on the grass in accordance with a practice that he considered one of the most effective remedies against nervous disorders "and especially on hot days . . . when the sun, on lifting its despotic hand over the meadow, falls conquered and there rises up, instantaneous, rhythmical, and unifying the victory chant of frogs and cicadas, that explosion of jubilant voices that join together to reach an ultrasonorous dimension with which to celebrate their recent liberation." He scarcely dined and only did so from time to time, on days when the poor state of his head obliged him to drink with moderation a stew of potatoes and carrots that he prepared for them both. He used the dinner as a medication that three or four times a week he saw himself obliged to swallow in order not to interrupt his drinking habits and to be able to prolong, day by day, his long night hours. He would go to bed very late, but almost all morning he would remain shut up in his room—not the slightest sound was heard in the house. He was accustomed to drinking only in the afternoon, sitting in the black leather armchair in front of the long dirty glass in which every day—within the supine and impenetrable ecstasy inspired not by the mystical union with the orb that surrounded him, but by contemplation of the principle of individuation, crystallized in the mother water of absurdity, futility, and ingratitude—were repeated the processes of the chaos represented in the slow and interminable ascension of the small bubbles toward the environment that will extinguish them to ask themselves— without any possibility of finding an answer—about those painful constants of memory that time, like the liquid, has imprisoned in a medium from which they can only emerge to be extinguished.

"These nights become long, very long. These nights— furthermore—in which the moon, with its moderate clarity, invites the patient to suspend temporarily the rancor he has stored up in order to contemplate the deceitful negative: those whispering poplars and birches and those silvery threshing floors, the faces and words of the past that return rid of wrath by a trick of the light; or even that violent and worthless appetite for forgiveness, rest, and beatitude that gratuitously takes over the soul—too comfortable, forgetful, and smug— when the land (in the same way that the platinated periwig magnified by a combination of shadows and the fever is transformed into a sinful and repeated nightmare in the insomniac's room) extends its ridges up to the windowsill or the bedspread to beg with a fawning and perverse gesture, a last gesture of hope that the next day rejects as an attack on dignity. It's hard to fight against it because it's easy to succumb; oh, that hemmed-in reason cannot find in the end any other refuge than the gambling den it always looked upon with disdain and horror; it's a question of honor, another contradiction. Because in it the whole capacity for resistance and protest has taken refuge, and even common sense, that child of reason that refuses to come out in defense of its elder when it sees it conquered. Because it's there, on the field of honor (never better put) that reason and passion fight their final combat to the death, like that pair of noble, brave, and skillful knights who went into the lists with their weapons gleaming and their own pride agitating the crest but who end up fighting with punches and bites, rolling on the ground covered with dust. What does it have in particular, after all, that from that moment on it should become so cruel and bloody?"

Sleeping, her face was more serene but also more mature. She had slipped off her coat and opened the neck of her dress, leaving the start of her throat uncovered, waxen colored, slightly mottled, foreshortened over the back of the chair with curvaceous negligence. The doctor turned off the light and in a while the room remained lighted by the opalescent glow of the moon on the limestone mountains, as if it were obeying those mutations of lights, tones, and shadows that in theatrical lumotechnics are considered necessary and sufficient to give room to evocation.

"What else?"

Suddenly he sensed her eyes open and then he saw them, shiny and black in the bluish half-shadows and struggling to free themselves from a contradictory submission, like those two jewels encrusted in an inexpressive and crude figure, which try uselessly to get out of it in order to speak of their superior status.

"What else?"

For the first time he understood that in such a situation, without being able to do anything against it and without any of his many reserves being able to come to his aid, a feeling of compassion could flower inside of him that—if she persisted in her withdrawn attitude, the long legs doubled and the arms folded at the waist, the head leaning against the back of the chair—could evolve toward any other that, entombed for many years, perhaps remained uncorrupted. He didn't want to know it and he was even afraid of questioning himself in that respect.

"Why don't you go on?"

He kept the liqueur in his bedroom, in a small cabinet set into the wall beside the head of the bed that, as on every day, unmade and messy, still held the smell of his sleep; he took the pillow, shook it, hollowed it, and put it in its place, spread a blanket over the whole bed and with a bottle of castillaza between his legs remained absorbed for a moment while he contemplated the habitual disorder of his bedroom, trying to remember what he had forgotten. The clothes, the packages of cotton, the shoes, the stethoscope peeped out of the half-opened drawers of the old bureau from his clinic days, filled with unbound books, more fitting for a student than a professional, bundles of outdated magazines, ancient yellow invoices, prescriptions, and samples that had impregnated the room with an intense and sour medicinal aroma. For a while he rummaged around in the drawers and shelves without feeling that he would find anything, but suddenly he drew out one of them, emptied its contents onto the floor, and, after pushing aside some knickknacks (he didn't seem to have been guided so much by his sight as by that instinct or identification that recognizes the object of its search before the senses perceive it), he took out a passport picture, wrinkled and yellowed, with its edges smoky, which bore witness to a long stay in darkness. He looked for a corkscrew—there was an old rusty jackknife under the night table—and, without taking his eyes off the photograph, he pulled out the cork with one tug, wounding himself slightly on the finger, and without too much attention applied a flow of liquor. He took a long drink, coughed, wiped his lips, and remained seated on the edge of the bed until he sensed that his guest, leaning against the door frame, was observing him from the threshold.

"What is it, Doctor?"

"These treacherous nights," he said at the same time as he put the photograph in his pocket. "All right," he had cleaned a glass that he had left within reach of his chair, on top of the table, half full of brandy.

"What I can assure you is that I never allowed myself the least license and that I have imposed the discipline of silence on myself ever since the war ended. If I understood anything it was that from then on two different women existed who must not be confused, if I wanted to preserve the integrity of a recluse; because each of the two had to defend herself from contamination by the other and a third one—much more logical, thoughtful, and respectable—would watch over and guarantee the cohabitation, independence, and personality of both. That third one—the referee—is perhaps the one who has come here and knocked at your door, not in search of her missing daughters, but of the penitence with which a mother overwhelmed by sorrow and remorse tries to find a cure for irreparable losses. Because if there was anything I learned during those days it was that the problems of my love were exclusively mine and that they would never come to be shared by the person I loved; and that doubtless she would have considered the slightest attempt on my part to make her a participant in them as an offense or a demonstration of selfishness. So that the many times I tried to go on a trip—oh, they were nothing but a fiction and none of the persons in the trinity, not even the recluse, intimidated before the others by a ridiculous prudishness, gave it any more importance than that of a juvenile running away, certain that it would never be carried out in any case; because it was a question of a fraudulent and arranged game, a kind of short holiday for the recluse (incommunicado since the end of the war), whom the other two—usufructuary and zealous—did well to tolerate with that mixture of parental severity and acceptance with which one observes and follows the attempt at flight by someone, victim of her desperation, who will attempt nothing in the end but a return

[134]

to the cell that frees her of so many impossible urges—I saw myself sitting in the end by the ditch of a deserted highway or on the platform of an absurd railway station before or after Macerta, confused, disturbed, and without the strength to prolong for one instant more a contraceptive decision and trying to explain to a drowsy clerk (cloaked in tears, the perfume of soot, and the aroma of wine) the final consequences and the first and most immediate remedy (all trains went through at midnight) for an illness acquired during the last days of the war in a labyrinth of chaotic passageways and flickering bulbs, narrow rooms and enormous beds, trips in trucks and filthy buckets and shots in the thickets, during that interminable trip through the heart of the mountains. One day, it was at the suggestion of that same unhinged and compassionate ticket clerk, or maybe it was a coachman who was waiting for me asleep in the driver's seat ever since the day of my conversion, when in my desperation I came to rent a shay that would take me to the Hotel Terminus in Ebrias where the Región local normally stopped. . . . I knew the hotel, I knew it only too well and I remembered it well enough to suspect that the moment I had sufficient strength to push open the door and make the bells on the door frame ring I would have managed to close the cycle of growth of a person who until then had only known how to bring into bloom an unhealthy flower in passionate and fetid fields. It was better to let her die. At the other end of the street and on the sidewalk opposite the other two were peacefully waiting, certain that a few steps before the door of the hotel her firm decision would fall apart; 'Poor thing; there's no hope.' Because it wasn't a decision that they lacked but faith, a modicum of confidence that what she was looking for in the lobby of the hotel would close (or open) the new parenthesis. Then I saw the hotel clerk through the door, only his white head was showing over the small counter, and with a pair of glasses on the tip of his nose he was reading a local newspaper in a cool, gloomy, and solitary lobby. . . . My God, who was that clerk? why, without taking his eyes off the paper, did he make me falter, make me feel the futility of my myth, and quickly return to the starting point, while the other two people at the end of the street turned their backs, triumphant and discreet, in order to hide their joy by making use of a gesture with which they took pity on my shame? Not even if it had been a question of a brothel would that impassable barrier that separated her in the end from decent behavior have managed to interpose itself between her and the two people waiting on the opposite sidewalk. No, there wasn't the slightest possibility of degradation, she didn't have the slightest faith in perversion, that's what the clerk was telling me facing the varnished wood staircase; there was no doubt that I didn't lack resolve to abandon decency, order, and scruples, but I lacked courage, a capacity for sacrifice, and the lucidity necessary to embrace the swinish credo of a depravation in which, willy-nilly, I was going to find myself alone, with no one to accompany me and no one to whom I could turn in the event of a failure. It was what the two of them were telling me by their attitude: we're not judging you, far from it, we're only warning you that after going through that door you won't see us again, that's all. I don't know a more difficult step to take and I suppose that all who live in a state like that have reached solitude through a slow and continuous process of decomposition and ascesis, because certainly a person isn't capable of tolerating that act of brutal and instantaneous surgery that, in reality and a few steps away from the hotel, I meant to undertake. The others didn't know it; there's no possibility of shaking off and freeing oneself from upbringing or norms or anything, except at an early age, which I had already passed; and the adult woman, much as it bothers her, has incorporated into her conduct a moral sediment that, no matter how much she tries, she can no longer root out without destroying her most intimate fibers. The terrible thing is that it's an unknown process. After a few years of calm—a passage in calm dominated by the temperate breeze of conscience—even the skeleton changes and refuses then to obey the whims of fantasy or to recognize the gilded evocations of memory. During that trip the soul changes and takes on a shape—consciously or unconsciously—with the true impetus out of which it was born, distracted by that instant of fulfillment, participating in it. It's not just that the soul is mortal, but, truly united to the body, it lives only two or three days, in a hotel of ill repute or in some bushes, how should I know when. When it was a child, when it was afraid. Only when the party's over and, after a period of expectation defined by its faith in its survival does the soul try to awaken and revive, find itself with a disciplined body that from its own insides dictates to it, forbidding it to transgress its norms: ten or fifteen years later it understands quite well; how the person emerges from the ooze of that youth totally clean, naked, and innocuous, the passive agent of a strange will that only distracted it but didn't transform it during those decisive instants that remain deposited in the memory of an absolute lack of recollection. When she understands that her soul is being extinguished—around the age of fifty now—it's necessary to recur to the image without a face or a voice or a name, reduced and crystallized in that faded ecstasy that keeps it uncorrupted. Because, at the limit of her strength, she tried, like Cinderella, to escape for the last and definitive time the vigilance of her sisters and look at herself in the mirror to see that faded face, and all she knew to do was to take that trip and knock on this door."

"A little more?" the doctor interrupted, in a loud voice.

"No, no thanks."

"It's a very clean drink; it will do you good."

"No, thank you very much. Later."

"Who knows, the hours pass quickly."

"Time and weather?"

"Then there's no doubt: it's fear."

"My father used to say: Time and weather? Where are they? You mean rain, the rain . . ."

"Your father?" the doctor asked.

"He never knew anything about me. He didn't worry too much about my person, for which I have to be very thankful. He didn't even pretend, and above everything else he rejected my photograph, a suitcase stuffed with maps and compasses. I can assure you that it only produces tranquillity in me, no resentment. But it's all the same. I don't know either whether it began in this room or whether it was on the second floor of the hotel in Ebrias, it's all the same too. One morning, close to noon already, I finally woke up surrounded by a silence and a calm that were abnormal, a cold field, peaceful and bright, sunk in that strange rural peace that can only come about in times of combat. My sleep had gone on much later than usual, filled with a laziness that's born of so many hours of idleness and bed, so many unmade beds and so much unwashed clothing and so many unaired sheets and which I was only able to overcome through the fault of that disquieting silence. When I opened the shutters—and the steps that hurried along the platform stairs and the echoes of the shots and the panting motors that still sounded in my ears—I forgot all my suspicions because my attention was distracted by a pair of beggar dogs who were mutually sniffing each other, beyond the stone wall that enclosed the small garden of the house in a meadow dulled in color by the cold, with small piles of frozen and dirty snow, where some newly washed clothing and some very white sheets had been laid out to dry. Without my knowing it, in a moment of distraction, I again found the tranquillity lost before a sinful fearfulness that had been brought to boil by an incomprehensible procedure: a piece of clothing laid out to dry that—and then I got the smell of our bedroom, closed up for so many days—was talking to me again of the Samaritan order that I thought I had escaped from forever. I can only say that at that crucial moment of the transformation, when my whole body seemed ready to leave the chrysalis after having gone through the foul and grotesque process that would transform by means of an illusion man-

[138]

qué adolescent mysteries and the great words of youth and imaginary desires and the deficit of passion into the receptacle of a suicidal instinct (and ridiculous perhaps but doubtless intranscendental), my whole reason found itself occupied by some dungheap dogs who were about to trample on some newly washed sheets. How long did I stay looking out into the midmorning cold, leaning on the windowsill observing how they were chasing each other, knocking each other down, and trying to bite and mount in a lewd and innocent game that doubtless attracted and fascinated me as much as the forbidden memory of a suddenly remote and virtually heroic age—one which remains, that is, registered in memory united and motivated by a heroic intent, even when it wasn't like that—like the unexpected mark of an instinct which—between people or between dogs—couldn't be either boorish or punishable except by the threat represented by the domestic order that was materialized in those ever so white sheets that reflected the shadow of the grass in blue. I want to remember the other things and I scarcely can: how—with great effort—a half-dozen animals were loaded up at sundown by the corner of the house across from the watchful eye of a man wrapped in a military cape and wearing a balaclava that only let the tip of his cigarette be seen; how with the first hours of evening they set out on the road into the mountains, headed by the sentinel, perhaps the same one who watched over and was presented with, still leaning on the ubiquitous threshold, my initiation into the mystery, his hands in his pockets, the cigarette in his mouth, and the carbine slung under the cape, and closed up by the drowsy peasant swaying on the last donkey. How long I remained absorbed and in a reverie, shut up in that house, unable to get out of my imagination that atrocious trip to who knows what distant bramble patch on the mountain, on icy January nights, unable to distract a thought, wounded but attracted and almost hypnotized by the horizontal scratch that the reinforced edge of the saddlebags and the staff of the mule-

teer—as if for the climb they needed those last instants of
contact with the house—dug into the crumbling whitewashed wall a yard above the ground; I'm sure that my consciousness—without confessing it—through the abysmal and
phosphorescent lights of the soul saw a similar scratch, at
the height of the lower stomach, produced by a caravan of
fugitives. Was I like the wall, would I be condemned to the
same quiet and abandonment, when nothing but a scratch is
the testimony of the men who inhabited it and fled? I'm also
sure that, amidst silent recriminations (like those explosions
of the early morning fights, which, since they have no accompanying noise, never seem to end) a conscience that clung
to customs tried to offend me and shame me with that horizontal scratch, the only sign of his passage through my body
but—what is worse—also the only thing that had been carried away, distractedly, by a few crumbs of dust and whitewash, in his long exile. And, abounding in it, feeling how
inside of me there was coming to fruition the seed of a dire
premonition that in the future would always dominate me
with a cowardly and swinish taste that doesn't need experience to hit the mark, with the consent of fate—and its urge
for irrevocability—and out of the sense of duty and decency
that opposes it—and thus justifies the harshness of its rule—
to the tendency that everybody has toward corruption, once
it has known the limit of its forces, until I decided to knock
on this door and ask:

" 'Are you the only man left on earth who has no intention of curing me or correcting me? Is it you, doctor?'

"And you answered me: It's possible, I'm not very sure,
but it's possible that that's how it is, as if you were too
ashamed to affirm it in some solid way. Maybe until that
very moment I had been obstinate in maintaining the only
credo that, invested with different names, tried to go beyond and overcome the crisis of the initiation of a body involuntarily bound to an upbringing in decency, bewitched
and enslaved forever by a turbulent and remote moment in

the cab of a truck or the hallway of a hotel of ill repute on
the road into the mountains. And yet I scarcely believed it:
I tried to defend myself or defend that part of the person
that was indifferent to hypocrisy and, in a certain way, independent with respect to that possessed body that no one
was able to exorcise, neither postwar officials nor domestic
peace, the affection and the kindness with which the order
to which I was restored tried to heal the wounds and affronts of captivity, not yet on the altar of adultery but neither in the aberrant fire of renunciations, sacrifice, and fidelity. When finally—sitting in that same chair perhaps, a
unique sunset with rain, what else could it do—I understood
thanks to fear that there was no such independence, that such
a split didn't exist in my body and that I had only taken advantage of a legacy the nuns had left me with their education—as much for the respect for the laws of decency as for
the habit of dissimulation and deceit with oneself—in order
to keep a vicious cult uncontaminated, I convinced myself
that I had grown old. I understood too that similar contradictions and hiatuses . . . alas, are nothing but an apparatus
of youth, the accidents that rise up couldn't be less in the
course of that game that fantasy and destiny have undertaken, excited like two rival musicians trying to keep alive
a macabre night of revelry, have plotted to distract the drive
of the only age that hides a sincere unselfish appetite. Who
can doubt but that it works for its own destruction. Is that
sufficient reason to lead a person to the cult of oneself? And
it's always that way; always, sooner or later the day will dawn
when the object that the hands yearned for the night before
takes on all its value not by itself, but because it is found in
those hands. Something ends then, an age that isn't measured in years perhaps—I repeat—but in the extinction of a
certain generosity. When does it end? It's the reason of the
successive—the ally of fear—which will dictate which desires are worthwhile, which are suicidal, which branch has
to be eliminated in order to straighten the trunk that . . .

you must know: can it be—I imagine—at the moment when, after twenty years of what?—marriage? innocence? abandonment? prostitution? hypocrisy? who can give it its proper name?—a woman seduced in the cab of a truck, taken in again into the bosom of a society that more than forgiving her has pitied her, understands—the same as the recidivist and incurable criminal—that her nature leans toward crime and first it will be necessary to pass over all effective codes in order to embrace the field of virtue; that—now that it's necessary to hate something—in what follows she will hate laws, order, and decency in order to live in conformity with a credo that will find its real *raison d'être* only in sins; a heap of coals that gives off more heat when the logs burn but which, alas, will never light up again. When I went over to that telephone lying on the little Moorish table and the nasal, impersonal voice, not belonging to anyone but to the enemy ether . . ."

"We've only got one tree," the doctor interrupted, "but have you seen how it glows?"

". . . not in war, but in peace. Because the war was only a pretext, a wile that destiny imposes, as on Iphigenia, in order to test her closeness to her father; and my father was even less than that terrible voice coming out of a magnetic plate . . ."

"It was something more than that, no doubt. The proof that we weren't right, that there was no logic in our acts or judgment in our predilections. It was necessary to return to the beginning, however, it was necessary to erase the last steps that had led to such a morass. In truth, if there was no longer any confidence in the future or a tie to the land or a true faith in beliefs, why not return to the terrain of hate? Only out of defeat could something new rise up; it hasn't been like that, but that doesn't take anything away from the fact that it would have been the best reason to wage war: to be able to lose it."

"That reminds me that . . . but why do you say that? He

said that but didn't believe it except because of a perverse intention. So I would understand that something was disappearing forever. But believing that is precisely to eternalize it, to live in the confidence that it exists—because it did—even though we'll never see it again. I've always known it and that's partly why I'm here. I only learned about that war when it was ending. Somewhat later, after something more than a week, I suffered all of its consequences: a father dead, a lover disappeared, an upbringing in shreds, a knowledge of love that incapacitated me for any future; before me, and in the bosom of a society ready to receive me as a martyr and a desirable article, no other possibility was open but that of deception, incapable of confessing my closeness to the enemy and renouncing (I no longer say denying) him. There was no other solution, because I had known the fate of those unfortunate beings who have been engendered one moment before the cataclysm and whose nature, inadequate for subsequent conditions, has no other future but a slow and mute extinction. I was born in a certain way in the year 1938, at the end of a continental age: my lungs opened up to oxygen when the continent decided—without thinking about me, it thought rather about my father and his promotion friends—to sink into that lethal sea which my system didn't find itself (it never had been) adequate for. They're regressions and transgressions that occur in a periodic but—as far as the life of man is concerned—chancy way. So this new continental period that seemingly is already being announced on the horizon will no longer be of any use whatever to me. On the other hand, what can my friends and my country matter to me if, as a consequence of that cataclysm, all I have left is my self-esteem? Not even a taste for vengeance is left, I only hold rancor for those who—acclimated to the conditions of these past years—we will soon see on the ground, twitching, smothered by the atmosphere that they tried to pollute. For them it must be harder because I, at least, was shaped— I had to submit—in a climate lacking any future. Not they;

[143]

they thought they would survive. During the war, love, like any other item, was interdicted and it had to be accomplished with that clandestine accomplice spirit, mixed with anxiety, haste, and roguery that pervades children playing hooky. It couldn't prevail, knowing that it had been born of and owed its existence to a state of affairs that would of needs not last; therefore, harassed by its futility, it tried to find its *raison d'être* in a sinful instinct, in a certain sense of mockery, in a comedy of the comedy, having decided not to prolong the show beyond that fleeting situation and renouncing ahead of time an ulterior and false continuity that sooner or later would adulterate it. We mocked everything, although a bit late; in a comedy like that the first thing that comes off poorly is not pride itself but the urge to generosity. On a certain occasion he told me—I think it was during a moment of truce, in that flight into the mountains, sitting by the door of a shack while he tossed stones onto the road—the same as you: that the best reason to prolong a fight was always a defeatist one and that in our case it was absolutely necessary to continue the war until we had won total defeat. Only defeat will make the postwar tolerable. . . . What was the name of that couple who worked on the Committee? He was a tall man, with dark glasses and an unhealthy look, who scarcely saw anything and spent the whole war walking nervously through the hallways of the Committee building, smoking incessantly. And it seemed that he hadn't smoked before the war because a single pack would have sent him to his grave. Robal? Rubal? His wife—I remember well—was also called Adela, Comrade Adela; she was small, robust, and behind an incipient softness a contained violence was hiding; it's possible that serving as a guide for her husband had innoculated her with a state of permanent alarm and a drive to violence with respect to everything that surrounded them. For more than a year, the last one of the war, I slept in the same room as she, when the economy of bedrooms imposed a separation of the sexes; I don't know if I grew to hate her. A few days before my father's troops occupied the city we saw them abandon the Committee building, holding hands: they went out into the air for the first time in a hundred or two hundred days and they didn't dare take a step, holding hands and looking at the main square with the same strangeness as if it were the country of the Tendre. What abandonment, what cruelty. I suppose that the troops must have surprised them sitting on a bench in the same square, lacking everything and incapable of thinking about their own situation, everything that had happened, and the fate that was presented them, paralyzed more by nothingness than by fear and without knowing—or being able to know—how to do anything but squeeze their hands mutually so as to retain that last and only property about which nobody—not even themselves—would question them. I remember that I kept watching them until a turn of the truck as it went around a corner hid them from view, impressed with a feeling that I don't dare classify in any way: a mixture of compassion, relief, envy, guilt, and disdain. Compassion for their abandonment and envy for their simplicity and joy, guilt, animosity, and many other things for the distance that separated me from them in all ways. But how did I know that after a few days their image would return to my memory haloed by an aura of fatality, because it was no longer a question of a fleeting picture but of a condition. Subject to the same condition I found myself at the door of that mountain hotel of ill repute, drying my hands on a kitchen towel after cleaning a pot while the column of Navarrese climbed along the road that led up to the house. I didn't realize it at that time; what I refused to believe, what my self-esteem tried to make public in order to force a change in my feelings, what my spite, fear, and shame began to deny was implicitly recognized by a memory that went back to the image of that unfortunate couple. Nor was it sympathy that brought them back to me after a few days, rather an affinity of a fateful kind, thanks to which, without daring or wanting to under-

[145]

stand them, I no longer felt them alien to my own nature. There was no outrage or deceit, that's the worst of it; when I finally left the house—I returned to Región wrapped in military capes and blankets in the company of a little boy petting a newborn kitten and an old deaf carter who didn't pay the slightest attention to control posts, columns of eva- cuees, and groups of ragged and taciturn prisoners—I was still overcome by the feeling of guilt and tardiness, as if I were leaving a party whose noise was still echoing in my ears in the form of fatigue, sleepiness, and satisfied displea- sure, comforted in my inner code by the emotions which, after a few hours of rest, were to be repeated. But it wasn't that way because doubtless my body—my distilled and fragile desolation—required more care than mere rest and needed other guarantees and other nourishment than the dream of waking up; not to mention that appearance of innocence that I carried away from a fratricidal escape and I tried to console myself with the word expiation, with the word guilt, and the word duty, and that last word, renunciation; as if words had the power to suture the wound and relax those tight muscles that in no way in the world wanted to return to their relaxed position or get out of that absorbing, shadowy, and idiotized ecstasy, lying on the schoolgirl bed and sur- rounded by innocent fetishes and rag dolls, where as soon as she began to understand that the only thing left in secret was the body she began to caress that solitude in order to practice a forbidden cult. Although I didn't want either to forgive or forget the testimony that I kept in my tabernacle, it was of that type that tries at all costs to break secrets and oaths to be professed one more time. In reality, what did I have to hide, apart from the deviation with regard to the normal and decent conduct of a girl my age and of my up- bringing? Wasn't the war nothing but the ample justification for the disorders of a body? Wasn't it sufficient in reference to the credulous and impertinent little girl, placed one step away from the subtle borderline that separates her from a

[146]

public woman? Weren't a couple of weeks at an inn of ill repute enough, a trip in a broken-down truck in the company of some people who, in a certain way, were in the right at the moment for raping or killing me? What other answer could they give my father? Wasn't it—and still is, the frenzy of my father and his friends—a matter of the greatest importance to think about the indiscretions of a daughter? Oh, if everything had been as simple as all that I would have come out innocent: I mean, I would have come out of the sacrifice mistress of myself. But why go into details? What do people, names, places, dates, the kind of misdeed matter? What does it matter what I chose, facing what was given me? Weren't they all fighting among themselves? So what? Does it matter that I was the first one interested in losing her virtue? And if I told you that if the holocaust hadn't come I would have lost it too? Don't you think, Doctor, that there are many ways of losing one's virginity?"

"I don't know for certain. In matters of knowledge I have always tried to limit myself to the field of my experience."

"Sir, there are still those who believe that when that fragile petal is plucked one acquires a new status. I suppose it's a strictly masculine mania, a kind of guarantee that the quality of the product depends on a label on the cork. But of what little good that seal is to a woman, how little the state of the cork matters. Not only does she hate it, but she takes pride when she can break it and forget forever a state of its cursed importance. True virginity comes after, with the seal broken. And innocence and chastity too. And then, even though I didn't want to confess it, I knew it, day and night, lying on that schoolgirl cot, surrounded by dolls and schoolday memories and trying as hard as I could to reconstruct the pain and the itch of the wound on the lower stomach because in all probability in those times my poor economics considered it cheaper to suppose that I had let myself be dragged toward a forgivable and correctable sin. But how little that lasted, how soon the true economics of the body imposes on the means and restrictions of upbring-ing which tries to cure a ruinous and pitiful state with a fic-titious purification; and the game starts up again, with the following misadventure; there's a whole long moment in which chances, disasters, hope are carried on an imaginary level determined by guilt and regeneration between which the person moves like a ball thrown from hand to hand by a juggler who keeps it in the air without its ever touching the ground. This is the most terrible thing for me: because without noticing it in those final days of the war, in the cab of the truck and in the room at the inn, I had touched the bottom of what has been given to be called existence. And then there was no need for words, or memory, or—even less—feelings: there was no guilt or misdeed or morality, there could be no sin or repentance or moratorium. From there having been something deceptive it was only a tricky fate that refused to interrupt the brief interval of our love with the presentation of that atrocious bill that at the end of the days nobody was able to pay. Then it passes and can be seen with wrath how the woman, the man, sincerity have been tricked, because in that way it has been changed into an ir-ritating and stupid end whose principal diversion doesn't consist of determining fate but only hiding it. . . . When there's no longer any way out, how many things are seen clearly; when after years have passed one asks oneself about the basis of that morality that aborted so many things—that would convert all the impulses of a conduct into a landscape in ruins . . . immoral? indecent? inopportune?—one cannot help but think up to what point the individual has more need for justification before himself than before the external order that considers him to blame. I can still remember that hall-way of shudders, from the bedroom to the bathroom and the stairs, painted pale blue, tile floor, and lighted by a sin-gle bulb above the back landing, which I crossed so many times, terrified and half naked, trembling with cold, fear, and furor. I remember that while he was sleeping—a few times he fell into the sleep of a child whom I envied and cursed because I felt jealous of that hidden and unfathomable nature so alien to me, who with such rapidity and smoothness knew how to slip out of the bonds of love and curl up in his sleep, of that deep, regular, and strange breathing, like the heaving of a horse or the nocturnal roar of the sea—I often had to get up and cross that hallway that was lighted all night long, not so much to keep watch on me as to dramatize with its brutal lumotechnics the steps of the apprentice over the abyss. I don't know how I knew that there, more than in the huge rustic bed, my test took place and that the consecration of my vows, not the chastity of a body that had already lost all desire for virtue but the sincerity of a conduct that was groping for the post-virginal pure chastity of an infinitesimal feeling lost among a crowd of passions and contradictory doubts, was to depend on the ease that I was to show covering the forty feet of hallway naked. And when I got back and locked the door of our room (the same darkness that enclosed a certain heat that fit the smell of his flesh, the pale glow of the bulbs, and the reflection of the calm water in the basin, that deep, rhythmical, and powerful breathing which—just like waves on the shore—seemed to break on the folds of the sheets) gave the sensation of returning not to the erotic shadows but to the hot morbidity of the maternal refuge after the short trip through the whispering and hostile shadows. I had to weep then, with my head against his chest, and suck in my own tears off that skin that was shaken by a breathing that seemed to wish to stop just from contact with my lashes. But with him asleep I couldn't hate him, yet I was beginning to mistrust and to notice that a part of his condition would always be far away from me and not because I was ashamed of the terrible role my body was playing in his comedy, not because a reticent self-esteem answered the disdain of his dearest audience with rancor, not because of anything but because a sordid, pusillanimous, and alert awareness felt that its beloved, in the arms of sleep, at the same time that he was going away was recovering his independence like that smuggler who from time to time would seek refuge in the craggy regions only known to those of his race. And the pampered young girl who, without knowing how, has managed to break the barriers imposed by her caste to have an adventure that attracts and horrifies all the gentle people, contemplates for the first time the real line on the horizon beyond which she will never see anything, no matter how great her daring: a skin wrapped up in the smell of softness and of sweat, a solemn and distant breathing, profiled in the shadows like the line of the mountain range where those people and that accursed race live; she will never be capable of getting there, of changing into another one of them, perhaps because the gentlefolk nucleus that was born with her has warned that a large part of her passion is based on a horror of herself and which—if she undertakes the trip—will accompany her up to those borderline regions too; up to the lands of that furrowed race where sooner or later the beloved will return when, more than the nostalgia for his land, into his breast hate and scorn for the gentlefolk will flow. It was an endless line of days and nights of trying not to leave that room at all costs; I don't know if it was another manifestation of shyness after the first shame, which changes its sign and feels drawn toward the corruption (the heat of his breath, the smell of the sheets) when the object of her defense has been conquered. Because she will always try to defend something and when virtue is conquered it will turn against its former ally to fight for the acquired vice; and when the latter has been ruined it will take refuge in fatigue or languor. It wasn't just an exercise of apprenticeship in the hallway of shivers: the same morning air, the song of the cocks and the boiling pots, the aroma of clean sheets come to be repugnant, filthy for the one who can no longer hope for regeneration (I can't speak about fear of punishment because I never felt it). But I'm inclined to believe that with that reclusion I was trying not to reflect in

[150]

order to get the specter of the day far away from me—that was how I feared it—the day when he would have to leave me; I didn't want to provide him at least with the excuse of an absence of mine. Maybe not; maybe I was the one who needed a clear accounting in order to test the character of an unmistakable balance at the end of the exercise. It was I who should have been convinced that day that there wasn't any maybe in between and that, with accounts settled, the last thing we had done was play at hiding from tomorrow. Fate doesn't exist, it's character that decides. I scarcely turned on the lights or opened the shutters for two weeks during which the sheets weren't aired or the bed made or was any care given to those clothes in which a recently liberated body, insinuating and strutting, had had fun by itself in its grace and its duplicity, like the horse that a Gypsy walks through a fair, to startle and offend an avaricious and incredulous conscience that resists considering it his in spite of his having brought out the amount stipulated. And I thought . . . the amount that the body—and only the body—has known how to earn, did it correspond to it exclusively? was it a question of a clean business, with things set like that? what good are the damages and benefits of morality? During the long hours—the cold, the size of the bed, the play of that naked and unharnessed body under the disordered clothes was all that stopped me from giving it an order and a cleanliness that horrified me—that I was alone (our nuptial sleep was interrupted so many times by knocks on the door, the sound of boots on the tiles under the weight of weapons and damp capes) all I did was try to explain to myself the complicated financial operation in whose logic conscience basically never believed: what was the capital moral interest expended and what the profit and what the amortization of that body used for a good part of its life. How was I to know then that the whole economy of love is dominated by that first investment whose result is translated almost always into definitive and irreparable bankruptcy. It seems to me that in our logic

[151]

we have lodged a secret and wily tribunal that knows it and keeps it quiet and which, informed by an ancestral knowledge, accepts in its time the education bequeathed by the nuns so that, knowing the fraud that is approaching, it loads all the responsibility onto a naked body before an obscene mirror. And it's even possible that all the deceptions of instinct—which nature has engendered only with an eye to success, alas, would be something else if an authentic unfortunate awareness really existed—come from a clandestine focal point that knows too well and ahead of time the futility of love and against which the body will always founder. Until his silhouette in the early morning was once more marked out in the doorway lighted by the bulb in the hallway, a triangular cape and a cloud-colored balaclava rolled up on his forehead. 'Still asleep?'—'Oh, Lord, sleep . . . how could anyone still believe it?'

"What did I do afterward? You can easily imagine. I never got to know how much time I stayed there; I've come to know what happened in the war afterward with difficulty, why you people were fighting, what impelled you to run away. Not even the time I was alone after you left, wanting to believe that it was a matter of one more separation, just like the ones before. I don't know if I got out of the bed, because under the blankets, behind the closed shutters, that juvenile, conceited, and lewd body was twisting and hugging itself in order to get the idea of deceit out of it, in order to invent a different and imaginary hesitation and remain deaf to the revelations with a cruel premonition. One morning I perceived that there was too much silence around me; education let me guess that finally I had been given that solitude which it had foretold so many times and then my body leaped up, left the bed, put on the first piece of clothing it found on the chair, and ran barefoot down the hall in search of proof to put the lie to it. The sun was out, but it was a very cold morning, and the fields were still covered with frost beyond the hedges; some hens were trying to shake off the cold by flapping their wings on the threshing floor and pecking by the sunlit gate, but neither in the house nor on the road nor on the bank of the brook could a soul be seen. Only the stew pot was boiling in the kitchen, the smell of which had reached two or three stray dogs who were chasing and sniffing each other and who fled from my presence with their tails between their legs. Then my body went back to the bedroom, closed the shutters again, took off the dress, brought to its nose the nightshirt that had been there, and got back into bed, naked and reclining, putting against its face and breast what still held in its folds the strong smell of its lost love-making. I don't know how many days—or if it was only a few hours—she remained like that, drying her tears on that piece of booty that in the end smelled of nothing but her own solitude; biting the absent neck and tearing the empty sleeves, consumed with fever, while conscience, looking at the rays of light on the ceiling, recognized with frightful lucidity that she had lost her first battle and that in the future it was necessary to make use of a less innocent method and more hypocritical conduct in order to bring off revenge. One noontime, finally, Muerte entered the room, with a black-tobacco cigarette in a filter holder, wearing a black dressing gown printed with large, multicolored flowers and a benevolent smile showing a gold tooth. She offered me a cigarette, taking a wrinkled and half-empty package out of her bosom; she had pale breasts crossed with blue veins, enormous, as if to feed starving children. I asked her where you were; I think it was no longer my body who had renounced the bad-smelling item, but that prosecutor and executioner conscience who, after having made public his sentence, allows the last moments to be sweetened with a charitable and humanitarian gesture for the gallery. She sat down on the bed, drew the dressing gown up over her knees, and asked me if I wanted anything for breakfast. I told her to open the shutters and she smiled again, showing the golden fang once more while she closed the robe about her breasts and blew the last puff of smoke toward the ceiling. She took the booty with two fingers and threw it onto the floor; she looked me up and down, shaking her head she contemplated the state of the room that she hadn't entered for the past few weeks, gave me a few quiet taps on the ankles, and, after crushing the butt on the tiles, stepping on it with the slipper with a red pom-pom, after some discreet looks through the cracks in the shutters, told me that she was going to bring up some warm milk and crackers for breakfast.

"Even though you might not believe it, I can assure you that the reproaches didn't begin then. They were quite late in coming—as you have to understand: it's probably because reproaches that can't be displayed are stillborn or because they had to wait for a more bitter certainty than that first one that 'time and absence together come to snuff in vain,' when the drive defeated in that adventure understands that in the future it must surrender to the only person who will be faithful to it. It was a rather serious defeat trying to avoid it with a court martial and a prisoner in revolt, a few pronouncements favorable to my integrity, my spirit, the virtues of my race, and the strength of my upbringing. I resist belief in that decision: I don't try to justify myself anymore but to make intelligible how the forces of the defeated faction refuse to collaborate with the new government and how a person will remain divided in the future into two irreconcilable sectors; an anxiety that will no longer try to legitimize its aspirations but will consume them with clandestinity and an education, a bearing—call it what you will—that through need or desire will renounce the restraint of passion forever; a drive to possess and a drive to surrender that will never be reconciled, under any circumstances, in any friend. From that moment on I understood that any reproach I tried to make against you would inevitably turn against my self-esteem and that every possible solution would accept such an excision. So that when Muerte tried to clarify the situation, the first one to be surprised was she. She had nothing to console, no forehead to stroke, no soul to uplift. She only had to hand over my bad-conduct certificate, the money I asked for when I was drinking my milk, looking at her over the edge of the glass. I don't know why we called her that and I suppose the nickname also came from you. When I first met her I guessed that it was a question of the same person who since my childhood had watched over my safety in the absence of my mother. There wasn't the slightest ingredient of vice in her nature; there was nothing but rigor, avarice, and a little cruelty although—truthfully—I can't reproach her for anything: she showed a certain consideration for me, she put me up in her house and finally (her fear was so great) she loaned me the money without talking to me at all about the date and form of repayment. It was the first vengeance that I savored; after all, I was only an orderly person like her, who, through imprudence of ambition had committed a sin. Now they had to pay for their laxness, the same is demanded by the small child warned by his nurse who has taken her eyes off him for a few minutes to speak to a passerby. And all my father's fault, and I wanted to wait for him there to ask him: 'What did you do with my photograph?' It's possible that a couple of years earlier it wouldn't have bothered him to go down to the nearby store and talk on the telephone to my guardian, but twenty-four hours and an order sending him to the front were enough to divorce him from the calf whose upbringing he had tried to use during my childhood to justify his withdrawal and cowardice. I can still see him in those days, packing his bag: he's folded the newly dusted off uniform in the bottom and at the last moment he notices that in order to close the suitcase he has to leave out the photograph: mine, dressed as a schoolgirl, because my mother's . . . had been thrown out a long time before. I think that I spent a whole hour contemplating that glass of pure milk, quiet inoffensive milk offered in houses of prostitution as a regenerative certificate, like the archaic vestige of a rite that precedes nuptial depradations, while my soul, far away from there—absent for a moment from the business that was of such interest to it—was still smelling in the red cushions, in the aroma of lotion that impregnated the pillow, in the vice-ridden shadows, and in the disorderly wrinkles in the sheets the omens of a new status for one who was discovering an evident vocation. That I had that vocation . . . you, as always, said so first. But it seems that a vocation is very little if it doesn't rise up from an outside stimulus, something that in addition to revealing the attractions for the state surround it with a glory unlike any other. With all the vestiges of heroism having evaporated forever that vocation had of necessity to be dominated by scorn. Doubtless it influenced my father when he went off to join his Headquarters while the portrait of his daughter was left behind under a closet. So I decided to wait for him in that house and to be able to be in that room and if possible in that bed, between those sheets, with the ill-smelling booty clutched against my breast. But Muerte said no; she had too much position and a lot of fear; those bawdy-house madams are, above all, friends of order and respectful of the law, all her business is based on her good relations with the agents of power. And, also, they don't like jokes; and mine was in the poorest taste: an outrage. So she had to pay in order not to go through it. Because, after you left, what need did I have for shame and pride? I only had traces of them, weaker and dirtier every day, like the handful of blackened certificates, wrinkled, torn, and taped together that the unemployed civil servant always carries in his pocket in order to believe in a previous and less lamentable status. When a couple of months later I found Tomé in the woodshed of the house I could no longer do anything, I couldn't even add anything to the desire for revenge, and as for pity, what little it had to do with his cot! Under other circumstances the proper thing would have been for him to have returned to me, because I was the only thing that could have cured all his remorse. . . . I'm exaggerating, yes. What can I do but exaggerate? What is there left for me except to try to raise up the former value of a coin so new and so quickly devaluated? As for Tomé, you knew him, who better than you can know how mistaken I was for a second time in trying to put the same hair shirt of fate on him. What a word! He couldn't understand that I was closed up in it; he didn't want to understand anything but a lot of remorse that he carried with him to the grave and that I'm sure I could have cured if I'd wanted to break the terms of my contract. Who better than you can know about the things he felt guilty about, why he stayed in Región, why he was silent, and why he died; why that fragile, changeable, and kaleidoscopic will can rise up at random to the surprise of consciousness, not to anticipate the direction of its steps as much as to pretend and hide the intention of an incongruous fate. Because it's the past that reflects and illuminates, with that flint glass lens that only with a determined direction polarizes the light in order to extract from a dememorized and stupefied present a whole series of routine proposals that in reality lack any temporal figuration. Because if the future is a trick of the sight, the present is leftover will, a remnant. When Muerte gave me the money—the imperceptible gesture that made the kaleidoscope spin—the past didn't vanish but recovered all its value: the body was covered again with that film of rancorous alkali that in the future will attract, absorb, and decompose any preparation of the will. I'm trying to tell you that the money barely amounted to anything but it formalized a contract that my body and I had established in your presence days before. All that was left was for it to be endorsed, and that's where my father came in: dressed in uniform and wearing all his medals, he had no need to put his glasses on to sign that summary order on one of those octagonal Moorish tables with iron braces, moldings, inlaid and encrusted with bones and stones, which military men always have to have close by when it's a matter of resolving business of the nation.

"I said good-bye to Muerte; she was the one who wanted to do it with all the solemnity necessary to give the ceremony a definitive character. 'Remember, you don't know this house,' she told me. 'What about the money?' 'It's all I've got. Now I've got to start out all over again.' 'All over again?' 'All right, get going, child.' 'We'll see each other again, won't we? When I have the money.' 'Get going now, pay attention to what I've told you.' 'I don't want to go back to my father.' 'Child, don't you understand? He's down there.' 'I don't want to go back; when I get the money together . . .' 'Nobody is to see you now.' 'I may be back before you think.' 'Will you get going, child?' and she pushed me outside where the cart was waiting.

"It was harder for me to go back than I had expected. From the amount of money she gave me—and where she got it from I don't know—I understood the fear that she had gone through. But, on the other hand, I didn't wait long to make it grow. You taught me not to wait and in that aspect the contract was clear and precise. You told me—if I remember rightly—with your head leaning against the glass of the shaking window and looking forward toward the ditch (not out of fatigue as you would remember to pretend on occasion but to give to understand that it didn't matter much to you either) that I was perhaps—of all the people in the republican zone—the only one who was going to come out ahead with the war. But I didn't want to hear it; I'd moved off your shoulder and did nothing but also look at the ditch illuminated by the headlights, with my eyes wrapped in a dusty mixture of sleep, tears, and fear. You knew that for three days I hadn't stopped crying and, nevertheless, you had no other words of consolation. It wasn't cruelty nor was it a relaxed formula to sweeten the upcoming ending for me, but a simple mere conviction. You had said (after the failure of your plans for surrender) that the best reason for pro-longing that war had to be sought among the compensations of defeat. That the war had to be lost, no matter what it cost, no longer to acquire a firmer conviction of the evil of the adversary as to lose once and for all any confidence in history and its future. You also told me that the fruit of this victory of my father and his friends could be relished by those who, like me, without having sought it, and without having any guilt at all, would come out of the conflict without confidence in their parents or faith in their religion or illusions about the future. On that occasion, as on so many others, how wrong you were."

When they got to Región, all the outskirts were smoking and when they crossed the bridge over the Torce a very fine rain began to fall. A few days after the conquest of the city a munitions deposit that the republicans had hidden in a store on the edge of town blew up. A boy dressed in baggy pants held up with a rope and wearing a ragged military tunic that came down to his knees ran ahead of them shouting, impelled by that unconscious determination that had allowed him to pass through fires, barbed wire, control points with no other safe-conduct pass than his vocal cords. At every corner—as if every street were a side of the pentagram—his shout lost a semitone that finally disappeared among the desolate vacant lots in a rosy cloud of fire, rain, and dust. Almost all doors were closed and the façades on the Calle Císter seemed to waver under the gust of rain and smoke, like the tetric curtain that has fallen on the stage after the last and prophetic pause. The streets were dirty and deserted; before nightfall a fire broke out in the district by the river, which, held back or reduced by the rain, lighted up the horizon with a quiet, opaline, and iridescent clarity that only seemed altered by the shouting of that boy, by the breaking of the silence provoked by a sound running out of control in an emulsion of rain, fire, and darkness. When night fell some shots were heard: nearby and meaningless shots that, when they found a wall, left a small dry echo in the air, a crackling of flatulent explosions, as if there on the outskirts the rain was falling onto a red-hot iron. The electricity had been cut off, almost all the windowpanes were broken in their frames. At midnight the sky began to clear and the glow of the fire was reflected on some low-lying clouds with purple and orange tints. The cart stopped at a corner near the house. The peasant barely moved: his head down and covered by a black felt hat, framed between the ears of the mule, which, at the end of its years, brings back to his memory what war was like: a motionless animal, its ears stiff, black against the glow of the fire and the head of a peasant as quiet as if he were meditating, among the broken placards and corpses of dogs, on the passage of time. The door was half open and the entranceway muddy, but at the end of the stairs, above the glimmer of cartridge casings, a line of light blinked from a carbide lamp. The stove was lighted and the same pot that had boiled on the mountain was boiling again there, without smell or sound. The same boy's shirts and the same aprons of two years before hung on a line over the fireplace to dry. A voice of age, female and hesitant, was speaking behind a closed door at the same time as the sound of a marble ran once more along a hallway in darkness, jumping at the joints of the parquet until it hit the baseboard, seemingly making ironical comments about the futility of that war, about the quick passage of so many months that had been enough to complete a cycle of disaster and death but had not been sufficient to get the child away from his marble game. She was thin, quite thin and white-haired, with her skin toasted by hunger. With the door partly open she was drying her hands on the apron, the same expression on her face that she had seen when she had left—some time before—led by two armed men:

"Child, where can you be coming from at this hour?" she asked her with a surprised, annoyed, and scolding accent of one who had done nothing else but care for children. Still heard on the outskirts—the figurations of a night in which fear didn't enter because there was nothing to expect from it—was the shouting of that ragged child who ran through the open fields, louder and more stubborn than the fall of the rain or the buzz of the fire. Almost all the house was in darkness, the furniture covered with white drapes. Only the kitchen, at the rear of the hall, was lighted and—from the other side of the door, with his nose stuck to the glass—the child was looking at her open mouthed, with the supine and indifferent expression of those eyes enlarged by glasses. It struck again—for the first time in several years—the hour on the clock in the vestibule; it was a macabre sound, perhaps the signal agreed upon to take the coverings off the furniture; only then did she understand that the war had ended.

3

"I don't know whether it was true or not, but you had very good reasons to say it, I imagine," the doctor said, filling up his glass again. "You've got to understand that there wasn't the slightest opportunity left for them and the war was nothing but the final and most logical act in a fateful process; something like a public announcement of a suspension of payments by a corporation which a former employee—who has bought the newspaper to read the help-wanted ads—reads in passing. That man doubtless receives—it doesn't do him much good—a last justification for the social machinery that has left him without anything to put into his mouth, but they didn't even get that. The war, the war . . . for those who saw themselves caught up in it, without having plotted or expected it, couldn't have been a matter for reflection, neither reflection nor anything else but fear. There was, however, a class of people for whom the war constituted the best opportunity to find peace with themselves. They'd been living in an emulsion for a long time: a dissimulated and deferred rancor, the long wait for a disaster that has been announced but which hasn't taken on a body yet, that deliquescent harmony in the passage of days with which orphanhood without means, a country laid waste by the ax, a stingy subsoil, an everyday life and a generation with no future have come to establish an order of things in the paternal patrimony. And the whole future hanging in the void by a thread that will break with the first attack, that desire for violence held back only by an old, mute gamekeeper, the incarnation of a will that sleeps out of doors, ready to awaken at the first strange sound. But with merely the announcement of the civil war the emulsion is broken and the neutral particles of memory suddenly take on a violent shape and coloration. Even the mortuary harmony of the streets is broken and the silence of the gardens is changed. Over the potato fields—all the windows were open and the shades pulled up, it was a very hot summer day and the radios, at full volume, were repeating the same news of sedition every quarter hour without changing a word—a nasal and guttural voice was pouring out and with a chthonic accent and stumbling syllables was announcing the end of the truce and the prelude of the revenge. There was a moment of perplexity, thanks to which even faces, the most familiar corners, took on a new slant and it might have been said that—hiding behind the corners—even the dead were terrorized in their graves by that terrible and atonal voice, to wander about at dusk with their shirts unbuttoned, looking for a lost silence. It was no longer a matter of memory because the radio wouldn't let anything be remembered. Unmemoried, they tried to find a principle of conduct amidst a tangle of feelings: vengeance and fear, scorn and zeal. They didn't look for them in memory, which, perhaps, is nothing but the stone that covers an anthill, which—once the infantile, murderous, or curious hand has raised it—doesn't know what to do except run in a contradictory frenzy, with no other protection between sky and colony than mutual fear. That's how it happens with individual memory and all the more so with the collective one: by means of a warehouse economy

[163]

it doesn't remember hatred, but stores up rancor and, when it's brought up to date, it doesn't seek what the soul holds but that feeling which, after the expansion, fills it again with rage or anger. The substantive escapes me: but in those days I saw, everywhere, the ghost of many instincts and the inopportune search for a confidence that had already lost all its articles of conviction and was trying to find them in the most unlikely places, the most futile things and the most ridiculous beliefs—the banks of the river and abandoned stores, attics crammed with spoils, family portraits, old disguises— as if that news, as if those half-dozen news items—repeated with an obsessive monotony—proceeding from the most remote barracks on the peninsula were nothing but an invitation to the dance offered from the bandstand to a reserved audience who still hadn't had time to grasp the true nature of the party or to overcome its public bashfulness. During the intermission—between obsolete military marches mingled with republican airs—a certain sense of prudence tried to put order into the emanations of memory, a palate made for sobriety was trying to dissolve the taste of an unsaturated, bitter, and sour mixture of rancor and surprise that flowed into the mouth after an inopportune gesture. It wasn't a question of fighting yet, but of understanding. It was necessary—that's what the radio said—to know; and the struggle will be—it also said—the only form of study tolerated. During the last days of July the streets remained deserted and the resonance of the radios increased; one alone, away in a doorway at the highest point of a garret, was enough to fill a sun-drenched street, smothered and deserted between the walls of two convents. It was fear of sniper fire perhaps that induced everybody to live in rear rooms that opened on the courtyard; there, behind rolled blinds, someone tried to understand: who's talking now, who's right, what's happening in Madrid, what's happening in Macerta . . . mixed with that ebullience of proper pomp that the radio involuntarily has unleashed: 'the family name,' 'enemies of the house,' 'the welfare of your own,' 'the wrath of God,' 'the good of the country,' 'hatred, hatred. . . .' There followed a moment of hesitation, more intimate than public; that people had spent so much time to bring about its choice. A civil war in a country in ruins is always like that: you have to wait—in the bosom of every surprised heart—for the reactions of anger, rancor, resentments, desire for vengeance, urge to valor to transform the emulsion of milky coagulation into a precipitate of violent coloration. Only after a few weeks—not so much of unrest as of uncertainty—are the first outbursts produced, running up into the attic, morning patrols, a bundle thrown into the river, a pile of papers burning in the dump. During those days the men I'm telling you about try in vain to understand; they try to learn not the kind of storm that's threatening the country, but the kind of men they are. Maybe it wasn't faith or confidence that they lacked but credentials; they'd grown up in a country covered by wall rocket, thyme, genista; all their lives they'd been nourished on ruins, they never came to see how a stone is laid; the abandoned farms, uncultivated rural estates, the sown fields lying fallow, the forests cut down, the thirsty meadows and the destructive torrents were not the work of chance or negligence for them but constituted the marrow of a land whose standard was scarcity, whose hymn was supplication, and whose most impregnable fortress was fear. And ever so far away—deaf, bloated, sibylline, reticent, and contemptuous, like an oriental magistrate—that representative of the bureaucracy, indifferent to the slow course of history. When the whole country was divided by the catalysis of 1936 they didn't know immediately which pole to seek, what the nature of their intimate charge was. Because how could one who respected Religion take the side of Father Eusebio? And what form of respect was one who felt himself republican because of his readings going to have for Rumbal? Later on they learned, yes, when they had to make an abstraction of everything they knew or thought they knew in order to change, consequently, into the truly defeated; I don't know, I'm talking about a substance immersed in the peaceful neutral liquid that after electrolysis has seen itself despoiled of all particles with a charge and which lacks, in the end, all reactive value. For those who had to wage war the hesitation was short, even for those—who were many, perhaps the majority—for whom polarity was defined by their proximity to the pole or by the flow of particles around it. I don't know what the agent was that turned the current on or who was the catalyzer; history will give its judgment in its own time, which is quite different from that of contemporaries, because we're incapable of being satisfied with a simplification. What I do believe is that when a society has reached the level of disorientation that even manages to annul its instinct for survival, it spontaneously creates for itself a balance of opposing forces that upon entering into collision destroy all their reserves of energy to seek a state of peace that is—in extinction—more permanent; in the same way that schoolboys, surprised by the unexpected absence of the teacher, split up into two soccer teams into whose formation affinity, friendship, or differences scarcely enter but, rather, a certain sense of balance of strength that permits them to maintain their interest in the game during that hour of parenthesis. I am sure that, ahead of reason, passion and fear had already made their choice. Because the first thing that rises up is doubtless annoyance. I remember my youth and my life as a student, and when I try to reconstruct the thread of my decisions, I always see it in the background, the *ultima ratio*. I see there too a night of gambling at the beginning of autumn, the supreme architect of a pile of iridescent mother-of-pearl chips, who, amidst chryselephantine sparkles, moves toward the middle of the cloth to conquer the coin that had resisted him all summer; and I see it too (it's not a blushing) lodged in those deep eyes, always heavy, which over the gloved hand she has raised to hide her flushed look toward the table of combat where she knows her fate is being decided as she

[166]

breathes and lifts her breast with a gesture of hope that silences the dry and paused beats of her agitated heart. I was beside him; and when he made that gesture—without waiting for the fate of the card, even at the moment when his shoulder went through the door, the air filled with silence and the vibration of the knife—with which he meant to confirm a decision of which we had spoken so much, I agreed. How wrong I was, how I learned that that mistake presupposed a life of debts. At the moment when one decides to abandon his own Judas, it isn't scorn, or a surge of pride, or a sudden assessment, but the purifying annoyance that will cleanse her of the rebuff forever. And there is no doubt that it looked like pride: on the table she left the small black open purse—from which a mirror and a gold chain fell and a handkerchief was showing—and with a calm step she left the room while everybody ran to the group where the military man's hand had been run through and joined to the table by a switchblade knife. And I can see it even after, in the bearing and in the look of all the pursuers who left in search of her—or in search of the pile of chips—and even in the nostrils of the horses and their wrathful breathing along the road to Mantua, those mornings that were so cold and damp in the mountain autumn. But if that annoyance increases in a climate of laxness which always precedes the tragedy, passion then blooms without need of the intervention of any agent. No, there was no such trick on the part of reason: that August was much too hot and the people of Región, with the development of certain events that, instead of being resolved every week, became more complicated and fearsome, decided to remain in their homes for fear of patrols and sacking. And, nevertheless, Región seemed deserted, abandoned to a committee of defense and a few armed militiamen who, every afternoon—when it grew cool—got into some requisitioned and gaudily painted cars, trucks, and broken-down buses in order—with the pretext of rushing to the Macerta front—to run about the plain; they would search two or three farms, sack a storeroom, and come back to town in the early hours with booty that usually consisted of an old windup phonograph and a corrupt and venal administrator who, with his hands tied behind his back, his pants half-fallen and his pajama jacket open, had already acquired that lack of expression and paleness of skin, the consequence of so much internal trembling, of a man who has already ceased to exist when he is led down to the basement of the guard post. The streets were empty and almost all the façades and walls were decorated with large letters and proletarian slogans painted with tar; there was no curfew but no one went out after hours; there were no militias or nightwatchmen or any lighting except for that at the end of an alley cut off by a cinder wall, of a small and agitated restaurant inside of which the republican bustle gathered every night: a few bottles of ordinary white wine and uncouth song sessions, with patriotic lyrics alluding to the rebels, sung around the Mausers and garrison caps while the bourgeoisie, in their large, closed, and darkened apartments ruminated in horror during their vigil, waiting for the arrival of the search squad that had stopped at the corner bar to toss down a drink and listen to a fandango. It was a summer without peace or sun for the affluent class, who spent it all in the rear rooms; the radios had been confiscated and they received no other news than the rumors gathered by the old and faithful cook—the only one who went out of the house—at a market stand. And as for the front . . . life there must have been healthier and the people more honorable, although, to tell the truth, there was no front until the following year. But the determined men didn't want to know anything about all that: Eugenio Mazón, who had no religious beliefs; not he either, indifferent to everything. Juan de Tomé, on the other hand, had them, I don't know why, and he hid them. They were the only three who could have declined all participation in the struggle without anyone's having any reason to shout fraud; and the three of them, once in it, could have escaped because they had known the Mantua roads ever since they were children. Nobody made the slightest gesture—unless at the end—of withdrawal, because, in his conscience, I know for myself, there were certain limits that they weren't prepared to transgress. The explanation . . . I don't know where you have to go to look for it, maybe to Mantua itself. They fought like everybody and even with more skill and awareness than their comrades in arms because they knew how to choose the field. It's the only thing they chose, the rest of it—the horror, the fratricidal fight, the mediocrity of the leaders, the hoax of doctrine, the lack of support and even of enthusiasm—was given them. So they played, knowing that the match was lost, what more could be asked of them? Because, as sincere people, you have to consider that if a couple of circumstances had been changed it's possible they would have fought on the other side. Maybe it was Father Eusebio who pushed them toward the left. Father Eusebio! Who couldn't that fellow push! I can still see him parading as regimental chaplain, anxious to show off his boots. And after the war, as was to be expected, he began to talk about slums, Christ's poverty, humility. But a moment before I can also see him throwing his cap into the air, celebrating victory, by the same cemetery walls where at dawn he gave absolution to the prisoners. Then we saw them kneel and lower the backs of their necks, with the muzzles of their rifles pointing to the firmament, so that the priest—his silhouette, with the surplice placed over his uniform, outlined against the line of the hill—could give his blessing over so many victorious and humiliated heads, over a silent earth, curved by the weight of an imposition that, with its stark and impassible topography, it had tried for two years to throw off. There's no doubt that in those days they had now learned what the summer of 1936 didn't know: what the cold and the trenches were like. That was their doctorate; on the following day they awakened in a sun-drenched kitchen to greeet the dawn of victory with a proletarian-patriotic tango chorused by five recruits and a quartermaster. And then, after a cup of coffee, he went to the outskirts to talk about charity, the forces of good, the fallen brothers who sit at the right hand of God the Father, of whose power and glory that victory was irrefutable proof. A power that had taken two years to win a hill, a love that didn't hesitate to kill in order to satisfy the frenzy of its obstinacy. Nowhere can I see an honorable result, a proof of anything. I see, as always, that the church is the most consoling and lasting edifice that man has invented. In my time, things, if they weren't certain, were at least simpler and more attractive. And, of course, although the confirmation was always sought, refutation was soon in coming. That is, honesty and seriousness. I'm referring to Numa, of course, not Father Eusebio. In my youth—soon after the death of my father—glory must have been very close to Retuerta; it's an inn that's called that, quite near to the hill of the same name. It's a notable place, located at a height of almost seven thousand feet and open to the winds from the north and the west; following its slope toward the south, the only way by which it is accessible, you reach the Cautiva cuts. But what am I saying? You must be quite familiar with it from what you've told me. It's lonely, yes, but in spring and summer it's customarily visited for pasture by those herds of small wild horses who are no good for hauling or plowing, but who every four or ten years provoke the commercial appetite of some dealer with Gypsy blood, more unbelieved than unremembered, who buys them by the dozen from the first peasant he finds sleeping among the broom. It's a strange obligation and an ominous although moderate inversion, so repeatedly useless and incomprehensible that you come to be surprised by the veracity of myths and how well-founded almost all our legends are. That fables like those of Father Eusebio may make good sense is something else again. For in those days it was well known that the pastureland that breed frequents suffers exceedingly from limestone and saline waters, that the air is infected with emanations of fire-damp, and that after the month of April, in the course of a week, the meadows, hillocks, and hedges are carpeted with a large red flower similar to bromelia, with fleshy leaves in the shape of a scabbard, slightly hairy and with a color a bit more bloody than a poppy, which come out joined together again in a bract, with brown spots, with an attractive and pernicious look. They are the chalices, the herdsmen say, that hold the blood of Father Abraham, King Sidonius, and the valiant Aviza—the young protester—and all the Christian knights who have fallen over the centuries in the battles of the Torce and on which that rural Dracula of the turn of the century fed in his youth—the vampire Atilano—who in the first days of June—when the flowers wither and open their dry berries, extending everywhere small, wrinkled, and dark balls like capers—would go down by night to the walls of Bocentellas, El Salvador, Etán, and Región, wrapped up to his head in a straw cape, his mouth colored with vegetable dye; it's also the blood of all those who fell in that region victims of their impatience and of the cruel and insatiable appetite for revenge of the old guardian of Mantua. It's the flower of uneasiness, of the unrest of the soul, of the contrasts of the spirit, of the impulsive urge that takes over the will to conquer the heights when the first temperate days scatter the clouds that have hidden them all winter, to enwrap them with a purple halo, the prelude of drought. . . . The peasant curses it, doesn't ever pick it or uproot it or dare bring animals to where it blooms. The day he distractedly steps on it, he leaps back, falls to his knees and crosses himself as many times as there are flowers in sight; and if he happens to crush it or break it, custom obliges him to make a small cut on his finger and, in order to redeem his sin and appease the annoyance of the trampled dead, pour some drops of his own blood over the cut stalk. Because it is always born where human remains are resting, a bone or a scapular that calls for vengeance, recall, and redemption from the world of the living. So considerable is the strength of the curse that on more than one occasion a peasant who has seen his fields carpeted by the sudden magenta bloom (a trembling and urticant fiber) doesn't think twice: without tears, desperation, or fuss, he gathers his stock and his family, calls on his neighbors to say good-bye, puts his belongings into a cart, and—depending on the magnitude of his blame or his remorse—closes the house and barns and leaves the place after setting fire to them. And it might also be the flower of Mithra that a certain Roman geographer speaks about, and which will later be sought in pilgrimages at the bottom of precipices and in the venerable grottoes of saints by those great sinners of the high Middle Ages for whom neither Rome nor asceticism was able to afford an adequate penitence. The gamblers of fate—all men of fortune—of the first quarter of the century, after that last and tragic bet that was to drive them to the mine, placed it ostentatiously in their buttonhole, very late at night, before leaving the house of sin. He no longer had any other patrimony left than half a pack of cigarettes—just enough to rid him of any idea of suicide— the silvery silhouette of El Monje, nights of full moon, and, in the brambles across the way, on a very dark slope, the twinkling lights of the old silica mine, similar to those of small fishing boats immobilized at that point where night and ocean mingle and which for the man overboard from the ocean liner who is suddenly sinking into the waves, represent the only possibility of salvation. In the same way that the dandy changed into a castaway by virtue of a discourtesy of the machine, the recently ruined gambler—with the flower in his buttonhole—(and just like the former he goes over the side after a fleeting look at the salon where the tables are already going) throws his cigarette into a potted hydrangea and (after a brief search for the woman who is keeping the group in the salon together without suspecting the results of the last bet) leaps over the railing to start running in search of salvation through the mists of those fields, which he had been so indifferent to on the previous evenings, where crickets chirp and—near the brook—frogs croak in accompaniment to the barely perceptible song of a miner. It was a vein lost in the ravine in the mountain, which in its years of greatest activity—during the 1914 war—couldn't have produced more than half a thousand tons a year of very fine and clean silica grain—with a ninety-eight percent purity. The product was carried by cart to Región and from there it was sent—it's not known by what means of transportation because of the absence of that railroad that never entered into service—to the glass and ceramic industry of the Basque region and the east coast, where it was much appreciated, it's not known whether for the purity and uniformity of the grains or the irregularity of the shipments. But in spite of all the difficulties, that industry—which never lost its age-old flavor, its corporative character, and its family prestige—was to a greater degree than the exploitation of magnetite in Ferrellan, the Formigoso anthracite, or the pyrites of San Pedro mountain, one of the highest exponents of the mining eminence and the active well-being that the country had known during the first fifteen years of the century and perhaps the last vestige of an industrial task that remained shut down—without having come to settle down, as evidenced by the abandoned tunnels and the works of art invaded by the vegetation that grows among the ties and rails of that line that knew no other traffic or trains than those of muleteers—during the first years of the Dictatorship. It had always been the property of a family of druggists from Región who, every four or five years, leased it out to an emancipated foreman whose wife inherited a small part, to a gambler with no fortune who—for his regeneration through work—appealed for the last time to his father, or to a skeptical—terribly skeptical—charcoal merchant that aspired to build a fortune not by profiting from the silica, but with the discovery of those coffers full of Ferdinand coins, which—according to what is believed with absolute conviction—are there, hidden in those spots that have a mysterious aroma. The silica—certainly—got a good price in the reduced commerce of Región; so good that it didn't even rise with World War II, not failing because of that to render an ample margin of profit to the one who knew how to exploit it, even though making use of archaic and manual procedures, with some continuity. Because what is certain is that he only turned to it when he used up his resources for bringing off the archeological excavation, which—apart from some spearhead or porous earthen jug—never brought to light the slightest trace of those supposed treasures. The personnel of the mine disdained the silica because the grain—as much because of its look and color as for the divine imposition—reminded them of a crumb of bread; they were personnel—not the foreman, but the workers—who had their airs and who only dug silica—because their calling was the black chest that never gave anything—in cases of extreme necessity, when mere subsistence (an empty pantry, bare feet, not even a sack of bad charcoal on the worst days of winter) constituted a problem that could only be resolved with the loading and shipping to Región of three or four cartloads of the unpleasant but necessary product. Only gambling allowed them to abandon such apathy, when—bored with innocent pastimes worthy of old maids—they decided to gather up a little money and start the nightly card sessions up again. Apart from the foreman—who lived alone in an isolated shack and cooked for himself—all year long eight or ten miners who were lodged in a wooden shed worked there. None was of low origins, they had no love for the shovel and didn't take too well to the pick, but—on the contrary—all had high-sounding surnames; more than one had a title and liked to carve his coat of arms, by knife point, at the head of his bunk. They weren't unfortunates; they didn't feed on rancor, at least to the same degree as the society that had brought them into the world. They felt a great deal of nostalgia, but not for their parents or their unjust, forgetful, and ambitious brothers and sisters. There was a common desire—but which wasn't one of vengeance—whose maintenance—in summer above all—became excessively fatiguing and unbearable (when the lights of the casino illuminated the night, announcing the beginning of the season) and which of necessity gave way in winter to a more silky feeling of nostalgia. It was the foreman himself, during good times, who would go over to a worker—embittered, indolent, gnawed by rancor—to ask him the cause of his troubles: 'What's the matter, son, why are you crying?' There was no other medicine than a small burlap pouch tied with a cord that he kept in his desk drawer. 'But be careful, very careful; and remember your brothers, the ones here, your real brothers.' And he himself, after recommending prudence (especially if he had the misfortune to have good luck at the table, because that also happened sometimes) would help him slip away in the night so as not to awaken the envy of his comrades, in the direction of the gambling house, with the bag, tied to a rear button on his pants, bouncing. Most of them had to return after a few days—if not that same night—disappointed but cured, and if it's true that he didn't see some of them again, it's also true that he heard of more than one who, after cleaning the table with a rather large bet, had crossed the Atlantic to invest his winnings in some mines in Peru or Brazil. You can see by such things the tremendous power of education. A yen for mining—I can assure you—ends up getting into the blood. And although there were no bars to admission in it— as work in distinguished clubs for example—no matter what might have been the character of the foreman or the intentions of the lessee (because the druggists of Región never wanted, or didn't dare, listen to his proposal of purchase) to enter to work in it, there had to be something: good manners, a well-known name, a proper education, and also a certain class spirit. Entry into the mine was the consequence of a large bet and wasn't within reach of just anyone; if the foreman—to a much larger degree than the croupier—demanded a minimum in the bet he wasn't borne by a spirit of class but because responsible people in the business knew quite well that a person who remained there would be tired and disillusioned by such a mentality and knew how to renounce it and not be one who, borne by a spirit of emulation, tried to acquire it through that subterfuge. Therefore it was necessary to guard himself as much as possible from people of little consequence, like those seasonal parvenus and climbers who, concealing some quite different intentions, come there with pants rolled up over the ankles and shoes stained with mud to ask for a risky job and gain the confidence of their comrades; a few days later they would try to get a leonine loan, pretend to buy a family jewel at a ridiculous price, or, during the winter, with all the establishments for their activities closed, claim that they only wanted to matriculate in that free school in order to learn some ways which were absolutely necessary for them if they were to triumph next season. You mustn't forget that some families—and it's not a matter of extravagance—renowned in Región sent an heir there, as much so that with a pick he would acquire a physical constitution so that contact with his companions would give him a stamp which in other circumstances you would have to look for in an English public school. It was, however, a suicidal act: the boy would return home at the end of the summer transformed . . . when he returned: detached from his parents, removed from homely pleasures, alienated by the spirit of the mine, the nights of gambling, the lights of the spa, the shots and legends of Mantua. See whether or not there are some eloquent examples: Eugenio Mazón, Juan de Tomé, Ruán, that ever so quiet Enrique Ruán. . . . Because education in strange lands always results, willy-nilly, in a confession of impotence, reclusion, and exile. I don't mean by all this that a season in the mine involved a perverse transformation in the individual. Or an evolution toward a state from which his previous age could only be contemplated as a prolongation of childhood, formed by all the links and myths that a child is subject to. It was that or it wasn't that; there must have been something there that attracted the worker by its very simplicity; perhaps the gambling table in the salon at the spa doesn't admit comparison, at the moment of measuring the pleasure that he seeks, with that Béjar blanket thrown over the bunk of a comrade whom he can insult when he draws a good card, with scattered dirty handkerchiefs, cigarette butts, and plugs of tobacco. Nor is it admitted between the best wine of the house and that midmorning drink from a bottle sheltered in the shade of a hollow in the front of the quarry where a thin stream of water runs. And why talk about a siesta? Which do you think will be better? If now you take away from man ambition, the instinct of emulation and competition, and the appetite for all the false goods that his parents and society teach him, tell me where he's capable of living better. But there's more to it: there is, no doubt, a pleasure in being lowered, a pleasure in bad luck and a delight in the misery that—for the prisoner who drags his boots along the path to captivity, for the convict who spits on his hands before picking up his shovel, for the gambler who curses the next to the last of his chips, and for the schoolboy who, alone in the classroom, contemplates, intoxicated and terrified, that wad of blank pages that he must fill with the hated proverb that he will never believe in anymore—are all the more tolerated and stimulating as they are unfamiliar with satiety or satisfaction or reward. The deposit is located on the left bank of the Tarrentino brook, a little over a mile upstream from where it joins the Torce, closed in between greenish, gray, and vertical parcels of Ordovician quartzite and Devonian sandstone, hidden between the ruggedness of a narrow and zigzagging valley covered in its reduced width by a mantle of grass, some rows of melancholy poplars, and a swift and noisy watercourse barely visible under the continuous hedgerow of willows, birches, and crabapples, hawthorns, wild pears, and maples, bordered on its two faces by those steep and gloomy slopes covered with heather, broom, straggly oaks, and giant ferns. The waters of the creek are clean and swift and on the banks there is an abundance of forget-me-nots, colchicum, and meadowsweets; but when some gentleman from Región (or some scoundrel) decides to bury his savings in the anthracite and pyrites of San Pedro Mountain, the waters of the brooks immediately become stained with the color of graphite, then the hedge, the wild hyacinth, the meadowsweet bloom through a fine covering of black slime, punctured by worm holes. There's no pack-animal trail up to the lode: the product has to be transported to the opposite bank of the Torce in bags and on shoulders. There's no bridge around there; the river has to be crossed in a small, black rowboat (whose bottom always holds four fingers of oily water), the property of an old boatwoman who moves it by pulling by hand an old mine cable—unraveled and dry like a vine stock, its loose wires aren't sharp enough to cut into those terrible hands—fastened at both ends to two bollards of rotten wood. It would seem that she doesn't charge anything for the service, but she doesn't refuse contributions either, although it's true that scarcely anyone gives any. It's not too well known what she lives on in a small hut on the right bank, the walls of which are made of a palisade of half-burned railroad ties, covered with a thatch of straw and brushwood. She has no fence or door but neither does she have anything else to do—apart from pulling the ferry—than gather worms and roots on the banks, with which she feeds a small frying pan where some terrible oils are permanently boiling. A person who comes to the place—his pants rolled up to the calves—only has to give a short whistle and immediately, hunched over and barefoot, wearing a black petticoat, she will come out of her lair with short steps—without looking at the neophyte—while she contains her laugh and drops some twigs that she breaks nervously on the bank. She always lowers her face in order to hide a malignant laugh. 'Get in, sir. Heh,

heh. Get in, get in. Heh, heh, it's all right there, you can believe that, all right. Heh, heh.' She stands in the bow with the aplomb of a harpooner, her legs apart and one hand—which follows the other—always gripping the cable that she pulls on. And she pulls with such vigor—giving an inquisitive look from time to time and showing a few Lupercalian fangs as she laughs—that she always manages to beach the rowboat on the shore of black slime with such a sharp and violent lurch that the unwary passenger necessarily falls back on his ass in the muddy bottom of the boat. It's the moment when she—the old witch—starts to run, leaping and sinking her horrendous feet in the *schlamm,* in order to reach dry land, and throws herself onto a patch of grass, rolling around with laughter, holding her kidneys and wiping the tears with the hem of her petticoat. I imagine that with such a trick the novice Traveler (who can say whether or not it was the first time he felt the dampness of his behind through his formal clothes) had by necessity to perceive that he had crossed the threshold of a new life, that a grotesque, waggish, wounding, and uncertain destiny had managed in a few hours to replace the coldness of the maturity educated by the passionate emotions of schoolboy age. As for the ferrywoman . . . everything seemed to indicate that it was a matter of a legend, an allegory of rot and folly, the living image of that perverse and gratuitous joy that flourishes in the realm of the accursed. And when the traveler who, as he goes off on the path to the mine, tries to recover his dignity—as he smooths his hair and his behind and lowers his pants to get the splinters out—looks back—more furtive than a dog being stoned—he still has a chance to enjoy all the blushing that his blood is capable of producing: sitting by the water she is still twisting with laughter while she signals him with lewd gestures, flapping her petticoat and kicking her feet up in the air. They didn't hate her at the mine, but they feared her. Sometimes they didn't fear her and then they hated her and all in a troop on Saturday nights they would go down to the bank of the stream to stone her hut—on the other side of the water—and cover her with savage insults; she would run around the planks like a caged animal startled by a group of wanton schoolboys, cursing and gesticulating; she would roll around on the grass and—amidst laughter, hiccups, and blasphemies—would tear her petticoat, take off her woolens to imitate the most obscene acts, the filthiest enjoyments, and the cruelest orgasms. One of them in particular made her suffer more than the others; he was a strange young man, attractive and vice-ridden, who arrived haloed with a past replete with tribulations and love affairs. Athletic, haughty, and disdainful, he liked to jump into the stream naked, rub himself with mud, and splash his body all over with water with the delight of an artist who knows the most suggestive and insignificant attractions of a fold and a muscle, while the poor old woman—taking refuge behind her boards, biting a black bundle—suffered indescribable torments. I don't know the date of the first claim too well; I was told that before the exploitation of the silica a layer of anthracite also existed there, which during the last century a few laborers from Región attempted to revive. It's possible that such anthracite didn't exist, but, rather, a few spurious sediments and a change in coloration in the Stephanian layers, but things were not valued only for their intrinsic properties in those times—and coal could be worth as much for the calories it drew from the miner as for the ones it gave to the stoker. A handful of men still ready to consider themselves in the realm of the living agreed to work there with zeal, no matter what the fruit of their labor might be; because it was mainly a question—and that was its greatest profit—of challenging the foreman and fooling their fathers, defrauding the owner and deceiving the management in such a way that the work—brought about without discipline or order, without responsibility or over-seer, without stimulation or rigor—began to render profits so disproportionate and unforeseen (new cuts were opened, silica was discovered, and the claim was expanded) that they had to impose limits, through order, to such a state of affairs. For the first time a foreman arrived there who built himself a hut that was apart—and at a good distance—from the barracks. He was concerned with nothing else; he was a man on in years, serious and conscientious but very sad; going on sixty, he seemed to live under the weight of a family tragedy that had happened to him when he was an adolescent, and he let hours, days, and winters pass, shut up in his den, sitting on a stool with his head in his hand while with the other he drummed on the boards of a pine table, when he didn't get into his bunk to weep tearfully. And yet, in spite of exercising such a moderate and easygoing command, his presence began to arouse suspicions among the personnel. From the mouth of that good-looking young man came the first words of vengeance, cowardice, indignation, liberation, and with such repetition (a night didn't pass during the gambling that he didn't speak of that 'humiliating state') that they soon recognized him as a ringleader. But leadership like that was good for only two things: to go down on Saturday evenings to cajole, reproach, and stone the old ferrywoman, and to go up on Sunday mornings to wake up the foreman, pull him out of his bunk, and make him dig with a pick in the cut (he, who had never held a pick in his hands and who hit his feet with it) while the whole work force around him laughed at his lack of skill. Arriving there one day—and without asking for explanations or permission from anyone occupying a bunk in the front—was a rather different worker; he looked more like a bank teller than a gambler; dressed in a ready-made suit—and a city hat that had never been seen in those latitudes—he carried a wooden valise, which produced a certain stupor and brought more than one of them to wonder if he might not be a recruit deceived by a trick of veterans. But it wasn't a question of an *agent provocateur,* that was clear to see. He was the weakest man in the barracks and also the cleanest, because, unlike the others, he not only shaved every morning but he kept a tin soap dish and a good turkish towel in his valise, with which every afternoon—coming back from the cut, while the others fell onto their bunks until time for the game—he would go down to the stream so as, behind some bushes, to soap his torso and wash his feet. He was accustomed to coming back when the game was already under way; never—during the first part of his stay there—did he take part in it; quite the contrary, he would take refuge in his corner, at the opposite end of the barracks, to write down some notes in a very fine and precise hand in a small notebook with oilcloth covers that he held on his thigh, lighted by a carbide lamp that he had brought with him. Then they learned that once a week he would go down to the Torce to give himself a full body bath in a pool that was out of the ferrywoman's sight."

"What are those shouts? Didn't you hear?" she interrupted, half opening her eyes.

"No, it's nothing. It's absolutely nothing. That is, it's everything. A person has to get used to it, that's all. Once you do, what importance does it have? A person has to get used to so many things! He was an ordinary man, no doubt, but well mannered and correct; he wasn't a wastrel or an *agent provocateur* or a deserter. What was it all about, then? They didn't pay too much attention to him either until one day his attitude and position within the community changed radically; it was a Saturday when he showed so much good breeding and firmness that from then on, without any need for giving orders or being obeyed, he was looked upon and respected as the first among them all. Maybe the jokes and the lewdness of the insolent young man had reached an intolerable limit; underneath every laugh, underneath every shout there was a protest, an aborted and unsatisfied gesture of shame, a feeling of sin. He was a young man—I told you—with an athletic but rather unappealing body, marked with the signs of feminine cruelty that he exhibited with a pride that sometimes produced pity and at other times irritation.

And he did nothing but get into the water, take him by the hand—it only came up to his shoulders—and (without the young man's putting up the slightest resistance, all his docility emanating from his surprise or his cowardice), pull him over to the fence, behind which the ferrywoman was taking refuge, and make him kneel naked before her until he received her pardon. A pardon that she gave willingly and lying down, with a broad sweep of her hand that flew over the head of the prostrated person to address—like a farewell—the whole group of men who, from the other side of the river, contemplated the scene, holding their breath. From that day on tricks against the ferrywoman ceased, no one dared humiliate the foreman again, who, taking refuge in his hut, alien to any initiative, never got to notice the favor that he had done him. His visits to the ferrywoman became more frequent; it wasn't rare to see him sitting on the grass on the bank, always beside the soap dish wrapped in the towel, in animated conversation with the old woman, who, kneeling at his feet, her face animated by an expression of incipient joy, moderated and subdued answered the traveler who tried to get her attention in order to obtain her services with a signal to calm down, by virtue of which he had to wait several hours and sometimes give up the crossing because night was coming on. They must have spoken a lot that winter, although I can't imagine about what; I suppose it was about love and politics. He said afterward—and not in a tone of confidence—that the old woman had explained to him that spring what pride was. One day they found out—it was doubtless one of those last afternoons of a sweet and golden September—that, sitting on a rock in the middle of the river and completely naked for a couple of long and pleasant hours during which the old woman tended him with the greatest care and kindness, he had been lathered and scrubbed by her. Someone arrived at the barracks and told about it, panting, and in a flash the heavy card game was canceled. At nightfall he arrived, calm but not strutting, with the soap dish in his right hand, wrapped in the wet towel, his hair combed. He took off his work clothes and, after taking a clean change and an ironed jacket (a polka-dot tie also) out of his valise, he got into his city clothes, not like a perfect gentleman, that is, but like any discreet and proper man with a certain refined and elaborate tendency toward vulgar taste. Maybe it was that vulgar negligence, that absence of affection, of care in details that brought them to the conviction that—without adequate clothes, without a cent in his pockets, and without too much assurance to present himself in that place whose strict rules they knew only too well—he was ready to attempt, that night, an assault on fortune under conditions which—by being so far removed from the usual—would of necessity have to be taken as outrageous and insufferable. So they watched him leave with scorn. For that very reason no one in the barracks dared call his attention to certain details which until that day had been considered, if not imperative, very important at least. And so—in passing—they avoided the necessity of giving him any advice. So when he closed the barracks door a feeling of relief that no one confessed spread out. Very late one night four or five days later (when scarcely anyone remembered him anymore) the door opened and an intense and unaccustomed light illuminated the threshold (all the bodies wriggled in the bunks like worms when a stone is lifted). Pale, gaunt, and scowling, there he was again with a sodium lamp held high in his right hand and a bundle in the left. He scarcely said hello, went through the double row of bunks while his companions rose up out of their beds to the rhythm of his steps (with that sudden, stupefied, and hieratic automatism of barracks puppets who rise up out of their tombs and urns as the visitor passes), took off his jacket and tie, and tossed the bundle that sounded like a collection of small hardware on the last bunk. He emptied his pockets of a good handful of crumpled bills and a lot of coins, among which was a watch, left everything on top of the bunk, took his towel and soap dish, and left the barracks again without anyone's being capable of asking a question or saying a word. That was a night of sighs and lamentations, of agitated dreams and nightmares, no one slept in peace. The following evening, combed and perfumed, wearing a striped shirt, lacking any timidity, he went over to a group of gamblers who quickly made room for him.

'Do you want a card?'

'What do you have to do?'

'You have to make nine. If you've got a good card, stand pat. If you pass, you lose. These here aren't worth anything and these have got their number. If you've got less than three you've got to give up a card. Then, you'll see. Do you want a card?'

'Deal me in.'

'That one's worth two. One more.'

'What went on with you down there?'

'I can't complain. What about this other one?'

'Did they let you into the parlor?'

'What parlor?'

'The gambling parlor, naturally.'

'What about this other one?'

'An eight, a two, ten. You're into the well, you lost the bet.'

'That's how you've got to get them, look at that nice little nine. What do you say?'

'Thief, how can you go like that?'

'Hit me, I haven't got much patience.'

'It's always like that at the start. You'll cool off soon; in a gentleman's game you always have to lose.'

'Another nine. Don't you ever deal out a lot of nines?'

'So, then, they let you in there?'

'What did you think about all that? Did you know about it?'

'No, I didn't. Come on, deal me a card.'

'They let you play?'

'That one, what's it worth?'

'Can't you see, it's a deuce.'

'Hold on, man, hold on. Don't forget your manners. A gentleman's game. . . . I said hold on.'

'What about that one?'

'Patience.'

'Come on, get up another bill, we're not going to eat you up. What do you think we're playing for?'

'It doesn't look like things went too bad for you.'

'What things? What about this one?'

'An ace. But did you gamble a lot?'

'Every night.'

'But did you have any money?'

'The others did, that's what gambling's all about, I think.'

'What did you say?'

'So you won?'

'Every night.'

'And did you end up winning a lot?'

'Everything they left there for me. Are you going to deal me a card or not?'

'Hold on, man, everything comes in time. Are you going to teach us how to play?'

'But every night? You mean every night?'

'Yes, every night and every game. I knew it ahead of time, there's nothing great about it, why are you all so surprised?'

'Shit.'

'What did you say?'

'I said shit. I said it in the spirit of admiration, not offense. You've got no reason to be offended.'

'Let's go, deal me a card. Or is the game over?'

'Patience, you devil, the night's long. There's your card. Good luck, gentlemen.'

'What about the women . . . did you take a look at the women there?'

'Will you please shut up?'

'OK, don't get mad; there's your card. Good luck, gentlemen.'

[186]

"They played until dawn and he lost everything—everything he'd brought back—with the exception of his patience and a coin that looked like gold and which, at daybreak, he kept looking at, lying in his bunk. He didn't seem upset or surprised by his bad luck. The following night he disappeared again, clothed in the same light-colored suit and he didn't return to the barracks until after a week, with the same weary look, dirty and grumpy, his pockets full of coins and wrinkled bank notes, folded pieces of paper with writing on them that he read carefully and tore into very small pieces with a look of disdain, boxes of chocolates that melted under his bunk, chains and rings and watches that he emptied into his valise with the ostensible negligence of a traveling salesman who opens a bundle full of knives, combs, and safety razors before a circle of inhibited and indecisive peasants. He lost it again in the course of one night, without getting upset or losing his poise because of it; on the contrary, he restrained his impatience and gained in composure. He didn't seem to be questioning himself about the immutable aspect of his luck that led him to lose in one night and without any return everything that he had brought from the gambling house. He doubtless felt that it entered into the order of things for him to have no reason to be a beneficiary but a mere agent. He never made the slightest protest or talked about his bad luck or—what was most notable—ever tried to drop out of the game if he had a coin left to lose. He only kept that beautiful gold coin the size of a pocket watch, which, every night, when he retired to his bunk, he would contemplate with fascination and polish with his handkerchief after breathing on it. It was a very heavy piece, of genuine gold and American coinage; how it had come to rest in his hands no one knew—even though it was supposed that it was an offering from the old ferrywoman in exchange for who knows what gifts—and never among his barracks mates did he put it on the gambling mat. They played over a long period, all that autumn and the following winter and almost all the following spring until the arrival of that violent, un-seasonable, and fleeting summer in which, along with its or-ange flashes and darkened cloud clusters, the echo of troops of horses and solitary shots, the whispering of birches and the croaking of the rooks around the dying mounts and maddened riders, a whole age without reason and a people without the slightest moderation in the consumption of its pride were to die. All that remained was a cry, the sound of steps on the first dead leaves, the illusory vision of a man running toward the river down a slope covered with heather, at the hour of dusk, crossing the stream with the water up to his waist and reviving again—at the very spot where leg-end has it that old Atilano knelt to drink—the red blood-stain of Aviza, King Sidonio, and the Carlist volunteers. As I told you before, a mile or so upstream from the ferry-woman's hut the Torce is joined on the right by the largest and most constant of its tributaries, the Tarrentino; its bed extends along the valley of the same name—12,000 acres of mountainside in a wild state of which it is said 'In it there are as many vales as there are days in the year'—and the foothills of the mountains of Mantua, El Monje, and the gloomy peak of San Pedro, always alone and grand. In shape the creek describes a wide crossbow, with its string pointing toward the south, in line with the edge of the first shield, those banks of somber Devonian sandstone and those tor-tured carboniferous crests that, with a wide belt of acidic rocks, seem to surround and protect the proud promontory of limestone that jutted out like a breakwater destroyed by its age-old combat with the ocean, appearing on the tertiary plateau to seek refuge among its continental followers. It is toward the south where the highest and whitest summits of the range—because by virtue of their status as captains of that decimated army, perhaps, the continent has shown them a hospitality that it denied the flat escarpments, condemned by the hard life of the shore to go on suffering the aggressive nearness of the sea—appear stiff, haughty, and arrogant, like those high-society ladies who, at a table protected by a canopy, ask alms of water for the thirsty plateau. The Torres, with its eighty-five thousand and something feet and its leaning needle; and the Acatón, with a heraldic profile and Graeco-Roman name that still seems to be seeking that mythology which a people poor in inventiveness has been unable to adorn; and the Malterra, squat and squalid, isolated like an homage tower on whose parapets the rooks nest and tea grows and which tries at all costs to open a dialogue with proud El Monje, who, with its white plume, reigns over the amphitheater of Región and likes to surround itself with a court of black dwarfs, small and sinister choristers, the plumes and tinklebells of Mantua. The brook is born on Dead Men's Hill, which, since time immemorial, no one has claimed to have climbed. Located there, the dividing line of the borders of Región, Macerta, and El Salvador is materialized in a beautiful milestone, a Saint Anthony's cross and an inscription that says: *'ego sum.'* Its name is modern, it would seem, and comes from a bloody battle during the first Carlist wars where many thousands of men lost their lives. It's also true that during the last of those wars a band of guerrilla fighters, having lost the Maestrazgo campaign, instead of continuing their exodus toward Seo de Urgel, preferred to retire along the Ebro valley with the aim of reaching the pockets of Basque resistance; but, isolated and repelled countless times, they saw themselves obliged to cross the whole north of Castile, fighting finally to seek refuge in that impenetrable wilderness where history or legend situates successively a Celtic fort, an encampment of the VIIth Legion established by Pilate's father, a Mithraic temple in which the forbidden cult and customs were probably prolonged even after the African invasion; a grove for penitents who left the road to Santiago de Compostela—because they probably hated the enchantments, pleasures, and shady gardens of the Spanish Thebaid—in order to sing the praises of the Lord surrounded by brambles, snow, and vermin; and Cistercian ruins, four towers, a wall, and a garden, surrounded by wild hazelnut trees where, on autumn mornings, you can hear the sibylline call of mating pheasants; and, finally, a rural powder factory, from the beginnings of the nineteenth century, by means of which the place returned to its guerrilla line during the Dupont campaigns. That was where refuge was sought by that Carlist band who—with no faith to preserve and no dynastic line to defend—opted for a life in the wilds over digging irrigation ditches or pulling grain barges across the thirsty plains of Bourbon Castile. The herdsmen and woodcutters who penetrate the valley of the Tarrentino tell that the woods are sown with large gravestones and plaques, coffins carved out of sandstone that still serve today as troughs and watering places, outcroppings that have not been affected by the weather and which preserve, as it were, the matter of another fossil, an indecipherable kufic inscription, incomprehensible dates carved in the quartzite and covered with wall rocket; between the tortured roots of a live oak tree or in the center of a clump of brambles, the rusty head of a spear suddenly rises up, still pointing toward the sky, bearing the faded and frayed standard of its distinctive regiment; the tombstones of so many bishops and abbots that, one might say, they had been elevated to the miter only so they might enjoy it as a decoration on their tombs; or the enigmatic symbol of a scalene triangle with a number inside it and a direction determined by its solemn vertex, pointing out a way lost in the underbrush of the mountain and measured in ancient rustic rods. For the unaware traveler who may be trying to reach the heart of the range—or who aspires to scale the summit of El Monje along its south slope—through the valley of the Tarrentino, everything seems to be inviting him on a promising excursion. The first four leagues, from the junction with the Torce to the merger of the two brooks that together almost form it, along the road that borders the streambed—and which the peasants take advantage of to bring their herds for pasture during the four hot months; to cut oak firewood in the first half of October and to fell beeches every four or ten years (whatever is necessary for the buyer of the wood to have forgotten the disasters of the previous contract); to fish for trout all summer long and hunt small game just before Christmas—don't look like any of the rest of the country because nature has been prodigal there with what it stored away everywhere else, with such providence that it is impossible to reduce it to the limits of cultivation and culture. But going beyond the Y formed by the two brooks, Dead Men's and the Tarrentino itself, things change: the face of the mountain that looks toward the south knows no other vegetation than the dwarf plants of oak and heather, somber and quite steep slopes that from time to time open up into a broader gully crowned on the horizon by a bluish limestone crest whose presence is made known by the penetrating and suffocating aroma of the nettles, by a diadem of small live oaks, or the solitary squawk of the grackles. Isolated among the heather the twisted skeletons of an old or calcinated willow rise up, deformed by the winds that blow off the summit and covered with fronds of different kinds of mistletoe, and with mildew. But on the northern face the forest goes on; from the streambed, closed by an almost impassable barrier of wild hazelnut trees, hawthorns, and thorn apples, the hedges of wild apple trees follow one another and spread out, those wild apple trees that bear a small and sour fruit, so resistant to freezes, on which the livestock feeds during years of rough weather; amidst them, whispering and inviting, rounded clumps of birches that stand out, with always trembling leaves that prelude the mirage of a breeze on the calmest of afternoons, sewn together by threads of maples; a paler green, that of the ash, is always accompanied by a shade tree similar to the acacia but more corpulent, the brambles, where the bustard nests, a bird that sings at night in imitation of the bleating of a goat. Above 4,000 feet the holly, which on Dead Men's Hill attains the stature of a timber tree, spreads out. The beech, the juniper, and the yew become more frequent as the slopes become more pronounced until, always in a sudden way, a thick hedge and a closed and impenetrable wood hide the view of the pass, interrupt the road and—with a sign or without—try hard to frustrate that intent of a climb. It's said that years ago there used to be a road up to the pass that has been lost today by a lack of upkeep and traffic, the advance of the beeches, the action of the water, and the fear of the peasants, which have given the slopes back their original state. So, then, the traveler animated by a tireless spirit relies on an exceptional fortitude and equipment, as if crossing through a jungle, will manage to get past the beech forest (at the expense of his reason, no doubt, because no one with a drop of sanity would risk himself in an enterprise that doesn't seem to be the most adequate for returning to sanity someone who has lost it) but not the lower mountain, that jungle of heather, brambles, and thistles, those trenches covered with rootlets and wild strawberries, those ditches camouflaged under cloaks of thorn and broom, hawthorn and poisonous foxgloves, mixed and arranged with that rigorous order that doesn't lack for a touch of merry sarcasm (the svelte, graceful, and unsteady bromelia that rises up in the center of a mishmash of thorns and branches; the violet butterfly that is lost and winks in the heat of the afternoon on top of a wall of holly and caryatids) that seems to insinuate that its arrangement is dictated by the proposition to defend itself from woodcutter, flock, path, and plow. Only fire reaches above it: some day or other, between August and September, a flame rises up that grows lively and in a couple of hours a whole broad section of woods is converted into a crackling bonfire, enlivened by the winds blowing out of Galicia, which three days later gives up and goes out on the southern hillsides, perhaps because its very frenzy now lacks the will to carry its devastation any farther. And yet, considerable as they may be, the obstacles that Nature puts up are not the ones that will drive the traveler to his own desperation. It's something difficult to explain, a bit unbelievable and mysterious, and which, nonetheless, always happens; a consequence of the lack of judgment, temerity, or a fear that is slowly taking over the field previously occupied by pride. The shrewd and persistent traveler, ready to advance a half a mile a day—cutting his way through the underbrush on the lower mountain with a machete, his head protected by a mesh helmet, the only weave capable of resisting the attacks of those swarms of huge mosquitoes, prepared to leave a trail of shreds of clothing, skin, and hair among the branches of that underbrush (that species of furze with a blackish stalk and long thorns which sticks to the skin with more tenacity than a court plaster)—what can he do at the tolling of the bells, the funeral chants with which the new day is sometimes announced? On occasion, at the end of a morning taken up with the scaling of a few outcroppings of rock covered with hostile vegetation, when the traveler sits down to contemplate the path he has covered and at the moment he lifts his canteen to quench his thirst with a drink of cool wine, a sound that is familiar to him comes to distract his attention immediately. He knows it but he can't place it and when he skeptically tries to get his drink down, memory obliges him to recognize what his disbelief rejects; there's no doubt about it, it's out of place, but it has to do with an internal combustion engine; he forgets his hunger and his thirst and, without leaving the place whose conquest has been so dear, he tries at all costs to locate the origin of the explosions. It's a sunny and dry day and the outline of the horizon disappears into the haze. There is silence again, and with it the tranquilizing sounds of the mountain return to his ears, the whisper of the leaves, the buzzing of the insects, the high cawing of the crows who are drawing a comprehensible boundary line in the sky. He tries to see if he has a fever or has suffered the effects of a fleeting dizziness, the consequence of the effort he has made; he wets his wrists, dampens his pulse and his forehead and when, comforted but weary, he lies down to rest after finding refuge for his head in the shade of a small grotto under a bush, he's again startled by that sound, which returns with an intolerable and grotesque clarity; he no longer has the slightest doubt that, hidden in some spot in the woods which the echo brings closer with incredible fidelity, a man is trying to start an internal combustion engine with a crank, and after a few revolutions it stops again with an unmistakable belch. And suddenly (while the traveler is breathing heavily) it starts up again, at excessive speed, silencing with its roar all the whispers of the forest and frightening a flock of hooded crows (objective evidence which the traveler can no longer cease to take into consideration) until, after a series of explosions decreasing in rhythm and sound—and which echo through the whole area with a sarcastic tone—it stops short to open a new rhythm for the calm of the forest. The traveler, who refuses to believe it, cannot help but accept it; he looks at the cloudless sky, then at his bruised boots; he looks everywhere for the smoke from the explosions until, disheartened but not conquered, he decides to forget about the matter so as to get some sleep and clear a head which, because of fatigue, the wine, or a mosquito bite, is letting himself be duped by a few falacious symptoms and repeated sounds. But sleep is hard to come by, the heat is unbearable, and the uneasiness impatient. A couple of hours later, without having succeeded in getting to sleep and on that borderline of dozing where all external sounds become assimilated with certain recurring images that succeed one another, one leaning on the other like the musical motifs of a potpourri, up again rises the brutal chain of motor explosions of an engine that has started up at full speed a few feet from his resting place. Then he gets up and starts to shout, it's going on evening. The sun has hidden behind the somber slate mountains and against a purplish sky a pair of eaglets are describing their high circles, seemingly unaffected by that strange contingency. When, exhausted and voiceless, he understands the uselessness of his gesture, silence has fallen again after a few failing and fateful snorts which last long enough to be convincing. He's not asleep, nor does he feel feverish and, since the light is dimming, he decides to backtrack before night comes on in order to inspect the surroundings. But he will never manage to find anything until, disconcerted and saddened, he will see himself obliged to spend the night on that same crag where, hours before, with quite a different state of mind, he'd decided to make a halt in that itinerary that was developing most auspiciously. So he makes a fire and before the small, blue flame of oak roots, with a few nibbles on his crackers and cheese—because he is now wary of the wine—his spirit is comforted and recovers a bit of that confidence, the loss of which he again attributes to fatigue, flies, or sun. The sky is starry and the crickets are singing about him; little by little he feels overcome by a sleep that seems to be restorative. How wrong you are, my good fellow! Shortly before midnight an unexpected light, accompanied by a rattling sound, dazzles him and wakes him up. Confused, obliged to protect his sight with his hands and crawl on his elbows to get out of the underbrush, he manages to lift his head. But what are you doing, damn you? Before a circle of phosphorescent light, in the center of which a red light wrapped in heady vapors blinks, disappears into the night with furious wing-flapping and croaking, a terrible and instantaneous barb sinks into his back at the level of his kidneys, knocking him to the ground again with cries of pain and tears of fright; and all night long he will stay there lying on the rock, quivering and shaking, biting his knuckles, stroking with fear and apprehension the burning shape that emerges from the bite, cursing his imprudence, insulting this land that won't let itself be trampled on and which only grants its hospitality to fallen angels . . . young Aviza, old Atilano, the Cayetano Corrals, Eugenio Mazóns, Enrique Ruáns, adversaries in victory and brothers in the fearful exile. It's also said that there exists around there—although the traveler will never come to know for certain—a degenerate species of bird of prey with dark plumage and short, sticky wings (a kind of barnyard crow, hypertrophied in the abdomen, with a strange heaviness and no intelligence) which seems to have lost the right of self-perpetuation and which, in its phase of extinction, can only manage to feed on nocturnal insects on clear nights, thanks to the stratagem of the light that reflects on its palate. They are—in a certain way—similar to those phosphorescent men and women who by chance—not by tradition—were accustomed to gathering in the summertime in a mansion on the upper banks of the Torce, which although lacking a spring, had been transformed into a spa in order to be able to gamble all night long during the first decade of the century. It was during those years when a certain license in the customs of the upper bourgeoisie had brought on such an increase in secret illnesses—which took on the name at that time—that almost every river brought out springs with curative powers."

"I think that around that time"—the doctor was to add, and if he didn't add it he could have—"summer was also invented. I don't know much about history, but I can't help thinking that a great number of things we consider natural today and which, at first sight, have always existed, are really a consequence of the steam engine: summer, the wedding night, and—to a large degree—horror. Or at least they took on a new importance and social intent of indubitable character then. My father was the prototype of a person born in a rustic milieu, dragged by his time into a quite different one and one which, in truth, he never came to understand. He was a telegrapher, but until well on into his youth he hadn't known any system of long-distance communication other than signal fires. Understand, for father, whether telegraphy had wires or not mattered little. What was important and incomprehensible enough was the first kind, the cursed wheel that spun at demonic speed and perforated on paper whatever might occur to some lunatic at the other end of the peninsula or even beyond. And that, for a person like my father, not only increased his trust in his country and his contemporaries, but left him with the little he had. That demonic civilization—useless and imposed, that is, given rather than chosen—had, in order to be attractive, to present its cross entry, and that's why it invented summer, pleasure trips, the emancipation of women, and so many other things that didn't in the least tempt anyone with the slightest bit of awareness. And, in order for all of it to be enjoyed, they also invented Región. They soon understood that since it was a question of a civilization whose greatest pride was that it was different from all previous ones, many things that had existed before (such as adultery, virtue, fraud, love of one's neighbor) had to adapt to the new circumstances and dress in the proper clothing. And among them—and not the least important—fear. It's already understood that since fear is always in reference to something, it changes very much with taste and fashion. Those machines and customs ended up with many fears of a minor—and almost familiar—character, which were a relief for a man, as came to be shown afterward, because from then on fear of himself and especially of his fellows rose up. And, nonetheless, I think they never properly noticed the trap into which they had fallen; it was a difficult moment, the country was at peace, banditry, political factionalism had passed into history, a few isolated cases of suicide or madness were not sufficient to dissipate the joy of that unconscious cohabitation. When I reached the age of reason, many men wore shaggy, smoke-colored beards; they looked tranquil, decent, rather cultivated, and sound. And I think they also enjoyed shorter but more complete health; that is, they were so healthy that they died quite young. It was a remarkable generation that disappeared—*spurlos versenkt*—in less than forty-five years and from which no one is remembered today. They still maintained the custom of going up into the mountains almost every week, carrying a city fear, armed with a club and a switchblade knife, for they never

[197]

came to accept the shotgun offered them by 'The Twentieth Century,' that pedantic store chock-full of fabrics, small hardware, and home grinding mills that was established in every town. They hid behind the bushes, called to each other by imitating the call of the lark or the pheasant, and, from time to time, they opened the head of a fox or a barber with one blow from a cudgel. They were accustomed to possess their women on Saturday afternoons—before the walk—and on Sunday mornings they bathed in an earthenware tub and replaced the cotton blouse with a strange ruffled shirt through whose folds and buttonholes peeped out—like something left over from another age—those dark and curly hairs. They would go to mass, to their walk, and to get-togethers always on their wives' arms: they were much more domesticated than civilized; in truth, it could be seen that those customs and that city life fit them and was just right, like the bellboy's uniform in which a monkey is dressed at intermission at the circus. Not only was it a lack of confidence that was glimpsed in the blinking of their eyes, it was fear, something of furor, a strange fluid which under each starched shirt-front vibrated and struggled to emerge from it, similar to the internal buzzing that can be perceived in electrical poles long before the first symptoms of the storm appear on the horizon. It was an anachronistic but not suicidal passion; it didn't take their children into account—that's quite true— nor did it stop to think about progress, because it hadn't come to believe in the end of rancor. The only thing that can progress is ingenuousness, that was well known at the time: those grandmothers, in whose wombs solitude was engendered and who, breathing in their own horror, wander about without direction or duration (neither boredom nor memory exists in that kind of sidereal limbo in which they oscillate) through the naked rooms where light hasn't entered for years in order not to certify the state of ruin; and that small garden where the July and September parties were held in olden times, which they have converted into a tiny vegetable patch, cultivated with spade and rake of the child who lived just long enough to die or go mad in the civil war, and from which they managed to produce a few gray potatoes, some beanstalks, and a number of Polish cabbages with which they used to feed livestock awaiting slaughter in better days and which, boiled with a little rock salt, make up the basic nourishment of the surviving generation; the large, pale leaves hung up to dry and turn yellow alongside the age-old palm trees on almost every regency balcony of the aristocratic quarter give Región, when one enters via the Aragón bridge, the peculiar look of a codfish drying yard. There is a small terrace where a few ears of corn are drying and a well from which the old woman, once a week, draws a bucket of water that will boil for six days over the fireplace fed by chair legs and parts of old rockers, piles of books, and ancestral portraits that in the hypostasis of the fire cast their last look of serene rancor on the shadows of survival; from the first hours of Sunday until dusk on Saturday it's not known whether to make the leaf of that thistle edible or whether to keep alive—by wafting the hand—the memorial flame of the deceased in an enormous and run-down kitchen converted into a shrine thanks to a smoky print that shows a Levantine holy man contemplating the crucifix he holds up in his hands with the same supine awe with which an ecstatic fisherman lifts up an item that he hadn't expected to catch. Next to the hearth a room in shadows—the windowpanes have fallen out and broken and the gaps are covered with paper and rags— still has some remaining furniture: the virginal bed that has lost its canopy but is decorated still with the rosary hanging at the head, the mirror whose quicksilver has been falling off, letting one see the stains and scales of the degenerate tin, and the small dressing table with a single bottle that holds only hardened dust on top of a dry and transparent substance like mineralized resin in which locked in and preserved a moth is left to materialize and preserve the image of flapping its wings without reason. Until relatively recently I continued visiting them, even when they weren't aware of my presence anymore: a thin, hard arm, pale as an Easter candle, covered with a skin mottled with ocher spots and spangles and curled veins where I would apply the instrument to verify once more that the hermetic and stubborn pulse, besieged by solitude and abandonment, was still beating with the same violent rhythm as on the day of its first lovemaking. And I couldn't understand; I tried a thousand and one times to the point of fury to understand the reason for that siege and for such resistance without having recourse to the most obvious answer: we only live for ourselves, all that's necessary is a soil of hate and rancor to feed and develop and make the human plant prevail. And that pulse is nothing mysterious, the rhythm of the rancor, maybe the same furor that vibrated in the starched shirt-fronts, those curly collars and cuffs that were left, stained with blood, hanging in shreds among the bushes of the forests of Mantua along a road marked by mother-of-pearl chips, the remains of mutilated bodies and skeletons that have been kept intact inside those caves, wearing frock coats and spats. It's so much that way that, without too much effort, one comes to wonder to what point is that curse true, to what point will the future (must we insist on calling it future, that summer of widows, boiled cabbage leaves, urticant reverberations of a past of Sundays?) continue being determined by the hard-headedness and marksmanship and insomnia of that old guard. Perhaps he no longer exists except as the crystallization of fear or the formula that describes (and justifies) the composition of the residue of a body from which all desires have been sublimated. Now we know how dearly they cost, a price that can't be compared to the small value of what we now enjoy; for the exorcism of that account it has been decided—believe me—that the curse must be prolonged for as long as possible. For that reason they were accustomed to go there every year, to hear the celestial shots of a Numa who, at least, never misses. He gives up nothing but, at least, he doesn't allow the slightest progress; he doesn't squeeze, he smothers. Don't look for a superstition in him; he's not a whim of nature or the result of a civil war; perhaps the whole organized process of a religion, joined to the growth, merges of necessity into it: a cowardly, selfish, and coarse people always prefers suppression to doubt; it might be said that the second is a privilege of the rich. I don't think it was always that way, but in these times it's difficult to realize how growth and progress—that accumulation of numbers and subterfuges with which history regales itself in order to take on a consoling look—have upset our original nature. What the devil am I saying? Well, all right, there's no doubt that so-called progress is attained at the price of something, perhaps of what can't progress; judgment, healthy judgment, is one of them, won't it be necessary to sacrifice that if we all march at the same pace? The illness gets closer. Numa is nothing but the prodrome. It's true that we were living in a backward way, and why shouldn't we have been? And now we're cramming ourselves into a disguise without knowing what the advantages of the old costume were, just because it's an antiquity. The same thing happens to man, he's another antiquity. When so much is written about him, it's because he scarcely matters, he's on the point of being relegated to attics and museums. What matters is his society, his religion, his state, and his silence; in my father's time they still believed it was necessary to care for and look after those things in order to serve the individual; and now, by and large, it's just the opposite. Man is an archeological item; in my father's time they thought it was possible to redeem him from his slavery and liberate him from the exploitation of his fellow man; and all this has come to rest upon the fact that no one exploits anymore but we're all exploited, by the state, by religion, by the common good, by whatever, and against which nobody can fight so that far from suppressing exploitation, what has been done is to transform it into an invulnerable and sacramental thing. And those who were retrograde before will be advanced today, and that's how it will always be in this world. What my father's generation didn't know is that the common force that was to free them from their oppressors was going, unconsciously, craftily, and mysteriously (and what's worse, with the consensus of all), to turn into an impersonal and elective instrument of exploitation against which, by its very nature, no struggle is possible. I imagine that it must be what the kingdom of heaven is like: we can barely perceive it and yet we are already crossing the threshold. And all from talking too much about men and their rights. But had they ever once worried about that word? did a common denomination imply rights? wasn't it enough to be called Sebastián or Mazón or Tomé to know the little there was in common among them? what rights could they enjoy in common, just because a word, whose meaning they denied every day, embraced them all in order to destroy that differential condition that had baptized them? So does the head of King Sidonio—as legend tells—leaping over the swirling waters of the Torce and going up along those currents to their hidden sources, point toward the all-encompassing power of a river and a mountain that admit no other hierarchy or state of things than the dictates of their whims? And will the madness of young Aviza, opening the insides of his father's corpse in order to purge him of the wine that killed him (and the clink of glasses is followed by that of outraged swords), shape forever the behavior of a dispossessed and degraded people driven toward decadence and backwardness in order to preserve its legitimate authority? Such is the enigma of these years, perhaps these days, which must be solved. When the curtain goes up to open the second act (or third or fourth . . . what difference does it make?), one notices at once that the set has changed: the stage presents, with conventional decor, a place similar to the previous one, but the state of the weather is much more peaceful than during the lucky days of the mine and the gambling house; a soft September breeze is blowing—it's not known what it is a prelude of—and the heather waves with a strange whisper; perhaps as a symbol of the lost peace, in the center, a shepherdess, her hair done up in country style, calms the flock that bleats fearlessly among the crags. I have never seen sheep graze with fear, but, my friend, what difference does it make? Suddenly an agitated swirl of gentlemen dressed in the fashion of 1925 appears on the right, some on horseback, those bringing up the rear on foot armed with all manner of equipment. On a second level, barely visible, some military men in their blue caps can be made out. The bleating of the sheep is followed by the barking of the pack and the sound of horns. When the crowd stops in center stage a cloud of dust rises up that lasts for several minutes—or long hours—and hides the confines of the mountain range while another hunting horn, much farther off, indicates that a second quad is riding along the banks of the Torce. A cornet—the spokesman for the gentlemen—dismounts and addresses the shepherdess in aggressive and urgent tones so that, without the slightest hesitation, she will point out the path the fugitive has followed to him. The shepherdess, indifferent, rearranges her skirt, shakes off the dust, and looks at him out of the corner of her eye. There are those who say it's only the old ferrywoman in one of her many impersonations. All the horses whinny at the same time and the group becomes impatient. The cornet warns her, in a menacing way, that her life is in danger, but the shepherdess, by way of reply, takes a shawm from under her skirts and plays an obscene song. Several horses rear and some riders, either not ready or unskilled, bite the dust. In the underbrush, with a parting of the branches, the malice-laden looks of the delighted jacquerie emerge. The cornet, vexed, threatens her verbally. Certain repressed laughs can be heard in the underbrush, agitated by a wind in the leaves. A shiver runs through the crowd, who, dauntless, their looks restrained, their hands clenched on their saddle horns, approve the sacrifice that the cornet, unsheathing a short, curved saber, goes forward to carry out. One of the spectators in particular is unable to repress his shivering; he is a military man who has lost his tunic, wearing a borrowed quilted jacket, in the folds of which, while he glances to the side, he hides a hand that is bandaged with a dirty blood-stained cloth. By that time he has already got the habit of biting his fingernails, even those on the wounded hand, which he lifts to his mouth with the help of the other. And at the moment when the cornet makes ready to sink his weapon into that virginal, broad, and mother-of-pearl breast, her brassiere becomes loose, a gust of wind lifts up the shepherdess's skirt, and an ivory chip with the number 50 pyrographed in the center falls to the ground, as if it were a matter of the most intimate item of virtue: the confusion is enormous, all try to pick it up: 'What about the coin? What about the coin?' an insistent and unbending voice rises up with overwhelming repetition while the members of the group fight among themselves and beat each other up; because the previous anxiety is followed now by a battle that can only be glimpsed through the dust, the flashing of knives, the shots, the splashing of blood, and the pawing of horses, the whinnying and lamentations of the dying, who, when the smoke clears, occupy the center of the stage, withdrawn and crawling, dragging along the ground in search of chip, coin, shame, or vengeance, of a mortuary chimera or a page of the code on which to vomit up the blood that is flooding their lungs. And in this respect I wish once again to call your attention to a certain particular: how the contradictions that a people engenders—and which one day or another will bring on its fall or its ruin—on many occasions take on material form and the body of tragedy around certain people or situations with which they only had an episodic relationship. The way destiny, in order to scourge a people who deserve it, suddenly chooses a passing actor, capable of catalyzing opposing passions and producing a climate of destruction while the interests that it keeps in an unstable balance in order to conjure it away are unable to intervene. Because, in sum, what are all those gentlemen rushing off in pursuit of a fugitive, incited by a pile of mother-of-pearl and ivory chips looking for, what were they after? They had scarcely noticed his presence the first day of his visit to the gambling house; only by his extreme vulgarity could he have called attention. He could have been taken for one of those clerks from a different era, who didn't even gamble on Sundays and if they did it was in the morning; who put a bank note in their lapel and strolled through the rooms with a pack of cigarettes they're not used to smoking and which they've picked up for that occasion, looking at the ceiling. Who seem indifferent to the women, because when they cross paths with them, they turn their heads and only look at them later on, from a distance and furtively. They have their passions too, no doubt, such complicated and pertinacious passions that when they burst forth . . . one never knows what provoked them. Scarcely anyone remembered his first visit, perhaps only that military man—the presumptive lover of María Timoner— who wagered his aunts' farms every night. After reconnoitering all the rooms, he sat down beside a card table, in a rear position, where he remained all evening without making a move, without moving a finger, but making a show of his cigarettes. When at the end of the round the gamblers had already got up to withdraw, he went over to the young lieutenant, who—after a lucky night—was arranging his chips in different piles according to size and color. He fished around in his pants pocket for a bit—in spite of the fact that it was obvious that it was the only thing he had in it—and took out a gold coin the size of a watch. 'I'll bet this,' he said. 'And what might that be?' the other asked with a touch of sarcasm. 'A gold coin, can't you see?' 'A gold coin? That size? Let me have a look.' 'You can look all you want if you win it.' 'Is it yours?' he asked. 'The cards will decide that,' he answered with a certain coolness. 'And what do you want to wager it against?' he asked while he bent over to look at it, because the other one was holding it between his forefinger and thumb the way you show the time to a passerby. 'Against one of those white chips.' 'One of those white chips . . . you haven't said anything small. Do you know what one of those chips is worth?' 'And do you know what that coin is worth?' the other asked with a provocative tone in reply. The ferrywoman had given it to him the previous afternoon after much advice; all afternoon she'd been rubbing her hands, looking at him out of the corner of her eye and showing gaps in her gums when she smiled, contracting her nose and shaking her head. Suddenly she slapped him on the chest, knocking him onto the grass, and ran off, taken by a convulsive laugh. Then she coughed for a long time; she sat down fatigued, far away from him and turning her back while she dried her tears on the hem of her petticoat; from under it she withdrew the gold piece, which she tossed into the air several times, counting when it came up heads and when tails, piling up some twigs and stones on either side. Suddenly a shout shook her whole body at the same time that she drew back and clutched her hair; in the same posture—but more serene—she shouted again, turning her head so as to send the sound off in several directions, like a cock on top of a stone. It was at the spot where the coin landed and she counted piles of stones and twigs again until she must have made sure of something. Leaning, she went over to him, grabbed him by the shirttails, and asked him:

'Is it you, then?'

'What is it I am?'

'It's you, it's you. Why didn't I see it before?'—and she kissed his hand for a long time, leaving on the palm the remains of saliva that the young man dried with his elbow. 'Fine; what's been said has been said. Take it, gamble it; don't worry and above all don't be prudent, don't ever be,' she put the coin in his hand and started to run; in her underdrawers she crossed the river, at its lowest level in those days.

'Fine,' the lieutenant said, 'and what do you want to play?'

'What you were playing.'

'Do you know the rules?'

'Don't you know them?'

He lost three times in a row. When he handed over the third chip he remained thoughtful, drumming on the mat while he looked at the coin and all his piles of chips, almost intact, at the same time.

'Let's try again, what do you say?' the lieutenant asked.

'I won't say no. How much?'

'The same as before,' the gambler said.

'Do you think a coin that's won three times is worth the same as one chip? If you want to play you've got to put up three chips, my friend.'

'Who says so?'

'I do. It's my coin, isn't it?'

'OK; there are the chips.'

'OK; deal the card.'

He lost again and swallowed. With an expert gesture he picked up a whole pile of white chips with two fingers and, after counting them with his eyes, dropped three of them onto the mat: 'Let's see how long you can last,' he said.

'Let's try again; all told it's three *duros,* what's that to me?'

'Three *duros?* Do you think a piece that wins six is only worth three *duros?* You've got to put up six if you want to play.'

He didn't want to insult him because he preferred beating him, trusting in the size of his piles. He took three more, grudgingly, looking at him angrily.

'You're playing smart. Do you think your luck will hold in every game? Don't be crazy. Can't you see everything I've got there? I can last a long time, until my luck changes. So . . . what is it?'

'So the bet's six, right?'

When he lost again he began to sweat. The gambler felt irritated with himself, not so much because of his bad luck as for not being able to get out of a childish game that was beginning to become serious and uncomfortable. They played like that for a long time, surrounded by dimmed lights and under the vigilance of a drowsy waiter. It was already quite late when the lieutenant got up with a fatigued air; with veiled irritation and manifest trembling, he gathered up the few chips of little value that remained on his side, not enough to make a bet.

'We'll continue tomorrow,' he said as he buttoned his collar, watching the other put the chips in his pockets.

'Tomorrow?'

'That's right; a gentleman always allows one to get even. Didn't you know that? Or haven't I been playing with a gentleman?'

'You learn something new every day,' the other one said.

During the following weeks the gold piece began to attract the attention of some of the habitués of the house. It always won; not just like that, with all the winnings it was looking for and which—one might say—seemed to enjoy an opposite virtue, because when he left one table with his pockets full and sat down at another to gamble with chips and with the object of not risking the key to his game, he always lost; so even when he'd won a lot—much more than what the piece must have been worth no matter what its price—he could only keep that part of his winnings that he knew enough not to risk. For that very reason the coin was even more attractive, so among the house's inhabitants few were capable of resisting the temptation to covet it. But without doubt the most persistent—since he was the most offended, the one who had been the first to covet it, considering himself by his position to enjoy certain rights to try— was the lieutenant, who discovered at other tables (and among gentlemen) how to get compensation for the losses brought on him by that coin, the acquisition of which began to obsess him. His fiancée (or his lover, or whatever) never went into the gambling salons, but from a distance—always surrounded by a circle of older men, studious and indifferent to the gambling—sensed and followed the whole adventure with growing uneasiness. The first time he saw her was one evening when, in less than a couple of hours, he left the officer without a single chip. He crossed the room with long strides and from the glass door made a discreet signal to her, which she obeyed, leaving the circle of admirers with laughing excuses. It was—I repeat—the first time that he saw her, leaning against the door frame, restless but not nervous, when, with one eyebrow slightly tilted, she watched—without trying to hide it or accepting it with blushes—how her betrothed was eagerly digging inside her small purse; it was the first glimpse of that serene and open look—neither happy nor melancholy—which, capable only of contemplation, was incapable of being moved; there was something amazed and reflective—and a bit puerile—in her that emanated from an apparently interrogative attitude but one that basically wasn't interested in any answer: on the contrary, in the view (and in the enchantment) of those large, beautiful, quiet eyes all answers seemed to be transformed into questions, or into conjectures at least. So that in a short while the officer sat down again across from him with a reduced pile of green chips placed on the mat. 'I think it's best to let it go for today,' he told him to dissuade him. 'That's no way for a gentleman to behave,' he answered him as he pushed the pile forward. 'It's getting late.' 'Late for what?' but she'd already disappeared from his sight, hidden among the groups in the next room. 'It must be late for many things,' he said, with a downcast tone. 'All right, I'll play with my own winnings,' he added, pushing forward a pile of chips the equivalent of the other's. 'Ah, that's something else again,' the officer said, dealing out the cards, 'I already noticed that your luck couldn't last forever.' 'Yours won't either,' replied the clerk. In a short time he had lost all his winnings, which had passed into the hands of the military man; they were alone in the salon now, in the next room—with almost all the lights out—only his fiancée remained, with that young doctor who

[209]

was continuing her treatment at the Sardú clinic and who was her escort on every gambling night. All he had left— once more—was the gold coin and the officer, with a satisfied disposition and arrogant gesture, got up from his chair: 'María, Daniel, come here, you've got to see this,' he said. The other one got up and put his coin away: 'It's very late, good night.' 'You've still got something left to gamble with.' 'It's my right to want to bet it and to fix its price,' he said. 'María, Daniel, come here.' And when they approached the table, with coolness and disdain, he grabbed a thick and disordered fistful of the highest chips and threw them into the center of the table. But the other one didn't change his expression; he took the coin out of his pocket again, pushed aside the other's handful and chose a single chip, the smallest and least valuable of all. 'That's its price this time and this is the last play. OK, deal the card.' 'That's the price?' 'OK, I said.' And he won: 'If you don't have any faith in keeping them, there are things you have no right to bet,' he said, and while he picked up the single chip he looked at those motionless and peaceful eyes, paying more attention to his steps than to the blocks of chips her fiancé was piling up. It was a long game, lasting all through a vague time, summer, autumn, winter, and spring merged around a small green lamp and with no other change than the dress worn by María, who, every night, on the doctor's arm, attended the last wager. One day it was a watch, with a miniature of her framed on the outer lid. A few weeks or a few months later a bracelet, which her lover took off her wrist, hiding behind the folds of a curtain. There was neither affront nor reproach in her attitude; without wishing to watch, she put her bare arm forward with the same voluntary obedience as if she were going to receive an injection. Only when she drew back her arm did she turn her eyes—impassive, indifferent, ignoring—toward the real author of the despoilment, over the shoulders of her lover who was already on his way to the table with the bracelet hanging from his forefinger. Now it was as if there were nobody there as the fringed lamp lighted up a circle on the mat so small that only their hands could be seen. But until well into spring it was always possible to find a trick to keep the coin out of play and give back what had come from her. And finally it was a ring, with a diamond, that made him understand that it was not just a matter of the jewel but of the promise it enclosed. The eyes—in their most passive, most unreflective, most condescending look—confirmed it with an expression that by not indicating anything anticipated its acceptance, but he—the gambler, with only his hands showing in the circle of light that the lamp gave off, the black nails and the shirt cuffs with frayed and dirty edges—refused an item like that and, in revenge, always arranged for the engagement ring to crown the disordered pile of chips, withdrawing the gold coin that was hidden under it without his rival's noticing. So coin and ring always won but never faced each other in the same bet during that vague and long stretch of the game's duration, which Time and not the Gambler plotted, desirous of finding its own end in the envious man. But one summer day it finally came to a close, not so much because the rival found how to make him leave the coin (he didn't have any chips to hide it with and he finally had to match it alone against the ring) as for that lingering look in the frame of the glass door that knew how to close its eyes at the precise moment, which the owner of the coin would interpret as a plea; because she already knew, I realized much later. And she closed her eyes to tell him: 'Please, get it over with. I know you're going to win. I can't accept it, I beg you, I beg you . . .' So he pushed forward his pile of chips, a rather considerable pile, and on top of it he placed the coin; there was nothing opposite it except the ring, and behind them, María; and behind María, the young and inexpert doctor. The officer dealt the cards and the other one got up without looking at them. The military man, under the fringe of the lamp, was opening the fan of his cards with studied slowness, looking only at the symbol in the margin. Then he turned toward the darkness of the adjoining room, showing the open fan in his hand: 'This time there's no doubt,' he said with a firm smile at the same time that the sound of heels induced the other one to go into the next room. He took her by the arm—and the doctor didn't know how to stop him—and told her: 'It's done now.' 'What difference does it make?' 'Until now it didn't make any difference. Now it's everything,' he answered her and didn't wait for her reply, but ran back to the gaming table—where the officer was piling up and counting his presumed winnings, surrounded by a few addicts who were joking around him—to tell him: 'In order to keep that, you have to beat these cards.' He held them out to him one by one, separated them again, incredulous, openmouthed, and panting, while she—behind him—squeezed her hands and tried to repress the quiver on her lips.' "

The doctor had become aware, some time back, of a change; not only did he find her more distant, not only was she accepting his company without the previous relaxation but with the resignation that all exclusion imposes, but her whole attitude toward people who surrounded and admired her seemed touched with a reserve that—the doctor knew quite well—could not be attributed just to fatigue or timidity. From the first day, when he had put up the ring as a wager, the doctor understood that for her part—and in a tacit way, therefore much more irremediable—one of the links joining her to her lover had been broken. Perhaps not affection, but respect, yes; not the promise or fidelity or obedience, but loyalty, yes. And the doctor needed but a single day to feel himself the third protagonist, called upon to replace the flighty captain, but he decided to advance across that terrain with a very prudent step, with his head on his shoulders and without letting himself be dragged along by María's attractions. She had entered the Sardú clinic a year earlier to cure a nervous ailment, which at first had given him cause for concern but which soon convinced him that it was a trivial matter if not pure playacting. It was an ailment that was rather vague and whimsical to justify her staying at the clinic while her fiancé put off his decision to marry at the gaming tables. She hadn't hidden from him, since the first days, the fact that it was a question of her lover, who, in addition to inducing her to move there so as to have her nearby and begin her incorporation into Región society, in no way wanted to see himself involved—out of consideration for his name, for the position his aunts occupied, and for the inheritance he expected from them—in the type of relationship which, if it were translated into scandal, might compromise all those items or pour him irremediably into marriage. For a case like that the clinic offered a safe solution and refuge; it not only justified, for reasons of health, the presence in town of an attractive and unknown young woman, who in a different place, even with a house of her own, would have given rise to gossip, but, after the passage of a few months of obedience to diet, she was crowned with an innocence and delicacy that was all the more worthy of respect the greater the irregularities, which, in a different context, her own state might have permitted. And, furthermore, "a delicate state of health" constituted the best pretext for all those delays, withdrawals, and separations which a careful lover needed so as to justify himself in social gatherings, always avid for parlor gossip. The doctor, however, discovered the weave of the comedy quite soon. Sardú, taken by her entangling and mischievous eyes, had entrusted the care of the patient to him from the first moment with an attention that for its zeal and meticulous manner went beyond the norms of the establishment. Perhaps Sardú, but not the doctor, was receiving a bonus from the military man for the expenses of the performance. On the other hand, the doctor, and at the insistence of his boss, saw himself obliged to invest an amount equal to his first month's salary in a tuxedo and correspondence-school dancing lessons in order to be able to accompany her as well as other older patients who only suffered from a fatal boredom to sessions at the casino and to a few parties in Región with all propriety. Six or eight months after her entry into the place, after the Christmas holidays, the doctor began to live in such a state of permanent anxiety and anguish that he was the only one in the whole establishment who seemed in need of a cure for his nerves; because he no longer knew what kind of woman the one who attracted him was, and, worst of all, not only what future awaited him but what kind of present it was possible to enjoy feeling himself attracted by a woman whose relationship he didn't mistrust as much as her promise every time that the many fluctuations her relations with her lover suffered made him conceive of so many hopes of reaching her via much cleaner and quicker routes than those to which she seemed accustomed, as they seemed to distance him—definitively and desperately—from a person in whom everything, even her conduct, was unknown, alien, and forbidden to him. That winter—the one that preceded last summer—the doctor had an encounter (or a vision, whatever you want to call it) that gave him much food for thought, affected his spirit, and transformed his anxiety into an uncontainable desire to resolve that situation and, in the company of María, leave that place. And it was what finally pushed him into a decision with respect to her that, with the risk of her frequent vacillations—and of the changes in fortune and attitude of her lover—wouldn't have come about. It was toward the end of winter, one of those rare nights that as harbingers of spring enjoy an incipient aroma that the climate will take care to abort later on; and her behavior—the ring still hadn't been placed on the gambling mat—was going through a steady and serene moment, somewhat removed from everything that revolved about her in those days. They had gone out after dinner to take the air under the elms on the highway; the doctor remembered that it was one of the first nights that he took her by the arm in order to tell her about a theme he

[214]

knew quite well, a meditation perhaps begun under the African sun, in a trench in the Rif; he was telling how—to his mind—self-esteem differed from pride, two very similar feelings with respect to all things of one's own and which only—if they degenerate into illness—can be cured by failure; the first is the one that's cured, the second the one that's aggravated, because failure gets to show a man that the thing of his own he loved so much, to the point of losing his lucidity, wasn't worthy of such love; while pride prefers to deny that evidence and, before placing love for something of one's own in interdiction, prefers to attribute the causes of failure to the mistakes of others and not his own stupidity . . . when at that moment someone whistled to him, a shadow that he perceived farther back—on the other side of the road—hiding behind a tree. He excused himself for a moment, went back a few steps (he had a chill), and asked aloud who was calling him. "Come here," a muffled voice said in a very crisp tone. He could only make out a head wrapped in shadows, surmised more by the reflection on the forehead and cheekbones, and a body whose clothing it was difficult to distinguish in spite of the clearness of the night; maybe he didn't have any hair and was protecting his baldness with a pale and gaseous veil that was tied under the chin at mouth level. "Sebastián, isn't it?" "That's right," he replied, but with a certain mistrust, "What do you want?" "That woman with you . . . ," it could have been said that under his cloak he was consulting a pocket notebook. He also thought he saw hands sheathed in black leather gloves on one of the fingers of which—and that surprised him more than any other detail—a ring was shining. "I would say that her name is . . . let's see . . ." The doctor waited. "Her name is . . . here it is: Gubernaël, that's it." "Gubernaël? Absolutely not, her name is Timoner, María Timoner." "Gubernaël, Timoner . . . what a childish mix-up; but quite understandable since they both have to do with rudders," he said with a broad smile. "How is she doing?" Not for a moment did it occur to the doctor to get away from that impertinent interrogation. He answered, "Fine, she's doing fine. No need for worry at all." "I'm so glad. I pray for her health and that those bothersome mix-ups won't be repeated," he added with an even sharper tone; a breath poured out of his mouth that wasn't hot or fetid but so dry that his words seemed to be coming from a clay instrument. "What about Gubernaël, don't you have a woman patient by that name?" "That's right." "And how is she doing?" "In delicate condition, she's going through a stationary period but her general state gives me hope . . ." "Don't tell me anything else, nothing else. She's probably sleeping now, right?" "No doubt, a couple of hours ago I gave her a tranquilizer." "Fine, fine. Don't stay out too long. These nights are treacherous. Good night, Dr. Sebastián . . . ," and he didn't see him leave. For the moment he seemed to notice that he was retracing his steps in the direction of the clinic, but he soon dismissed that idea. On the way back with María he was held back by the feeling that he'd experienced a mirage, one of those involuntary spasms that memory initiates but which reality doesn't ratify or recollection makes shadowy, and which from then on will remain suspended in a no man's time, an aborted instant and a past without sanction or registry. He didn't say anything to her, avoided her questions, and tried to shorten the stroll. Early that morning, in the clinic, an old woman died, Gubernaël by name, of Flemish ancestry, who had spent several years in the institution stricken with a nervous ailment that had no cure but whose state hadn't led one to fear a quick release either. María told him a few days later that on the night of the stroll she'd had some nightmares—one in particular that insisted on and repeated the same theme; wrapped up to be shipped, she was unwrapped and wrapped up again a thousand times because of a lot of deficiencies and counterorders—and that, protected by a very superficial sleep, she'd had the feeling that somebody was coming to visit her room early in the morning. The person had reached the head of her bed and had lifted the sheets, but on recognizing her, withdrew stealthily, ashamed of his own indiscretion or confused by the same mistake that the nightmare was revealing. The doctor remained very thoughtful: the mix-up in names the night before, the disbelieving attitude of the shadow, the death of the Gubernaël woman, and the news of the visitor who came to lift the folds of her sheets and was sensed only by his breath . . . all that led him to think that, thanks to an order sent out by mistake, a mechanism with its goal set on María had been put into effect and it wasn't going to halt except at the head of her bed, thanks to . . . During the weeks that followed his unrest grew; he didn't want to go out for the evening strolls, he lavished all manner of exaggerated care on her, and, with the absence of Sardú and the pretext of a sudden attack of anemia, he put her under a regime whose rigor came to arouse suspicions from that fiancé who at no moment would believe in the pretended illness, even when, in those days, the only thing that really mattered to him was the gold coin of that middle-class gambler. It was one reason, and not the least, why she'd been absent during the greater part of that long and uncertain game of cards in which, starting with the moment when her engagement ring entered into play, she herself, by her own tacit will, became a pawn. Because she hadn't forgotten either his gesture or his parting phrase when, with an expert hand, he snatched the coin from her. The game went on for a long time, on an almost deserted stage; and with the arrival of good weather the doctor's fears lessened, so they went to the casino more often to witness the outcome that those two men, absorbed and furious, incapable of overcoming with tenacity and time the laws of a few numbers that seemed to have been conjured up to destroy them, had decided upon without taking them (and here we have to include the doctor) into consideration. And for the last two months they no longer left the table; she, paler, more reserved and serene, watched immutably (and scarcely hopeful, perhaps), without a moment of weakness or a change in the direction of fate, how her fiancé would lose his fortune, which only momentarily passed into the hands of the other one—also immutable, serious and paradoxical, always wearing the same ready-made suit and the same shirt with dirty cuffs, the same plaid tie, shapeless now and knotted about his neck like the cord of a penitent, sitting at the gaming table with the persistent and unalterable discretion of an upright, reserved, and punctual clerk—to evaporate in an excrescence of pasteboard and a hypostasis of mother-of-pearl, the last sublimation of money that never appeared but which, one day, reduced to a wrinkled and folded piece of paper and the engagement ring that remained in the center of the mat, was aware of its extinction.

The doctor never came to know exactly how the deal was made. It's possible that there wasn't any deal at all, but over so many months—and through so many vicissitudes—both gamblers understood that the woman, represented by the ring, was included in the pot. And she corroborated it, sure of the power of the coin, with that closing of the eyes with which—besides conveying her agreement—she made the other understand what it was really all about. So it was she—not the officer who, all things considered, would feel her lost but not won by the other—who decided the fate of the three; of the four, rather. Because the doctor was also wrong, convinced that the whole game only represented a humiliation for her, a despoilment and a deception; he didn't know enough to take into consideration the presence of the rival who, as careful of his game as of his duty, without dropping his discreet and resolute stance, scarcely gave her a look. Therefore, the doctor calculated and measured his actions very well, but without perceiving that the only one who was to draw any advantage from them was the one whom nobody was looking at, dazzled by his gold piece; without making any declaration, obviated from the beginning by a behavior that led him at every turn to hide the state of his feelings so as to spare her, in those circumstances, greater mortification and unpleasantness, when he suggested the idea of the trip to her (and he did it without revealing his intention of accompanying her, but only as a cure for all the upsets brought on by the continuation of the game), he only received a tacit and weary agreement, a "later, later," the exponent of so many painful moments during the last few days that had come to be transformed into an attitude of anxiety and expectation and recognition of a manifest inclination toward the gambler—not mitigated by the anger of a wounded pride—independent of the thanks she owed the man who had known how to comfort her and of the annoyance aroused by the one who had only known how to humiliate her. From then on the doctor knew which way to go; he knew, of course, that before the end of the game the decision wouldn't come from her—or from that pride in a convalescent state, from that ingenuous aplomb not backed by reflection or interest but by other more simple and, to put it that way, natural virtues—paralyzed in a somewhat expectant and astonished moment—hands half raised, eyes turned to a corner—like a doll that has wound down before the dance is over. It could be said that, forgotten by the hand that had wound her up, she was incapable of picking up the movement until another equally skilled hand noticed the mechanism that the other had suddenly forgotten. All that was needed then—according to the doctor's calculations—was a little tact; he decided—she merely agreed, almost paralyzed by the latest humiliation and alienated by a psychic shame that still sought the engagement ring on her finger, on one of the first nights in September and one of the last of the game. He arranged his affairs at the clinic, packed his bags, and, in order not to arouse rumors, went to an inn on the outskirts of Región, an isolated inn located at a crossroads where a taxi—which was to pick up María first—would come get him in midafternoon. And they decided to go to the session for the last time, even though the doctor wasn't completely confident;

he suspected that—without giving it the character of an ul-
timatum—it was a question of bringing about a final and almost involuntary—dominated by inertia and indecision, just
as the gambler, sick of losing, feels incapable of getting up
from the table, of curbing his curiosity about an outcome in
which intrigue and hope, never boredom and weariness, are
mingled—intent to restore the order subverted by chance.
He was almost cleaned out and the other one had accumulated a considerable pile of chips of different colors; no sooner
did he see them enter than, spurred by a wink from Time,
who, running along a neighboring hallway and half opening
a door, made evident the nature of his haste, decided to risk
the final bet. From his jacket pocket he took out a wrinkled
envelope that he placed on the square marked on the mat;
then, carefully, he leaned back in his chair and picked up his
hand with a questioning and impertinent look at the other
one. It was the envelope that held the ring and with it the
disclaimer, but the doctor didn't know that; in order to know
that he would have to wait a few years. "And that, how much
is it worth?" the other one asked, with a certain coolness.
"You know only too well; let's not pretend at this point."
He was playing in a more relaxed way now, he'd learned
how to count a pile and evaluate a bet with a simple glance;
he pushed forward all the chips that he had in front of him,
but, leaning comfortably back, he shook his head and made
a sign with his chin; he didn't delay, he didn't want to look
behind and—without wanting any discussion, without
showing the slightest wish to pass up a decision that had been
given him—he took the coin out of his pants pocket and
tossed it into the center of the table. Then he crosᵥed his arms
and waited for the cards the way someone at a window in a
government office waits for a certificate. He didn't uncover
his cards, he didn't see the officer's gesture; he got up and
only after exchanging some words with her remembered that
he had to return to the table, not to withdraw his winnings—that he was sure of—but to receive the certificate. That

[220]

was when the doctor—absorbed in her walk—heard the sound of the chair as it fell; it seemed to him that the other one wanted to flee but before his body could start running fear had already made a reflex. And he threw himself onto the table because he understood that under those circumstances he no longer had time to explain that he wasn't responsible for the deception, that there was no theft therefore but a question of an appropriation that Time had sanctioned and sanctified by obliging him to accept the rules. Because there had been no bet on his part, only the mere acceptance of a stake and a function that chance was now trying to cheat him out of. It was Time who united the two independent acts: a hand that contradicted and invalidated all previous ones and the compromise acquired along with them. It wasn't his intention to rob the officer—much less wound him—but to oblige him to renounce his play and restore order, on which the salvation of that woman depended, for he had changed his luck just to show, one more time, that his mastery would prevail. There wasn't any fraud therefore. It was Time who, as the stingy and willful distributor of His own decisions, was transforming into fraudulent action the respect for His acquired compromises before those whom He had to answer every time He induced them to transform the game into law. But the very agent of time—he'd begun to put the piles in order so as to take inventory—had no other instructions but to carry the execution forward; he threw himself onto the table as soon as he understood that it was useless to explain it to him (as useless as an attempt to discuss the spirit of the law with a tax collector), because he had no time for it every time a gambling mentality wouldn't accept the explanations of a causal thought and because—consequently— he needed an extension that the sentence was denying him, in order to present his appeal and try to invalidate the judgment; and above all because she'd already left. Before the other one could pick up the envelope the extension had already been granted, the hand remained halted on the mat and joined to it by a knife stuck between its bones and which, spattered with blood, was still vibrating with the decreasing diapason of its vengeful justice, until the flow of blood, running with surprise at its own liberation, halted the fascinating tremor of the steel to announce pain and blame. Then he saw the piles of mother-of-pearl chips and the gold coin, which he picked up by the handful to empty into his pockets, a gesture that formed part of the mechanism that the knife put into action once the will had decided to appeal and memory had obliged him to accept all the facts in the summation. Immediately they all turned around; it could have been said that they'd been rehearsing a scene repeated a thousand times and that, having reached a certain perfection, they could go on to the next one; and then they hesitated because they could scarcely remember what the gesture, the expression, and the tone required by the next one were. "The third act—or whatever it is—refers to the misadventures of the squad," the doctor will say later on, "from the first moments of its formation around the gaming table where we have left the gambler's hand nailed down (on stage the breath of nemesis is announced; all the ancient sins are going to find their correlatives in the apparatus of ruin) to the fearsome bivouacs in the heart of the mountains, the infantlike wailing of the wind in the draws, the presentiments of punishment, the premonitory warnings of the guard, whose steps resound in the fallen leaves. Consumed by fever and burning with a desire for vengeance, a man—with a three-day beard, he chews on the nails of a hand held by a tourniquet—watches with mistrust his comrades in the advance as they try to distract themselves playing cards on a night of ill omens. He no longer knows what he wants, because vengeance, woman, and fortune are mixed up in his furor, livened by the impotence that overwhelms him facing the immenseness of the mountain; the sight of the mother-of-pearl, whose futility someone mentions in order to justify the withdrawal, clouds his mind. Once more knives flash, bodies begin to fight, the cry is followed by running, the running by . . . a solitary shot in the confines of Mantua. A scene from a play is converted into the end of an epoch and a few inexpert amateurs have to play the same role as Cato at times; the curtain of an anachronistic light comedy of manners rises to reveal a set in ruins, and during the intermission, while the extras change disguises and the actors smoke in the hallways, the civil war breaks out. Those who have arrived late for the performance barely realize what kind of play we've been called upon to see . . ."

"But what about those shouts? Didn't you hear shouts? They seem to be inside the house . . ."

"Yes, I heard them, but I don't listen to them," the doctor answered. And he added: "It's what's left over from those days, shouts, sighs, a few shots at the end of summer . . . it's all the food of our postwar; we live on rumor and feed ourselves on intrigues, but our moment has passed now, passed forever. . . . The present has already passed and all that's left for us is the fact that one day hasn't passed; the past isn't what it was either, but what it wasn't; only the future, what's left for us, is what's already been; in that last kitchen inhabited by a heroine of yesteryear—even the flies have abandoned it—only the hands of a cheap clock move to indicate a mistaken hour, not so much to measure that immeasurable and gratuitous time that the Gambler has bequeathed to us with infinite length as if to materialize with its interminable circular movement the nature of the void that enfolds us, the silence that succeeds an ultrasonorous Past whose echoes resound in the area of the ruins, the last bugle calls, the pounding on the street of hooves that among the gray colors of the afternoon frustrated by door hinges and the weak whispers of the frayed curtains and the long sighs— belches of a hard-to-swallow and indigestible time—try to rise up out of a gaseous yesterday into a today without memory to fall time and again, like that scarab informed by a stubborn and grotesque will that leaves no place for reflec-

[223]

tion, which returns to the ground feet up every time it tries to climb up a base, not in forgetfulness but in a lack of interest, and which are only revived with the distant death rattle of a motor coming closer along a dusty road, behind which hasten—uniforms turned into dust cloaks, beards made of cotton and netting, all the pride, the dash, and the wardrobe of the troop reduced to the limits of a distressful caravan of country actors, their looks hypnotized by a point beyond here—to take refuge in the delirious hospitality of the survivors, the specters of a tantalized yesterday. But the premonition is exact; after so many years of resignation the unmistakable sound of the motor (it would have made the most patient person curse) returns once more to put their faith to the test or to alleviate their purgatory, who can they be? are there a few or a lot of them? are they young too, like our fathers? or, on the contrary, have they reached our age? . . . And from the other side, do they still remember us? do they intend to remain? are they going to war? do they intend to burn everything once and for all? are they headed for the mountains? is the old man waiting for them? are they coming or going? As the sound approaches it grows darker in the room, it's always that way. The shutters, the latches are closed; the candles are lighted and the reflector glows, the other specters come out of the boxes, the dusty cards, the prints in missals, the photographs draped in velvet. The light of the headlamps of a car obliged to maneuver a village crossroads shines furtively through the cracks and holes in the boards onto that morbid setting: all the walls suffer from dampness, there are no chairs left, run-down ceilings, the light hesitates and grows, along a narrow hall a shape attacked by photophobia runs, needing only to push open a door to seek refuge in the basement of moans. Then the phenomenon of light and sound operates, time is broken, to run toward that instant in which it remained in suspense; I know now that it wasn't an instant and that probably that ominous latch never made a sound, just as there was no sound from the horses' hooves or the bugles and shots from Mantua, but what wasn't yesterday has to have been today; since there was no greatness today, ruins are necessary, those families that today are piled up in their tombs and shrines barely existed, nor was there the wealth that justifies the decay that mounts up today, nor do the weariness, the lack of appetite proceed from disillusionment because the famous promise was never kept; so they never came to say the words that today ceilings and hallways return, converted into yearning. It's true that memory adulterates, enlarges, and exaggerates, but it's not just that; it also invents in order to give an appearance something that had lived and gone away to what the present denies. In a cloud of dust you come to see a desperate father, how many times does a crack in the wall represent a figure in an act of offering? There's a particular vase in the bottom of which he sings a whole summer's afternoon, marked by the voices of children playing beside a pool. And yet no such pool existed. Sometimes he's quiet: he listens in silence to the testimony of a wounded self-esteem (self-esteem is always wounded, that's why its existence is known) that tries in vain to justify the behavior that vanity extols; who knows, I repeat, whether or not that father existed, that fiancé; but doubtless there are thirty or forty years of desolation, of euthanasic disdain for the street and the morning and his fellows whose offenses he doesn't wish to forgive and about whose mysteries he doesn't wish to ask himself any questions because his adulterous concubinage with the specter of her intimacy forces her to forget and deform her only legitimate link. It was something also combined with the light, as if light and mirror had tried to distract her attention with a chance reflection so that she wouldn't notice the last sound of the latch, much farther below. Then she will return to him, transformed now into a mythomaniacal grandmother, to share with him that medley of illicit loves and cloistered grandeur which, at the same time that he beats on the door, is magnified by the same impulse of wrath or shame to take

[225]

on a haughty pose before the bedroom mirror. How she would talk to him about the play that was put on before that mirror—that monster of duplicity and alienation—in whose frozen interior there will develop in all the following years the whole filthy decomposition of a frustrated appetite, amidst whose furtive glimmers will be produced the complete inversion of an order that, lacking a single particle of love, will have no other way out but to devour itself in order to restore the stability of the rottenness, the ruin, the unreason, and the pride! I think that it knew at once how to deceive her with a false image that only took the demented half of her passion while the other half resisted—in the silent hallways and the basement in shadows—believing in that fateful sound, the terrible click that sounded there below scarcely more perceptible than the dropping of a pin or the snap of a relay that stopped the mechanism of the house, which broke the fragile precinct that preserved our nymph age from the vengeances, vicissitudes, and contradictions of a slothful and cajoling time. It was the good-bye; the young woman who in front of the mirror makes up her face and fixes her hair surmises at once—in the same way that the expert foreman perceives, over the buzz of the powerhouse, the discharge of a valve—the hours of old age and solitude that approach after the sound of the latch. Barely dressed, she will run downstairs, break locks and windows, pound on doors and go down all the hallways until suddenly (the echo of abandonment has spread everywhere) the sane half will find itself enclosed in a new gaseous chrysalis of abandonment while the other half, indifferent and sarcastic, practices the dance steps to the rhythm of her own whistling. Under those circumstances renunciation is rarely produced, what comes, rather, is a kind of accommodation with misery—mitigated by fables—of the same type as that degrading and insolent clinging to well-being; it's the clinging that bears up, that doesn't tolerate changes, that on those rare nights at summer's end will light a candle to look once

[226]

more at photographs of the past and beg, amidst tears, hic-cupping, gagging, and tremolos, Numa for a radical re-venge. A spot exists quite close to the one you're looking for that we could call the tabernacle of ruin. I'll tell you where it is: beyond Burgo Mediano, a town fallen apart since the war, you have to take the road that goes up to Mantua and stop in a village called El Salvador. You can well imagine why they call it that. Actually, only the tower of its church remains standing. It was a village, nonetheless, located in a unique spot on a pleasant and fertile flat stuck in the center of the encircling mountains; so that from the tower the whole Región range appears as if within reach of your hand; in the center and due north, El Monje, whose enigmatic presence can be seen on even the darkest nights; and to the east, much farther away in appearance and always fringed with clouds, Malterra . . . really, I don't know what I'm surprised at. Those nights I'm talking about (and it's usually in Septem-ber) a couple of days after the car had been seen on the Re-gión road, several people who can no longer live except at the expense of sacrifice come to the belfry. The journey is a long one, doubtless, to be made on foot, but the reward is compensation for everything. Don't forget that what's in play is a kind of survival; nothing less. As soon as they get there, and although the nights are hot and cloudless around the tower—which the hooded crows abandon on such occa-sions, the way the inhabitants and landowners of a village invaded by summer people do—all that can be heard are in-vocations and laments, that senile crackling of a thousand desires aborted half a century before which bloom on their lips to rise up to heaven in an interminable fumarole of whispers. For there, in Mantua, hidden among the burning thorns, the vervain and lavender, sleeps our last hope; or maybe not, perhaps it never sleeps; he's clumsy, old, and one-eyed and—according to the common people—from his car-tridge belt hangs a whole rosary made from the gold teeth he's pulled out of his victims; with the arrival of autumn,

when he considers his hunting season over, it's his custom
to sing a very long and very sad song that can get to last ten
or twenty days, which tells the unfortunate story of the Carlist
unit that took refuge in the valley, and which, trivialized,
divested of its hypnotic power, adjusted to ordinary lyrics—
'for a crust of bread' or 'you, people of steel'—is sung by an
out-of-tune voice on all the inhabited terraces of Región on
mornings of relief. In winter he dresses like a taiga herdsman, a pyramid of raw wool crowned by a morion made of
fox and rabbit skins, wound in spirals, and underneath his
small, black, and lively eyes are moving constantly, with no
need to look in order to know where someone is walking,
where the fallen leaves are being stirred, and where the underbrush shakes. His story—or his legend—is multiple and
contradictory; on one side it's asserted that it's a matter of a
Carlist survivor who—over a hundred and some odd years
old—from his hatred of women and Bourbons draws new
strength every year to defend the inviolability of the forest;
on the other side, also widespread, is the belief that his existence goes back many years and decades in the past: a monk,
swollen with vanity, who abandons his order when intransigent and moderating reform tries to restrict the consolation of wine. . . . It's also claimed that it's only a question
of a military man whom we all knew and who, having loved
a woman to the point of madness, fled out of spite and
withdrew there to hide his voluntary mutilations and to wreak
vengeance on the bodies of those who follow him. It doesn't
seem unlikely; I'm not saying that such things can't happen
in this century too, but I do affirm that then, I mean before,
they had more fateful consequences. What does seem true is
that he always waits for night before going into action. Some
become interminable, the ear cocked in the direction of the
horizon where the glow of headlights was glimpsed for the
last time; it's a wait for the confirmation of the limit that
poverty has imposed on survival in order to consecrate his
condition on a landing of the belfry staircase. On some oc-

casions—when, for example, a party of Belgians tried to get there with the help of a lot of scientific apparatuses—he made them wait several nights, but Numa always responds in the end. All right, I kill you. Don't ask me for anything more, I kill you and that's that. In that way your conscience will still be at peace and the forest will still be mine. That's what you wanted, wasn't it? Don't worry anymore, that's how it goes, satisfied? You can all go back in peace, nobody can come here, I see to that. I already understand that your misery wouldn't be tolerable if you knew that anybody could come here; so this is the best thing for everybody, I understand. The pay . . . you know only too well: no disturbance at all and, above all, nobody harbors any hope other than that of punishment of the transgressors, not to mention the ambitions. A peace, no matter how awful it may be, is still a peace. I'm careful to maintain it just the way you people see to it down there. Agreed? That's how it goes. What do you say about the condition? And the future? What do you lack from the future? Reflect: a future only opens up to threats, all the rest is a lot of talk. Go back home; don't call yourselves cowards or base, there's no place for that, because a whole science of destiny is hidden in your baseness. Yes, there's no doubt, it's Time that we still haven't managed to understand; it's in time that we haven't learned to exist and it's behind time—not after desperation—that we resist accepting death. The Gambler was right: he hadn't set any trap, it was time who refused to accept the validity of his reasons and accepted, in exchange, a stupid combination of cards. So it's he, what shall we do to him? I wonder how it's possible for us to persist in maintaining such an abuse: in making it the repository of our hope when it's it—and only it—that sets out to defraud it. There are those who've become accustomed to having a future before them and there are also those who, in their shamelessness, assert that the most important and decisive part of life is what hasn't yet been lived. Let them ask us about it! I must have told that one

[229]

already how in Región on the following morning peace is made again and a mitigated joy, sung by the boiling of the teakettles, laughter in the garrets, and out-of-tune songs on the terraces, of an age-old and ridiculous frivolity, come to replace the squeaking of the rats, the creaking of the beams warped with lichens. Framed in a high window, a smiling and peaceful and slightly propped-up face seems to give it-self over to the recreative contemplation of a sunny morn-ing with the indifference of someone used to the supernat-ural echoes, of the same nature as those peasants who—on the Bayeux tapestry—plow their fields without paying any attention to the celestial phenomena and apparitions that people the firmament behind them. Why that peace? Doubt-less because they don't figure on the future, Numa had just said that same dawn: 'Let things stay the way they are, shit on the future.' No trace of hope, in this land of disappoint-ments, has prevailed since the time it was stamped with the click of the latch or the shot in Mantua; nothing better for our health could have happened; nor will it prevail—I can assure you—while there yet remains a postcard, a yellow photograph like the one you carry, a memory of any kind with which to plumb the abyss of a today that's nothing but a was, a something that hasn't ever existed because what ex-ists was and what was hasn't been. The latch sounded—and as if obeying a stage mechanism—the blind was closed, the street disappeared, darkness fell and the voices of the chil-dren grew silent and everything remained—like that happy colony of insects who, in children's stories, go from sum-mer bustle to the rigors and penuries of winter—in the state you see it in now. I've spent my life among them; all my science has been taken up with trying to preserve that last remainder of a pulse that beats in their arms without know-ing why, in the name of what? I think that the life of man is divided into three ages: the first is the age of impulse, in which everything that moves us and matters to us needs no justification, rather, we feel attracted toward all that—a

[230]

woman, a profession, a place to live—thanks to an impulsive intuition that never compares; everything is so obvious that it's worth something by itself and the only thing that counts is the capacity to attain it. In the second age, what we chose in the first has normally been spent, is no longer worth anything by itself and needs a justification that a reasonable man concedes with pleasure, with the help of his heart, of course; it's maturity, it's the moment in which, in order to emerge gracefully from the comparisons and contradictory possibilities that everything that he observes offers him, he brings off the intellectual effort thanks to which a course chosen by instinct is justified a posteriori by reflection. In the third age, not only have the motives that he chose in the first one been worn out and invalidated, but also the reasons with which he supported his behavior in the second. It's alienation, the repudiation of everything his life has been, for which he no longer finds motivation or excuse. In order to live in peace a person has to refuse to enter that third stage; no matter how artificial it may seem, he must make an effort with his will to remain in the second; because drifting is something else. So, I'll say one thing to you, one thing: my people, my folk, my generation barely glimpsed the first age; we were immediately given everything, we could choose almost nothing. By means of an effort more considerable than was thought, we managed to survive thanks to an incomplete, illogical, and defective but sufficient justification. And it didn't last very long; in truth, we haven't known anything but drift or maybe running aground, running aground, that is, on a coast so sordid, so desertlike and hostile that we've dared to get out of the boat that brought us there. And yet, I'll tell you something else . . ."

But he didn't tell her how on that afternoon toward the end of September he'd lost María Timoner. He hadn't found her at the clinic the same night as the scandal. He hadn't found her baggage or any notes or reasons at the desk. He went to the inn where his bags were locked up; he didn't find out anything about her there either. But the arrangement still stood, at a crossroads that his eyes could reach if he went out onto the balcony of his room. And standing on the balcony he let a couple of hours, three or four pass. The car he'd spoken for arrived, he put in all his bags except one and went on to the crossroads where he waited sitting on a wall until nightfall. Near midnight he was unable to wait any longer; he got into the back seat and told the driver: "Go ahead, I'll tell you where." He made him leave the main roads, cross streambeds, follow horse paths. "Go ahead, go ahead," he said, sitting in the back seat, his arms resting on the back of the front one. After three days he understood the truth, the car stopped in a field beside the Tarrentino, and perhaps from the lips of that ferrywoman came what made him stop and abandon the search. "Forget about it; forget about it and go back to Región," she was able to tell him, with her feet in the black water. The doctor understood then that there's a kind of duty that can only be paid off with spite, sacrifice isn't enough. He scarcely knew the family that lived in the small house; he had the car stop in front of the railroad barrier—which since it never ran was always closed—and told the driver that since it would be a short stop it wasn't worth turning the motor off. The parents looked at each other, so surprised that they scarcely knew what to answer: "She's your daughter, isn't she? She's of age, isn't she? She accepts me as a husband, doesn't she? What are we waiting for then?" He didn't even know her name. He only asked her three questions: what her name was, if there was a well in the small house, and if she liked cabbage soup.

"But, right now?" the father asked.

"Right now. Why should we wait for tomorrow?" Then he said what resolved all the hesitation of the parents. "I've got a cab waiting at the door."

"A horse-cab?"

"No horses. It's a modern cab that's waiting at the door."

"Then we'll all go, if the doctor doesn't mind."

"Naturally," the doctor said.

They scarcely had anything to take. The object of greatest value was a sewing basket, which they put up on the baggage rack along with a suitcase tied with cord. The three settled in the back seat, startled and stiff, without even daring to close the doors.

"Región," the doctor said.

"How lucky you are, daughter; riding in a car at such a young age," the mother said.

"It doesn't happen twice," said the father with a sententious tone.

"Let's hope not," the doctor answered. And added: "Región, hurry up."

They rode with their mouths open, not moving a finger. The young girl sat between her parents, motionless and pale, her look was staring and her expression was absorbed, a bit eager. When the car stopped they could only look at the doctor with a questioning expression and a certain fear; they didn't even dare open the doors.

"You don't have to get out. It's only a matter of a moment," the doctor said in front of the town hall.

"What luck, child, at your age and in a car."

"Have we arrived already?"

The next stop was at the parish house.

"Have we arrived already?"

"Get out now, it will only take a minute. You too," he told the driver.

It took something like a half hour; the parents were impatient to get back into the car. Only when the doctor took the young woman by the arm did the mother seem to understand the purpose of the trip.

"What's going to happen to us now?" she asked.

"You people are going home."

"What's going to become of us?"

"And how can we get home at this hour?"

"You'll go back in the car," the doctor replied. "You'll take them right now, you already know where it is," he repeated, addressing the driver.

"That's something else again," the father said.

"That's something to see, a drive in a car."

"Two, woman, two," the father said laconically. They weren't even capable of turning their heads when the car went off; they'd forgotten to say good-bye to her and kiss her and they were taking back the small trousseau, the sewing basket tied to the baggage rack.

He didn't take her to the new house that night. He did it the next day, in the afternoon; he pushed her into the room where his mother was sewing, sitting in a high wooden armchair, very sturdy, especially constructed for her rheumatism and which the doctor had had made by a local cabinetmaker. He said nothing but the introduction: "I would like to introduce you to Mrs. Sebastián," and he left.

"I'm going to tell you in a few words what I think time is," the doctor said that same night: "It's the dimension in which a human being can only be unfortunate, it can't be otherwise. Time only appears in misfortune and therefore memory is only a register of pain. It only knows how to speak of fate, not what a man is to be but how different from what he would like to be. That's why the future doesn't exist and of all the present only an infinitesimal part isn't past; it's what wasn't. That's why it can only be what your imagination didn't foresee. Imagination is a faculty that is only given to creatures who are fated not to fight against it but to deny it to themselves. I want to see how at one moment in our history our parents went to sleep, a sleep of well-brought-up people. Twenty or thirty years later they woke up to the clamor of radios and the announcement of war. When they were sunken in that sleep and the first symptoms of Ruin crept in, it must have been understood that fate and time had once more refused to finance an investment that could only be amortized in Teruel, along the Ebro, or at Doña Cautiva Bridge. Under such circumstances isn't it more sensible to let Numa fulfill such a logical task? Since the future doesn't exist, let's see if, once and for all, it gets rid of the past."

4

I don't know—she could have replied. But the night had begun to grow cool; she'd opened the curtain again and the glow of the garden in the moonlight brought a certain phosphorescence into the room. Without the doctor's helping her, with quite a bit of effort she managed to open the window. It's true—she thought on looking at the abandoned garden—how during those last days of September the aroma changes and suddenly, after the wild tumult of summer, the countryside quiets down. The way it seems to withdraw into itself and become immobilized into caution, mesmerized by the threat of winter. It could be said that even the black poplars hold their breath at the chill that will tear their foliage off. What a strange and contradictory sensation of calm and truce for a soul that has sacrificed everything—not the body—to feel once more a reminiscence of that rash feeling that had been born in these places; and what wouldn't that soul give to change memory—transformed into an obsession by an unjust reason—into just enough juices to reproduce the untimely blooming of that dizzying present, so timeless, fleeting, and passionate, which could never be transformed into past.

"Don't you think you're exaggerating, Doctor?"

A discreet burst of laughter rose up from among the bushes, disappearing in the silvery glimmer of the night into a thousand fleeting sparkles which seemed to go with it and in the moment of their instantaneous fusion to light her up (a pale, loose-fitting suit with which to detemporalize herself in the desexed autumn of an abandoned garden) with the iridescent innocence of a vision, paradoxically lasting and passing, lacking in stigmas and in age.

"These nights are treacherous. That trip . . . you can see that I don't advise it."

"I think you're exaggerating, Doctor. If you'd lived that present that you don't believe in now, you wouldn't be afraid now. Maybe fear is the least of it: there's something before it and it can seek the strength to leap over it. Or forget it. Or something that isn't fear but that's shouting for it. There's something true in what you're saying but that's not the terrible part; the terrible part is that the payment for a present, which wasn't time, must be made with age. Or maybe it's the value of a single currency in two different coins, one very strong, the other . . . scarcely worth more than the paper that stands for it. I don't know. It seems that the body should have learned to assimilate the pace of the days" (from in front of the garden in shadows to the other side of the window her voice seemed to be accompanied by a subtle and emotive fluorescence that lighted up her face when the word stuck in her throat) "up to a point where it would be superfluous to fill them with a feeling, a duty, or a memory. The present is really a very small thing: almost everything was. I try to remember that at the time I hadn't reached the age of twenty. The civil war had caught us in a moment from which—I don't know why—it was proper to expect more joy than what that age usually brings with it. No, it wasn't insouciance. Two or three years earlier I'd left the Black Ladies' boarding school and that period is more than enough to understand that everything they'd taught us to respect, avoid, or fear was something exclusively ours. Because a young woman leaving a religious school has to face up to a world before which upbringing has rarely been removed, if she doesn't join the bourgeois order by way of marriage, she can at least conform to the received values. Nor was it rebellion, not even nonconformity, but in any case a kind of pedagogical insufficiency that began with the vocabulary and would be translated into that credulous and smiling doltishness that can be seen in the most uncouth pig farmer, feted and shown about the capital by virtue of some rural contest. Because on leaving that school we were nothing more than provincial young ladies who were opening their eyes to a world quite different from the one offered by that education; that lack of focus creates a kind of social strabismus in the adolescent that will impede him at first from realizing his situation in a period that he might never come to understand. That was certainly what it brought on in me, until well into the war, that feeling of being in the midst of a company of great temperamental actors, a worthy group, shrill and shouting, who, incapable of shaking loose from their own inhibitions, will never come to understand the plot of a comedy whose situations and jokes they know by heart. A woman at that age and in that milieu rarely finds herself placed in a society where she is accustomed to look at herself and run into herself, as in a mirror. But in my case I lacked that society, the mirror only showed a disfigured and grotesque image, which, because it was true, could only show a clown's role. I didn't go back to my father but to an aunt of his, ten or twelve years older than he, who still lived in the house of their forefathers. My father had also lived in that house as a student and he returned there—when there were only two aunts left—one summer in 19__to show off his first cadet's uniform. I was born there and my mother died there. Although I always lived apart from him I needed very little effort to understand how the career of a military man, brought up within those walls and under those looks, must sooner or later turn into spite, an appetite for regeneration that the country would go about transforming into vengeance and destruction. But what my father went out to find one morning of hunting in 1925 when I had left school gave no reason even to organize a masked ball of retrospective character. I mean that even though brought up in the same milieu and with the same blood flowing in our veins, what made up the essence of their pride and code of honor for my father's generation for us was nothing but an object of mockery. The education that, out of spite as well as any other way, had come to form a part of my father for me was but a useless and annoying shell that I had to get rid of at any cost in order to receive the sun of my time. Nor do I have to say that sexual relations, or the manner in facing up to them, make up the first chapter of the new manual; nor do I have to say that the Región I knew at the age of seventeen was a much simpler town than the one my parents had known, rid of that strange, abundant garb with which the archaic order had adorned its usages. I think that twenty years earlier it wouldn't have been the same at all, friendship with Juan de Tomé had no reason to have emerged as the preamble of a sexual adventure; but in my time that was the way it was, the new relationship between the sexes meant nothing but the elimination of all those rites and sacrifices that would doubtless lead to marriage, but neither were they replaced by anything else. So that friendship was impossible if it didn't lead, the same as before but without rites or solemnity, to marriage. It was a rather blind moment; the young man who thought himself liberated didn't know now what to do with his hands or with a freedom that had not concerned itself with finding anything for him to do. Or were the car rides and Sundays in a country house the whole prize of that new freedom? Because in the end that's all there was: a privileged person's car, like that monster Eugenio Mazón had got from no one knows where, lunch under the live oak trees, a house in the hills where an old couple who took care of him lived, and always the phantom, only the phantom, of our sexual freedom underneath. When I saw him for the first time, that summer when the war broke out, he was a kind of sad satyr taking refuge in his Sabine woods, lacking everything except protection and—it might be said—tormented by the recent eruption of masculinity. I don't know if you realize how a young woman who has barely been out in the world two years tries to learn how to dissipate the heat that she's been accumulating in her ignorance while education and the family environment are silent, that whole society without canons, those lives without direction, and all those desires lacking in ambition, with no other aim than that of being consumed in the moment and the place where they're born, will prevail in their spirits with much more enthusiasm than the sensible rules of bourgeois reason. Deep pits and antinomies like that can only be produced in adolescence, that age 'in which, to our minds, it's enough to name a thing in order to create it,' but what's created is only what intoxicates the soul and what's named is frequently only what isn't known. What isn't known . . . all the imaginary, fascinating, and dizzying horror that fate places in front of juvenile perplexity with the sole object of frustrating its ulterior experience, of defrauding its prospects with the aim of succeeding over the years in drawing out of a squandered youth a complete person formed from a heap of deceptions. So with the outbreak of the civil war I found myself plunged into that combination of curiosity, urge, and fear that gets into a person in sordid alleys, looking at posters and obscene symbols of vice, as before the den where the horrors of genesis are exhibited, the aberrations of nature, and the horrendous enigma of perpetuation. Years later, on the threshold of a whorehouse room dimly lighted by the opalescent reflections from ambiguous hallways, the soul will recognize with singular and cruel lucidity that a single fear, a single pride, and a single selfishness have come to weave all those heterogeneous circumstances to provoke disgust and return the castles of an innocent age to the sand. Because as soon as it's discovered there's no questioning or hesitation. Just waiting. I'm talking about desire: I can't refer to it without associating it with the period of the war and tying it in with the leather jackets, the broken panes held together by gummed paper and protected by strips of adhesive tape, the nights in the Defense Committee building, enlivened by the machine guns on the plain or in the mountains. . . .

"You told me before that the present had never happened. You've closed the windows so as not to hear the cries of a drunkard or a patient who's run off into the woods for several weeks. You don't know very well why. Everything you've told me increases my confidence, I must confess to you. When I found out that all his fun consisted in hanging stray dogs I got to thinking that it might have been the case of an old acquaintance of mine, attacked by the same illness that was translated into a different fury. But what little difference there is, how close I can see myself to the incomprehensible limit that separates us. You don't see me as having the strength to continue the trip and I don't see myself as having the health to abandon it; once again because we're witnessing the same circumstance from two rather different points of view. Both are situated in fear, it's something both have in common; but I'm sure my fear is nothing but a package containing a conviction while the one you speak to me about is nothing but the last state before desperation. Or vice versa. All that continuity in tedium, repugnance, and selfishness that I was talking to you about before, don't you think, doctor, that it obeys something? don't you think it's a question of that hidden and bitter humor that segregates the soul vice ridden by an improper function in order to defend and preserve its last pure nucleus? what is it trying to maintain virgin, that fury that leads him to kill the dogs? where did it really want to go? The same I tell you; you, however, must have understood that beneath that secret hides the only cure for a health that is gradually ceasing to believe in everything. If I've taken this trip, if I have ended my marriage with it, it won't be to hear a few pieces of advice concerning the common cold. Or hear talk about the glow of the walnut tree on autumn nights. I've gotten too old; to put it better I've made everything old, even what surrounds me and I've finally decided to try at any cost to return a little warmth to the years I've got ahead of me. I've decided to stay at Muerte's hotel; I plan to get there tonight or tomorrow morning. I don't know what might have become of her, I don't know if she's still alive, if she's still living there and running the same establishment and making her living in the same business. I haven't seen her again since, already married, I went back to her place to return the money she'd loaned me. You must already imagine what it was really for. It wasn't I, it was my husband who didn't have the slightest desire to find out about that. But in my conscience an impatient desire burned not only to tell him the story but to tell it with pride. To make him know about my pride and—it was an anticipated form of vengeance—my faithfulness. Poor man, he didn't have the words to say no and— after a year of marriage, I'd spoken to him about a hostel on the mountain to enjoy Easter vacation—I dragged him there like a steer to slaughter. I don't know what happened, Muerte was still running the hotel but perhaps, warned in advance of our coming, she'd decided to whitewash it for the space of our stay. But there are things—that hotel at least—that don't let themselves be whitewashed easily. It was a violent week, silent and difficult, that wasn't good for anything. No one learned anything more than what he already knew, nobody could overcome the doubts about what he already suspected so that stay of six or seven days only served to define with greater clarity the mutual mistrust and suspicions and to engender all the troubles and difficulties that—without leaving a latent state—will break up a union that wasn't based on anything more than a reciprocal appreciation. Let's not talk about memories now, please. If they were only what is meant by that word at least! I would have known what to be guided by; I would have known, however, how to translate yesterday's glory into today's loneliness and to reconstruct that tortuous process of adulteration that transforms a young girl ready for all sacrifices into a wife who knows how to take care of her husband's guests at noon and deceives him in the afternoon with a lower-class lover. But I don't know how to do it, there's the drama; I don't know how, coming out at that point, you reach the other, I don't know what happened in between. I no doubt lost the thread of the discourse in the cab of the truck that in those winter days of 1938 took us from Región to El Salvador, and from there to Muerte's hotel, for ten, twenty, or thirty days, oh, too terrible and too turbulent to be unforgettable. Because that's precisely what's forgotten in those days when memory isn't present. I think that only the body is present and maybe manacled, gagged, and stupefied. A body that for moments like that needs to be alone and refuses the company of those inopportune companions, memory, conscience, upbringing, and all the rest. Then the body won't be capable of remembering anything, like the drunkard brought back into domestic life after a night of wild carousing. I scarcely saw him during the first two years of war. Toward the end of 1936 I'd been called to give testimony before the Defense Committee where, thanks to the intervention of Juan de Tomé, who had friends with a certain influence there, I was treated with some deference. It was a matter of finding out my father's whereabouts at that time and his attitude toward the war, but even when his career as well as his nonappearance obliged one to presume such answers, they didn't become evident until the summer of 1937 when it came to be known that my father had been assigned to the General Staff of the invading army. In August or September of that year, I don't remember well, we were called in again, but my aunt came out after three or four days of internment, I don't know whether because of the small value of her person as a hostage, the disdain to which fear had brought her to speak of my father, or fear of the custom of a daily rosary that the Committee guessed would be produced if they kept my aunt in their basement. Juan de Tomé came to visit me; he told me that it was a matter of a voluntary—but under guard—confinement, not in the status of a hostage but in order to avoid any harm that might come to me for being the daughter of whom I was. Later he told me that, through government offices, he had proposed an exchange to my father, which, in accordance with previous arrangements, would be carried out during the current year. I don't know why, but that proposal came to suggest a change in my status; I left the basement and without leaving the building was transferred to the top floor, the servants' quarters of the old palace, and they gave me decent lodgings and even a job in the office, under the vigilance of that famous comrade (Adela). She was a small woman, intransigent and standoffish, who couldn't hide her displeasure when some soldiers of the Committee brought some dresses from my house along with some personal articles that I kept in a locked suitcase under the bed to which she didn't have access. It seemed that the Committee had placed a lot of hope in my exchange. The comrade (Adela) would frequently interrupt my work and, with ostensible annoyance, make me go with her to an office downstairs where, after I went in, the door would be closed in her face. Juan de Tomé, always in civilian clothes, accompanied by two or three other military men, was accustomed to wait for me there: 'It looks like your leaving will happen any minute. Everything's arranged and all that's missing is a small detail that depends on your father himself. But now it's a matter of knowing how far we can trust you . . .' Almost everything was a string of abstract words for me and I was scarcely able to make out their ultimate meaning. In the first place because I could barely remember my father or because I still had a schoolgirl's picture of him. All that wasn't really too different from those calls at school when

[244]

a couple of times during each term they would have me leave the classroom or the ranks to follow a sister to the mother superior's office: 'I've had a letter from your father. He's quite concerned about your deportment and your grades and he asks me . . .' Such was my childhood connection and such it continued to be in my youth. I began to think that my father was ashamed of me and that, afraid of a meeting, he was trying by all means to maintain someone else's tutelage and discipline from a distance. The childish mind translates all that into indifference, alienation, abstract feelings . . . spite. I supposed that they're only the consequences of being an orphan and that a father and a daughter, with the link of the mother lost, can't remain united except by means of a paradoxical and inflexible separation. I remember perfectly well a passageway with mosaics with great sunny windows through an inner courtyard and the moment in which, led by the arm of the nun, the schoolgirl leaves the line of her companions to be led to the visitors' room where a corpulent gentleman, almost a stranger, is chatting animatedly with the mother superior. I remember the kiss, the recognition; the face that isn't remembered except in abstract lines (love doesn't inform memory therefore) that suddenly seems identical to oneself, making the chasm that separates it from its nonaffective image deeper, that contact with a cheek that gives off an unfamiliar aroma of shaving lotion, that kind of confused and invincible timidity with which the childish soul, when the strange paternal hand strokes its hair or squeezes its waist, defends itself from a pursuit that has no relation to the facts in its memory. I remember perfectly the return to the courtyard where my classmates are having recess with a box of candy, not daring to turn my eyes to that corner of the cloister where mother superior and father—toward where the looks of all the girls converge—are stopping for a last instant: 'It's my father' with that false and insecure tone of abandonment that tries to rehabilitate one's pride with a ploy. Because the child always harbors a precocious kind of fear that the paternal balance might fall apart and that in certain cubbyholes of his intimacy all that's needed is a minimum of stimulus to make it a certainty. It's possible, therefore, that when she says, 'It's my father,' she scarcely believes it anymore, scarcely believes in that word, devoid of value, which is supposed to serve only for the audience and which, at the moment of going to bed in the communal dormitory, freed of the compromises and frauds that her self-esteem has imposed on her in the courtyard, is transformed into weeping and sorrow as the girl's mind plumbs the depths of her own abandonment and, in a contradictory and destructive upset, learns to trust only in her own fears and tears. I assure you that the life of an orphan schoolgirl isn't translated into great resentments; it's cold-blooded rather if you want to understand by that a lack of affection, interests, and misgivings of one who is ready to go out into the world without great things to defend or many debts to be felt bound to. My father, in one part of its meaning, had ceased to exist before his death, bequeathing to me a legacy of impatience, failure, and anticipation: because a great part of my life—you'll soon see—will cease to exist at the end of the civil war. After the war we'll see so much of it that we won't even be surprised at the rapidity and the haste with which so many bourgeois households will abandon the moral precepts on which they were formed as a consequence of the death of the head of the family, the pillaging of a country place, or the loss of the dining room silver. It had happened to me a few years earlier, that's all, I didn't have to wait for the war to see myself bereft of father, home, moral principles, and place in society. It so happened—I don't know if the republican lines were already breaking up—that from an office in the Defense Committee they managed to establish telephone communication with his headquarters. Is that possible? Maybe it was a trick, I don't know, but I don't understand its object unless to work in its power an X ray of my filial sentiments. It was a small parlor that gave the impression of an

[246]

imminent move; all the chairs were piled with files and papers and the floor with bundles and typewriters. When I went
in, a soldier squatting by a small night table was trying at
times to reconnect a difficult telephonic conversation. I don't
remember who else was there, Juan of course. A few of them,
obeying a signal, left the room in a body and went to the
small switchboard where a communications officer was trying
to reestablish the connection. I think I remember that I was
biting my nails, sitting on the frayed edge of a chair while,
leaning against the door frame, wearing an unbuttoned khaki
tunic that revealed a white shirt, he was watching me in a
provocative and bold way, mingling enjoyment with vigilance. The telephone began to howl, giving off mechanical
sounds that mingled with the curt shouts of the officer and
a whole Committee on the eve of exile or captivity, ready
to believe that on the other end of the wire a Pilate of the
cavalry would accede with pleasure to a concession of pardon in exchange for an item who, fearful, orphaned, and
timid, not letting herself be intoxicated by her own urges,
was drawing back in horror toward the fearsome instant when
the game would be over: it was the state of the child who,
after the Sunday uproar in the company of his friends in the
game room of a house where he's been invited, in an instant
of silence catches in the hallway the voice of the nursemaid
come to fetch him; how the familiar voice in the strange milieu where he has been given freedom that the discipline of
his house doesn't tolerate suddenly becomes hateful, the agent
of an authority that cuts off his freedom, restricts his enthusiasm, and subrogates his desires. And then, from that corner, from an ashtray piled high with butts, and from a receiver left on the table there came that impersonal, nasal, and
authoritarian voice that quickly made me retreat to certain
solitary and bitter moments, the whispered admonitions, the
songs of resignation, the porchways of the cloister. You can
imagine the complex chemical that was developing inside me
under the influence of those two antagonistic agents: the

[247]

spasms of the intermittent voice that was coming from the telephone with the unhealthy and high-pitched tone that a magician uses to reach the subconscious of his medium, drawing to it all the particles of my being that were floating like a colloid in fear awaiting punishment, confinement, or forgiveness, and that unoccupied, somewhat indolent un-preoccupation with which—in spite of his youth and his sit-uation—making a lighter that wouldn't light click number-less times, he was looking over the disorder of that room, the papers and files in the chairs, the shrill telephone that was unable to coordinate the orders between the beyond and the hostage—or whatever she was—confused and trembling. The flame wouldn't light, all that was ignited was an inflamma-ble mixture of fear, contempt, and desire of flight inside of me, a mixture of battling particles, each of which, before obeying the perverse catalyst, tried in one last and intimate instant to maintain itself in the previous suspension so as not to fall into a deathly and hated balance. He made a very par-ticular gesture, twisting his mouth, winking in disdain at the wrathful receiver. Then, without my knowing why, he put his hand on my shoulder and squeezed my collarbone at the same time that he shrugged his shoulders, indicating to me not to worry about those wild and ridiculous sounds; I don't know if he realized that—just like the child who with an in-stantaneous touch of his finger takes delight in breaking the rotation of a top—the whole contradictory catalysis would be resolved with the simple contact of his hand to deposit on its anode—he squeezed my collarbone again and then the base of my neck—all the particles of my restiveness. That's how it must have been: in my awareness I think I can re-member the retreat, the abandonment of fear, toward a hid-den refuge where femininity hides and where it awaits with strange confidence—no longer tinged by annoyance, it's more like predestination—the moment when the battle of the hy-men is unleashed. Then he disappeared, making the lighter click at the same time as the telephone fell silent and in that disorderly room the silence that follows the fulfillment of all tests fell. The test had been made—there's no doubt—my body had shown its polarity. I won't see him again until many days later—at the inn on the highway—and, still, in spite of the many vicissitudes it would know in the meantime, my virtue was lost in that brief episode. Maybe he knew it and so ratified it. A month later the same certain and indolent look—but which wasn't interested at all in the results of its motion—seemed aimed toward that mutual secret and that tacit complicity which since the moment of the test had brought us together on the terrain of those who knew only too well: 'You see how little effort was needed.' You see how at the opportune moment a hand on the shoulder is enough to open the eyes of a person in a situation like that, as if nothing were more natural than that sober and efficient method, as if nothing were easier and more puerile than that combat which, ever since childhood—it could be said—he had known how to unleash with ease, tranquility, and even courtesy. Now, on the other hand, I'm referring to the attraction indirectly. It's likely that it was the real remedy, not the epicene gratitude of a knightly exploit; I'm also referring to that insouciance, wrapped in the skin of an insuperable and impenetrable reserve which, just as it let him make the test so economically, would accredit him in the end, with no other credentials needed, for the collection of his honorarium: 'My name is so-and-so, I've never liked to waste time.' That's how I see it now: a whole archaic and awful power that was advancing toward us through the unjust triumph of its arms and which, adding disdain to arrogance and iniquity to rapine, aimed to incorporate me into its cause at the end of the struggle through the intervention of the spurious and vicarious spokesman, halted in an instant by an unconcerned and virile gesture, a hand that squeezed my neck, while on the small Moorish table the open telephone was crying on its back like a defeated animal—parading its power in order to reduce me to obedience—to open my eyes, dishonor my suspicious virtue, and point the way for my rebel vocation. Then I understood that without having anticipated or risked anything, I had acquired a nature, not a second one—as people say—but the only one my body could shelter and which, in the shadowy cloisters, with the whispered admonitions, they had tried to hide from me and which was worthy now of a rehabilitation and an indemnification after so many years of an unjust sentence. But we were already in October by then, in a Región invaded by darkness at all hours, bombarded from all the outskirts and inhabited by a few dreamy survivors who ran unexpectedly from every cellar to load the last carts with mattresses and blankets and escape along the road into the mountains. The man in command there was named Julián Fernández, an energetic man— the son of a Región housemaid—but not very clear minded and who, in order to get out of that morass, could only think of locking people up; Mr. Robal in one room, and Adela and me in another, and in another poor Juan de Tomé who, with his dirty topcoat, was trying to convince him to organize a junta to surrender the town to my father under the most honorable conditions. He had never moved out of Región and he didn't know how to leave it; those who knew how were fighting in other places at that time: Ruán and the Germans on the flats of El Quintán, old Constantino at the Doña Cautiva Bridge, and still farther north, between El Salvador and Muerte's hotel, the only one who really knew the mountain . . . he and Mazón and that, what was his name? . . . Asián, I think, but who really seemed only concerned about their own salvation. That was, in the last instance, what moved Fernández, not the clumsy negotiations of poor Tomé, convinced that none of his former companions were going to sacrifice their safety to lend us a hand. It was no longer a matter of compassion—I think—but of loyalty to a principle common to all of them and whose frail reality would be clearly shown in the coming weeks. If that was so, why that war . . . ?"

"But what is that principle? Why the only ones? What kind of safety is that? What do compassion or loyalty have to do here? Who put that into your head?"*

* The doctor knew quite well what she was referring to and could, with a certain causal knowledge, make patent certain reserves to which he evidently wanted to withdraw. But as a doctor and as accidental mentor he couldn't help questioning himself—and questioning her—about a conduct that, having left so many points obscure, was no justification for so serious a decision as her trip. Even at times when it was a question of a legend and other times of reality, what was certain was that an estate existed that in times past had been the property of Alejandro Cayo Mazón; a photograph of his ward also existed and a requisition—that could be verified in any newspaper morgue—from the Court of Región demanding the appearance of those criminals in revolt. The sentence wasn't made public; just Mr. Rubal, the only one of them who had been caught, was sentenced to capital punishment and disappeared into the shadows of the postwar a short time after the war was over, carrying with him the secrets of the proceedings. But in that sentence for rebellion—and ultimately in the photograph that wasn't from the time of the war—implicit was the survival of some outlaws who, twenty years afterward, were considered dead. Apart from the legend of Numa there also existed the shots and—as a confirming consequence—the inviolability of the woods beginning at an evocative bend in the road that the doctor knew very well through an unerasable image: once he was to follow the guard (similar to the print of a pious wayfarer, a pilgrim's broad-brimmed hat and a back bent by his many years or the weight of an immense overcoat) up to a strange place, located in the bottom of a valley, a few stark stone houses roofed with slate and straw hidden in the grove where smoke was coming from, to attend the childbirth of a lady who concealed her identity behind a black veil. They'd probably seen him return at the end of a summer, two or three years later, without guard or mule or saddlebags or basket, suddenly thin, his face gaunt and his clothes in tatters, although with a firmer step and a stronger bearing. When on the return from that trip he entered his house and saw his mother—the widow had waited all summer for him, sitting at his father's desk, which still smelled of gummed paper, her fist resting on an unpaid bill on the desk and, with a haughty smile of triumph, her look fastened on the door that sooner or later had to open—he may have made his decision. But it's also likely that that attitude determined him to close the door again and return to Región to hire a car; forty-eight hours later he will open the door once more, push a very timid and humble girl inside, and tell her: "Here is the mistress of the house," closing the door behind her. Every year, around the same time and in fulfillment of an agreement, he made that double trip to visit the child and take care of his health and to cure his lungs of that atmosphere of gummed paper and formaldehyde that he had breathed all year long. The child lived in the guards' house, separated from the other one. They were accustomed to arrive at nightfall and to spend the night in the house. On the following morning he looked at his throat, his eyes, and listened to his heart. He didn't seem to grow day by day but a certain amount each year in the space of one night. Then the guard woman would wash him and comb his

[251]

"I don't know. I've never known. I've only tried to explain to myself some things that happened in line with some principles that at the time must have been valid. In any other way I don't understand the meaning of that war, what they were defending, how they were different from my father. As I told you, they locked us up on the top floor, in a servant's room stacked with the useless furniture of the old palace. A soldier stood guard on the landing. There we were, not leaving for a month (comrade Adela and I). The comrade (Adela) was a robust woman, disciplined and intransigent, who, all during the war, didn't change a black skirt and a white sleeveless blouse that left a pair of enormous arms

hair, put him into a Sunday suit and both, around noon now, would go up to see his mother in the other house. It was a short visit that didn't last more than a quarter of an hour, in a huge empty parlor, with a warped floor, at the end of which was the lady in mourning, her face covered with a black veil sitting in a large wicker chair located on the other side of a window to hide from its sight and the rays of light that came through. "Good morning, Doctor, how was your trip? How do you find the boy?" "The boy is strong, it's obvious that the mountain air is good for him." "A little pale, don't you think?" "He hasn't gone out much during the winter; some bronchial trouble, a couple of bad colds." "But nothing serious, right?" "No, nothing serious." "What about his education, does he know his rules?" "Education . . . maybe it would be best . . . ." "Good day, Doctor, thank you very much for your visit." He was a child who scarcely spoke but in whose look there wasn't the least indication of weakness, or the slightest entreaty: impenetrable, enigmatic, and standoffish, he seemed to be as far from asking for help as from reproaching him for his incapacity to give it because he was incapable of understanding the compassion with which the doctor could look at him since, never having left there, he didn't have the same idea concerning loneliness. The last time he'd had the feeling that someone—along the edge of the woods as the horizon was turned a bit orange by the silent and distant storm that was breaking in the mountains—had been following him, hiding behind the trees. It was a feeling already lived but not remembered, one of those stimuli that—like the meteors that cross the stratosphere and melt as they rub against it—enter the dense field of memory but never get to fall into it, leaving a wake of doubtful light in a convex and somber zone of reason, which will be joined afterward to that almost forgotten vision, a temperate night outside a clinic, a few words of baleful augury, and the breeze of a hot and violent summer. A hidden presence, buzzing and ungraspable, that seemed to delight in making certain blinks of light and some barely perceptible cuckooing comes to him all along the road to show him that it was ready to follow him to that secret place. The doctor didn't know if it was the eighth or ninth anniversary but it was before the coming of the Republic. He saw him first going out in the air, unaffected by the winter. It could have been said that she'd been born for that situation: a single change of clothing, a single room, and a single and permanent annoyance. Sometimes I've wondered if it wasn't a new incarnation, hidden under a new disguise, of that migratory person who has exercised such an unfortunate influence over me with the weight of her immeasurable censure. (Adela), I'm sure of it, was being won over by the proletarian revolution and incorporated into the Defense Committee in order to watch over my steps, just as in boarding school. A few weeks later, under the weight of the defeat, she will be changed into Muerte, to settle up with the profits of a brothel the

down the stairs with a tranquil and resolute bearing, the same day as his arrival, one last afternoon of a precocious springtime, dressed in the dark Sunday suit; but when he saw him he started to run, went past him without looking toward the guards' house and the gate to the estate. Then he heard a single and weak sob on the upper floor. In the reception room, barely illuminated by the sunset light, his mother was lying on the floor below the furniture, studying (her veil had been removed from her face for the first time) the ceiling of the room with the supine, mute, and absorbed attention of someone who, in the reflections of the light, continues the avatars of a game in which she has lost all her wagers and used up her resources. He didn't see him again until well into the war, ten or eleven years later, in a hallway of the Defense Committee, wearing a military tunic with a captain's insignia and a pistol on his waist. He didn't know what had happened in the meantime, maybe between those two moments there had been nothing but flight; as if when he left the house he had kept on running until the year 1938, coming to a halt in the only building where he fit. It is certainly fate that—taking advantage of an unbalanced instant and the weak sight of eyes covered by a black veil—will impel those childish steps on top of the dresser that held the famous medal to follow the career of an orphan, a rebel leader, and a deserter. From under the piece of furniture all that emerged was a small and wrinkled head, like that of a tortoise who, in an overturned position, no longer struggles to straighten up and conserves all movement in order to prolong a certain death agony; she had taken off her veil and—up on the dresser—María's son saw the face of his mother for the first and the last time: nothing but two huge, greenish, and hallucinating eyes lodged in the pile of putrefaction on which they fed. Then three steps, three furious kicks, and a stupefied shout will be enough to launch him into that headlong and fateful running, that interminable trip into the night of hatred and solitude to flee from everything around him and forget his mother's face, buried under the dresser, her hand clutching the gold coin, converted by illness into a bloody skull sprinkled with blackish bites, two luminous balls over an opening that gave off an intense stench of mucosity.

[253]

debt that she contracted with the society of the victors. A short time later she is transformed into my mother-in-law—an authoritarian and laconic lady—to become reconciled once and for all with those law-and-order people whom she had never renounced in the depths of her soul. If all those people are not one single person and only one it seems to me a waste of nature and society to employ so many people to fulfill a single function: watching over my behavior and trying by all means to keep me subject to the order they embody. I don't know where she (Adela) got the idea to take me with them, in the suspicion that my presence and my testimony could bring about grave consequences in the recently conquered town at the moment of repression. But that suspicion unfortunately also extended to Juan de Tomé and others in the sense that their last-minute good offices were interpreted as an act of treason. Later on I came to perceive that I had been their bait and their last recourse of appeal. It was through that same telephone line and it was doubtless his voice, calling me in anguish to help him, coming to dissuade me from a duty and an affection that no longer meant anything to me. I didn't know it but even if I had known I wouldn't have come either. That's the tragic part, that's what was probably elevated at that moment on the highest altars of criminal selfishness, which has dragged me into that false martyrdom through which—paradoxically—I will recover because of duplicity the position in society to which I had no right. It was a single communication that decided both fates; I can picture him, dressed in his dirty topcoat and his hands tied behind his back, surrounded by pistols and leather jackets, and the attentive look at the officer who with the earphones on was only shouting to demand silence. I suppose that he too was witness to the same scene, I suppose that he didn't need any recourse to jealousy or anything else in order to slip out of the den and come to the office where I was waiting to squeeze my shoulder, make a gesture of what-the-hell and try distractedly to light his lighter. But of that I came to convince myself very much later, when, purified by my false martyrdom, the flock of the conquerors tried—on a student cot in a childish room replete with rag dolls and university trophies—to make me forget all the stations of that imagined calvary. It was at tea during that first postwar year, in the company of those thick-necked and racy captains who had served with my father and who, therefore, thought they had the right to three months of vacation, frivolity, and flirtation, before taking up their privileged positions, when I came to understand that not even knowing it was Juan's voice would I have been capable of altering the decision provoked by a malignant movement of shoulders which (but then, under the influence of the new uniforms, the taste of the white bread and the Guinea coffee, the horrendous innocence that those dolls seemed to exude in order to return me during sleep to a white childhood, his image had flown into a zone dominated by disbelief, the impossible and the nonreversible, to remain preserved by a preparation that fate and love put together so as to immunize it from all the attacks of an ineffective and inoperable certainty) wanted to seal his fate. Because when the certainty comes to her—in a tearoom, during a parenthesis between the commonplaces with which, after three years of the trenches, those officers knew how to amuse a woman—that it was a matter of Tomé's killer no less, there is a whole imperishable register that will no longer make her pay attention and which prefers to load that blame onto itself or to alter the only image that will remain fixed in the bosom of her depravity. A few days later—although they were calm days the uncertainty was no less; the panic was never greater, not even when we crossed the lines, for during those afternoons, shut up in the small bedroom with the windowpanes lined with paper, unable to use the electric light, with ears attentive to the bustle of all those people preparing to flee, fearing at every instant that the unhappy and spontaneous decision to join them might be forgotten, betrayed and abandoned in a locked room where they would find her, humiliated and defrauded, witnesses of her disgrace—the last contingents who were defending the Torce plain abandoned their positions to take refuge in Región and join the Committee's exodus. Some of them slept in the same house, among others those two German brothers, probably the last survivors of the Theobald Battalion, which had been fighting without cease since the end of 1936. They arrived almost barefoot, their leggings open; they finally took us out of the room and our beds were occupied by the wounded. They scattered us about town, I drew (far from Adela at last) the couch in a parlor all covered with mattresses where more than twenty people slept, watched over by a sentry who, sitting by the door, made his cigarette last all night, putting it out and sticking it in his pocket after every puff. I don't know how long we were there, more than a week surely. Every day a caravan of fugitives would leave town at dusk, making use of any means of transport, but in every case—I don't know why—without daring to give up their mattresses. I've seen mattresses travel in the most unlikely ways, but the results must have always been the same: when I returned to Región from Muerte's hotel, the whole highway was sprinkled with the remains of mattresses, lining, and stuffing, much more resistant and lasting than their fragile owners, who had disappeared from the face of the earth. The house was slowly depopulated until the only ones left were the sentry—it seemed that he only had one cigarette a night, a cigarette that got smaller each day until it was a roll of paper the size of a toothpick—the younger of the Germans, and I. He was an attractive and timid young man who carried tragedy in his eyes; he would disappear during the day, wouldn't leave the submachine gun, to come back to sleep each night with more dust on him; that German's dust was like his hair, different from that of Spaniards, greenish in color. There were no more mattresses left and although I suppose that there must have been a lot of empty beds in

Región he always came to sleep in the same corner on the floor, lying against the baseboard facing the wall and covered by a gray blanket. Doctor, in that corner on the floor, under that gray blanket, the German ate my flower.

"Was the sentry present? I don't know, but I wouldn't be surprised if that's how it was. Otherwise it wasn't too important because, as it turned out, that obligatory witness to my first night of love had the same awareness as those dolls dressed like Hindus who squat in the display windows of coffee stores, alternately lifting a cup to their lips with the right hand and a cigar with the left. Except he didn't have a cup, instead of a turban he was wearing a beret, and instead of the Havana cigar all he could raise to his lips was a thin roll of cigarette paper. And although I wouldn't remember his name for many years, one day—without thinking about him much—it came back to me with certainty: his name was Gerd, he was my height and must have been four or five years older. His eyes had a greenish, indefinable color, like stagnant water. The first night we only slept in each other's arms under the two blankets in order to take advantage of our mutual warmth. But the second night we slept in each other's arms and made love. I couldn't look into his face without feeling great sorrow. He spoke very little, he'd lost a brother a month before but the desire for vengeance didn't appear on his face. He must have believed in predestination and was waiting for the same fate as his brother, without impatience or desperation, as the end of an adventure that offered no other solution. He was in no hurry to abandon Región nor did he have the least desire to join one of those caravans, but, on the contrary, during the two days we were together in that room, he only worried about maintaining order and cleanliness in that small space around him; he shook off the dust, we sewed his leggings, he washed, cleaned his weapon, and gave me a German knife that I was unable to hang on to. That first night he barely moved, face down, looking at his watch from time to time and scratching on

[257]

the wall with the tip of his knife. 'How sorry I am for you, Gerd'—I couldn't help thinking that as I watched him out of the corner of my eye—'how little those eyes will shine. What a peaceful face you have: what a pity, Gerd, how soon they'll give you a burst in the chest.' So on that second night, without saying or asking for anything, he turned his head toward me, I kissed him on the mouth, and we made love. I don't think it was different from the first embrace, from the kiss on the mouth or the impulse that incites the sleepless cheek to seek the beating of that close and harmonious chest, but when the accent is placed on that isolated act so much, without considering what precedes it or what follows, it's with an object to put in relief the importance of a thing that the man probably wished underneath it didn't have. On the other hand, in that look of indifference while the telephone was howling, in the brief pinch that discovered a new nature upon breaking the gaseous chrysalis where the larva had developed, no one is going to be aware and yet everything begins there. I think that in my brief German romance, apart from the pity and the desire for profession of the catechumen, there was a great deal of importance in the fear that the first fruit would be picked by Julián Fernández and my interest in deceiving him ahead of time and defending my chastity with an earlier surrender. The difficult situation was interrupted by a marching order that a civilian came to bring us peremptorily at a moment when we were busy mending a coat. It was only for me and, clearly, had been given by Fernández himself; I scarcely had time to throw those last remnants of a trousseau into my bag—two blouses, an overcoat, a skirt, and a faded and mended slip—maintained for possible use, which the despoiled fugitive holds onto in her long road into exile. We left Región that same night, in a khaki-painted car occupied by Julián and his people and an army truck covered with camouflaged canvas into whose cab they put me along with four soldiers. We went along very slowly, with the lights out, and as we passed by the last houses I saw him running along the ditch holding the submachine gun. He made no signal for us to stop, threw his rifle into the back, and then leaped in. They tried to put him out, they stopped the truck and approached him with arms at the ready. Behind my head I heard the sound of a bolt; he said only four words in a barely comprehensible Spanish and they all returned to the cab immediately. A bit farther on, the car that was going along ahead of us stopped and I don't know why, but we remained halted for a long time. They started back again and we entered Región once more, where we spent the whole night and the morning of the next day. Julián Fernández had come to see me in the shed where we spent the night, but, surprised by the presence of the German, he limited himself to telling me that under no pretext was I to leave the cab of the truck. Sitting in the back and leaning up against the other side of my seat Gerd spent the whole night close to me, so close that through the wooden partition I could hear him cutting and filing his nails with a pocket instrument. They decided to leave in broad daylight the afternoon of the next day. It was a sunny day, quite clear and rather cold. It had been an eternity since I'd seen the street so close up and with the sun shining. When the truck started up I turned my head back to look through the rear window at the house where they had kept me for almost a year; four or five men were coming out the main door at that moment—and that Robal couple among them— with that air of peaceful resignation and limited pleasure with which the patients of a charity hospital come out to enjoy the winter sun. And then, knowing that a trip lay before me, a long one and one without commitments, I felt free, transported, I even daresay happy. The trip didn't have many incidents at first; those in the truck had no other interest but to see themselves far from Región and to recognize those scattered and indefinable people whom we passed on the highway from time to time. It was said that the car in front wanted to reach El Salvador without going by the bridge, using a road that left the river, went up onto the slopes of its left bank, and which evidently must have been in the hands of Constantino's people. At a crossroads we stopped again and Julián, in person, came back to us. He was wearing civilian clothes, with half boots and a military cape. With him came a white-haired man, wrapped in a topcoat buttoned up to the neck, who let himself be led like a blind man. They helped him into the cab while two other soldiers and I saw ourselves obliged to move to the back and settle among the crates, the boxes of ammunition, and the blankets, and we started the trip again along that dirt road through some deserted fields behind the cloud of dust of Julián's car, which was quickly lost from our sight. I soon fell asleep with my head resting on his shoulder, sitting against the partition in the back, with my knees held by his left hand between mine, the one decent form of being free that the little girl had foreseen already in the communal dormitory at boarding school. We made infinite stops, I don't know how many punctures, because the load was too heavy, the engine overheated on those desolate inclines. A noise woke me up—not a glow— an unusual drumroll followed by the smell of burning cloth. Gerd had fired four or five shots from under the blanket and, in the darkness, the smoking barrel was peeping out under the hole in that position the viper has lying in wait after having bitten and injected his poison, sticking his head out from under the stone in order to verify the results. Opposite me a soldier who was blinking with a single eye was trying, lowering his head and throwing his shoulders back like a drunkard, to keep an impossible balance, until he fell on top of the blankets that covered the ammunition cases. When they lifted him up to throw him out, I no longer wanted to look at him, his head had fallen onto his chest, with the smell of gunpowder in the folds of the blanket. It was a long and painful trip; quite late at night we got out to rest in some abandoned buildings and pens in a fallow dale among terraces beside the river. Facing us and not far away the river-bed was lighted up by the glow of the battle, the noise of which was with us during all those difficult hours of sleep."

It was a question of the battle that the 42nd Division was waging during the first fortnight of November under the command of old Constantino to clear the bridgehead that the enemy had managed to establish at the point of Doña Cautiva, having cut the highway to the mountain. Constantino's troops, reinforced by the fugitives who were arriving every day from Región, initiated the counterattack on the 5th in a south to north direction without the support that Mazón's few people could have given them if they had decided to break off from the volunteers stationed at Ferrellan and El Salvador and run to the aid of their comrades following the course of the river. Between both forces no other communication existed except that brought off, following instructions from Fernández, by a few contingents that had escaped from Región, avoiding the skirmish at the bridge by making use of that road. The battle, which lasted until the first days of 1939, was the last waged by the two armies, for after it the war was reduced to those search and destroy operations against scattered bands of the republican army that had opted for taking refuge in the mountains, hiding weapons and burying ammunition, and which became suddenly paralyzed before the final victory by the sudden death of General Gamallo. It was one of those massive counterattacks, launched with unsuspected drive and maintained with courage, which even when they lead nowhere—not even with victorious tactics—have to be organized and executed during the final hours of a campaign whose results could not be altered by anything anymore. Its immediate objective was the recapture of Doña Cautiva Bridge and ultimately the elimination of all enemy forces on the right bank of the river with an object to regrouping and shaping up a reduced nucleus of resistance upstream from that point, in order to contemporize until the arrival of an honorable peace. But it was an idea that the victor was not disposed to share in. During that same month of November the first objective was reached, the bridge was retaken—in the bloodiest battle waged in the province during the whole war—and the republican troops managed a penetration of several miles along the Burgo Mediano road. And that was all. Gamallo, the rebel general, without a shot being fired, occupied a Región abandoned during the first days of December and, sure now that he had bottled up the remnants of the government army between the mountain and the main body of his forces, began a profitable campaign with no concern for territorial winnings, prepared to reach with mortar and rifle fire the most remote brambles and plant his flag at the top of El Monje. But in that last campaign of annihilation the forces of the Republic would show that on the eve of their extinction they had learned how to blend into an army, that they knew how to defend a position as well as their adversary and were ready to make him pay very dearly for his last whim. It will go on longer than expected and through a new irony in that delirious war an unforeseen accident will frustrate his aim, will impede total annihilation of the conquered, and will detain the victorious infantry with its foot raised and ready to be planted on virgin mountainsides.

Toward the end of November, after the reconquest of the bridge, almost all the republican captains who had been fighting in isolation since the end of summer met and came together again. Under the supreme command of Constantino a plan of withdrawal toward the north was decided upon, which consisted of accepting the battle of annihilation and moving the army, with the main force in permanent contact with the enemy at the same time that other detachments, captained by those who knew the terrain, would break off from it in order to clear and keep open the road into the mountains. The plan was not executed because Constantino's obstinacy and resistance changed that withdrawal into an immobile battle in which, besides being completely annihilated, they saw themselves surrounded and lost by maintaining connection and continuity over such extended territory and which the old man didn't want to shorten because so many of those mobile groups could find their salvation in the mountains. So in the end only a couple of very reduced groups, twenty or thirty people all told, succeeded in watching the final day of the battle standing on a crag (arms hidden in some rocky terrain), watching with binoculars those sun-drenched, distant, and smoking plains where the conqueror was bringing forth and imposing his law.

When on the night of November 17th the small column of Mazón's detachment, which the fugitives had joined, tried to ford the river some eight miles upstream from the bridge alongside the mill where the course of the water is divided into several branches and a dam, among marshes and vetch, at a point where they no longer expected to find an enemy, not even any inhabitants, they were surprised by a rain of blue flares fired from the opposite bank that broke the darkness to reveal fleetingly that secret, imperturbable, and sinister peace of the mountain, scarcely disturbed by the destructive dispute of the mortars and the shouting of the Moors. Almost half the column was stopped with the water up to their waists and shot down before they could reach the shore; the rest, dazzled by the fleeting illumination, ran to take cover by the walls of the mill like insects to the baseboards when the revealing light suddenly goes on, holding their breath, their looks like the antennae in an imitation of death, finger on the trigger in an expectant pose. A bit later, from the darkness of the shore, the fire of the howitzers began to reach the mill, which was nothing but a pile of stone the following morning with no other movement but the falling of dust and the collapse and creaking of the beams of calcinated wood. All day on the 18th they remained—Eugenio Mazón, the Germans, and a hundred of their people—hidden among the heather, among the gray quartz outcroppings that normally come down to the river like sawteeth, guarding the cars camouflaged with branches and spying for any movement on the opposite bank while they piled up their cartridge clips and rubbed the rifle barrels with saliva in the manner of gamekeepers. With the arrival of night, from bush to bush, the order for withdrawal was transmitted, all ready to continue on foot after reaching and getting past the hill with the Navarrese and the Moors. The flares rained down on them again, the spaced, dry, and flatulent explosions that marked their ascent like the creaking of an ancient and rotting staircase. For two days the battle lasted, with mortar and heavy machine gun fire between the two combatants who were hiding on opposite slopes. On the night of the 19th the Moors crossed the river at the same spot where Mazón had tried and, protected by the lobbing fire of the howitzers, established their positions there for an attack on the mill. But around that time the republican penetration along the bridge-Burgo Mediano road had reached its height and the Navarrese advance forces who were operating north of that spot began to fear a possible cutoff in communication, because of which they delayed the attack in order to pay more attention to watching their lines. The intensity of the fighting at the bridge also obliged Mazón to disengage his defense and look to the south and the unexpected arrival of both forces in the vicinity of a Roman bridge only increased the confusion—exaggerated by the successive crossings of the river that both bands brought off—of those battles that lasted until the last days of the year. Two days after Gamallo launched his counterattack from Burgo Mediano the Navarrese advance forces—who enjoyed a certain autonomy, spurred on by the impetus of the volunteer—made their own; but poorly led and weakened by the vigilance of a broad sector they were thrown back by the ruins of the mill. The difficulties in communication among the different sectors and the apparent ease of the enemy's means in such a reverse led the nationalist command to believe that the forces of Mazón, Julián Fernández, and Constantino had come into contact along

[264]

a continuous line that covered more than three miles of front. Their firmness by the Roman bridge and the mill confirmed a hypothesis which, in accordance with the principles of a battle of annihilation, was translated into the reinforcement of the advance force by a brigade of Moors and several Schneider 15.5 pieces. On December 5th the attack on the mill was resumed along two converging lines that came out of the positions by the Roman bridge. At nightfall on the 7th the Moors crossed the river again on some underwater rocks while the Germans, who were holding the Región road, were attacked frontally and obliged to retreat along the same path that Mazón had used two weeks before. It was a clear and cold evening when the sun went down behind the peaks after a great explosion that seemed to dissipate the war: a gust of wind had carried off—definitively and toward the south—the echo of the shots and bursts, restoring the sound of the water and (while the zephyr made fallen capes flutter) the barking, "unreal, sonorous, and regular, stamped by that sad and resigned desolation"* with which the dogs were calling to each other and seeking, from field to field and ruin to ruin, to start up again the dialogue that the firing had momentarily interrupted. The Germans were resting behind some bushes when they heard from very far off—perhaps farther away than reality because the muffled sound that seemed to float on its own hanging echo came stamped by a distance different from that of the far off—beyond the evening hills and beyond the imaginary instant that was broken and mutilated by a thousand past explosions, voices and shouts and the remnants of unrecognizable songs that seemed to be climbing up to the heights in a fugitive minuend, the last echo of the death throes which the old and unmoving phonograph turning the wrong way had drawn out of the whispering waters and the sibilant branches, the silvery sleep of the pebbles, and the murmurs of the passes, the breath of

*Faulkner

[265]

that warlike mountain range which after ten centuries was being trod by the same intruders who had come to cut up the blond knights with their curved swords and their spears of ash and who today were repeating their same gibberish, with the sound of armor and slum music, to accompany the final death throes. The skirmishing went on all night: advances by Moors in their broad capes, knowing only how to run in a crouch and whom the night vomited up, drunk on cognac and shouting, abandoning them by the walls of the mill, cut down by the burst of a Vickers, and after the first instant of confusion giving them back the serene restfulness of death. Bunches of two or three who tried to reach the main door, shielding themselves with the corpses of their comrades, piled on top of them like sacks of grain on the threshing floor in the moonlight flailed by the German's rifle. Until at the hour of dawn everything was quiet again, voices, shooting, the very echo of the war that seemed to be coming out of the earth itself rather than from the rifles, as it tried to take part in the uproar, like the loud-voiced barker of an obscene sideshow, giving way to that astonished instant of calm which (to the rhythm of the bitter, distant, and off-key accents of the old phonograph—the gurgling of the water joined to the reveille of the last birds of the year hidden among the willows) it is possible to enjoy only in the bosom of a war. They weren't shrapnel but penetrating rounds (the rapid-fire Schneiders that no one knew where they were coming from or why) that bounced peacefully upon the stubborn and immovable topography too fast asleep to be awakened by such a superficial din, beginning to fall on the terrain recently conquered by their legions. On the following morning, behind a covering knoll, drunk on cheap cognac and heartened by the frequent and useless artillery support, they tried once more to force an entry into the ruins and dislodge the Germans and Mazón's men—cheered by a few swigs of alcohol and some tobacco plugs that they found in the breeches of the corpses—from their redoubt. A tight group of them—yellow turbans, hanging capes, light steps— advanced toward it, casting an invisible but palpable stare; he fired a full burst, not even looking, pressing his head against the butt, seeking the orgasm of swift lead whose trajectory—and trepidation—could almost be felt, until the bullets were lost in the hanging cloth; but when he lifted his eyes again the group was coming on together, toward the hot barrel like an emanation and materialization of the magic smoke. He fired again twice, lowering his sights, making the earth leap thirty yards away but when the erethism ceased, when the cloud of smoke cleared, the whitish group appeared, the five hunched figures with the same imperturbable, perhaps static and contradictory position of advance. Then he began to shout; he stood up, holding the Bren; a few last bullets, like the last death rattle of an animal trying to stand up after the collapse, came out of the barrel to stick in the ground near their feet, until he let go of the weapon and started running toward them, dragging his feet and shouting in German, tripping over the capes, the heads, and the foreshortened looks, which after death continued asking about a grotesque and ridiculous I. When dawn broke on the 9th, with the snort of a slow-motion engine that was waiting on the highway, the figure of a ragged and dirty man appeared with a submachine gun under his arm on the ruins of the mill. With tired but unhurried steps—on the highway another one appeared who whistled and waved his arms to call him—he was lifting the corpses with the tip of his boot, turning them over and going over them, careful not to step on them, separating the stones of the demolished walls—almost transparent was that first virgin color of day, which after twelve hours of nocturnal rest manages to clear the age-old dust. The corpse was stretched out on the bank and covered with mud, its feet in the water. A famished dog the color of wool was sniffing between its pant legs with its snout. The dog whined, a brief moan disappeared in the empty greenness of the water and the dawn. He took him

[267]

out of the water, turned his head over, and laid him on the icy grass. He washed his face with some river water, scraped off the mud, and combed his hair. He tried to straighten his arms and close his eyes; then, going close to his ear he told him something in a very low voice, in German. His face had lightened; with the lowered jaw and the half-open mouth, his expression had become shadowy and his green and hazy eyes had lost their serenity, contemplating, hypnotized— slanted by that secret and supine acquiescence with death— the vertigo where it had disappeared. He turned his head to find the slanted look face on but his eyes avoided its direction, glassy and fastened on the fixed point that death had assigned them. Again he spoke to him in German and wanted to kiss him, but couldn't feel that he was near or manage to get his thoughts close to him. Then he caught the stench the dog had left on the corpse. He got up calmly, after running his hand over his face, released the safety on the submachine gun and turned toward the river, giving a long and sustained whistle. The dog lifted up its ears, held for an instant between interested and wary, not knowing whether or not to believe the new and dubious friend. Then he gave a leap; rising and falling backward, landing face up with the whole charge in his shoulder, while the rattle was repeated in a graver tone, climbing up the slopes with the vapor of the waters.

"I had stopped trembling but I was on the point of bursting into tears because before I got to sleep I saw him many times on a riverbank, riddled with bullets and covered with blood and dirt up to his chest. I think that was the first time in my life and maybe the only time that I didn't cry for myself but for him, because without having grown to love him I didn't think of him as lost for me but for himself, abandoned, wasted, and forlorn, like a new Joseph who, alienated from fraternal love, had chosen sacrifice without paying any heed to his feelings for himself, without even letting them speak, and that must be why the tears were unable to come forth.

"I think we got to El Salvador that same night; our stay there was very brief, two or three days at most, just enough without the German's protection for Julián Fernández to make me his lover in that high-backed bed under the portrait of that gentleman. The more we withdrew the more suspicious he was of his comrades; here we were practically alone with the drivers and a few soldiers he had turned into his personal guard. They must have laid a trap for him in El Salvador; I never found out what happened and the only thing I could make out was that he planned to halt there as little time as possible, convinced that Mazón and Asián and all the others were waiting for him. What he didn't know was that Constantino was there too, wounded in the head and leg, having been carried there from the bridge on a stretcher. I didn't even get out of the truck; they stopped us by the church and made him get out. A stranger got into the driver's seat much later and put the vehicle by the entrance to the inn where we were lodged for several days, men and women mixed in together, sleeping in hallways, rooms, and stairs. There are things that since there's no use in remembering them memory keeps in a ragbag convinced that they'll never be of any use again or that they'll only be good for patchwork. I think I found out that same night, but I couldn't get to feel myself close to him or missing him because all my strength and my feelings seemed driven to maintain the heat of my oven as if they feared the approaching extinction of the flame that kept it lighted. But my vocation was also telling me that all I'd done was to begin, something less than dressing myself in the unpolluted garb of the neophyte who is to be introduced into the mysteries he has chosen; there was something inside me that was repelled by that situation because not wishing to confess it to itself, it was afraid that the true mysteries wouldn't reach any level except that of the initiation ceremonies, but I myself—not in vain was I educated at a religious school and in a certain way intoxicated by a mentality that defends itself from what it doesn't know with disdain—attributed it to fear and the fleeting nature of a passion that admitted no other balance or other temperature than those of the oven. There was something that feared a deep disordering—something that couldn't stop lamenting the kind of weeping that followed Gerd's death and which by not being muffled and silenced by submission to sexual desire stopped feeling sincere, clean, and decent, the true tabernacle where the oils to feed the flame are kept—and which I couldn't see behind the luxuriant sparkle of incandescent particles (vapors vitiated by desire, hopes submerged in passion, ideals retracted by appetite), except for some tissues torn red by the masculine flame and which on retreating from that horrendous torch which had cut them at its whim would show by their shapeless wounds and by their fragments impossible to recompose the destructive nature of the test. It was a moral conscience again, a decent and integral conscience, but just as inoperative for holding back the catastrophe as those committees of conscientious objectors who try to oppose a worldwide conflagration, perhaps the only part of the body that knows itself and which in addition to anticipating the future harm—without knowing how to cure it—is pleased to accuse and liven the pain of the flesh where the conflict is developing. There is no doubt that it's the only thing that—without withdrawing, without abandoning the flesh that gives it lodging—doesn't stumble when everything else begins to hesitate: at the same time that the residues of that education are transferred, in the face of the approaching conflagration, to the subcellar of resentments, the old destroyed fabric, the walls of the oven covered with refractory soot, and the fragments of a person who thought herself formed divided now into her simple and inert components, try to recompose their nature with an infantilization, a return—as it were—to the nymph age with no memory that knew how to assimilate the most complete helplessness, the most bitter disillusionment, and the blackest oblivion in an intemporal limbo, an anodyne trance in a moment—for the organism that has everything in the future—dislodged from time. I have never understood why love comes so late for its appointment with a person and why, consequently, it takes pleasure so many times in destroying, with the blow of an insolent and extratemporal hand, a whole previous organization. It must be because the process foreseen by nature places love before sexual desire in the same way that the roast that wasn't salted when it was in the oven won't render its proper taste no matter how much salt is put on it on the plate. It's the purgatory of those of us who transgress its rule, and we'll never know its taste or free ourselves of the vice in order to calm our hunger with atrocious food. I understood it much later, after my marriage; love and sexual desire are mutually exclusive after the first test; desire and the sexual act make up the only defense against the threat of a love that in adolescence already has disfigured its physiognomy, torn its tissues, and destroyed the integrity of its person. I imagine that a person who knows how to preserve a portion of that love—if that mixture of poison and explosives admits any preservation—must suffer a reciprocal and inverse action, taking refuge in pleasant and aberrant chastity. I find that the girl prepares herself in secret for that sacrifice because a certain arcane premonition teaches her to expect everything from the nubile age and to subtract any importance from the events of youth; that's why she's calmer, wiser, and . . . more hypocritical; and all the ceremonies and rites that precede the loss of her virginity are only the abbreviated preparation for that return to childhood—if she is a mother the same as if she isn't—into which her course is translated when she reaches the climax of the sacrifice. There is an instant in it, a defense mechanism that nature has set up in secret to cut off the effects of a possible destruction; it isn't just the infantilization but also a return to certain unconscious refuges that the child created in another age and to the shelter of the amorous struggle, where she hides her failure and cloisters her sorrows every time the orgasm comes to disperse those purely illusory aspirations to masculine fusion. Every age has its delimited terrain, its aspirations, its dangers, and its climate, speaking in masculine terms; but when there is an attempt—and woman always attempts it, lacking a precise delimitation—to go from one unsaturated age to another where the spirit wasn't taken advantage of, ridiculed and lashed by a series of slaps, she retreats even more to an ambiguous, epicene, and puerile age, peopled only by fun at the beach; but then time has really passed, the leap isn't measured by time but by the terrain it's tried to land in. I've come to think that my first lovemaking had no other effect than to pull me out of my age into a kind of anachronistic and lascivious lightness, a premature senility—if senility is that, boredom, hopelessness, a lack of curiosity—that only knew its own horror when it saw itself accompanied by wrinkles. Or is it perhaps that loss of fear which—one might say—is the only thing that subjects us to age and curtails that crazy curiosity? We were living—living, huh!—in Muerte's hotel several miles from the firing line when we were unexpectedly attacked by a reconnaissance patrol that doubtless didn't know that the remnants of the enemy army had taken refuge in the small and hidden chalet. Some shots rang out and we ran to the cellar, Muerte and I and a couple of other women, while they went out the back door loading their rifles. Because the rest of the time all they did was gamble. Once, a while before, after knocking I had timidly opened the door and stuck my head into that secret room where women didn't enter, where the former and the new members of the Committee almost always gathered at night after returning from the field. There was so much smoke that at first I couldn't see anything, the rectangles of the carbide lamp hanging from a hook over the foot-warmer table where old Constantino, his head bandaged and one eye covered with a black patch, was playing solitaire. But there was money on the table and other loose cards, the signs of an interrupted game. Eugenio Mazón, stretched out on a cot near the door was sleeping and snoring on his back, his hand fallen to the floor on top of a cheap novel. Asián, who was coming from the bathroom with a towel around his neck and a glass in his hand, opened the door behind me: 'What are you doing there? What were you looking at?' 'I wanted to see if he'd come back . . . Last night.' 'And if he hasn't come back, what of it?' In the back of the room, over a basin, he began to gargle. After emptying each cheek he turned to look at me to repeat that: 'What'll happen if he doesn't come back, eh? What do you think will happen?' Then when he finished gargling he went over to the mirror to look at his eyeballs and the marks on his face while I, frightened and openmouthed, couldn't move a finger, stock-still on the threshold until the old man turned his only eye on me: 'Would you please close that door and get the hell out of here?'

"But he told me that in order to conquer fear there was no need for courage or calmness or lucidity; it was a matter of solitude. The cycle the child had started there with the telephone conversation, between uncertainty and hopes, the look of the old man closed with a new certainty and a much more urgent necessity to conquer fear than to reach love because fear is always real and love . . . a speculative invention to overcome the former without wishing to fight it. It was a very brief battle, they surrounded them on all sides and cut them down like rabbits, but a few must have escaped, leaving four or five corpses near the house; because of which, that same night, foreseeing a new attack, we left the hotel in the vehicles to take refuge on the mountain paths for a few wary days. I remember the time I stayed huddled against the rear wall of the house, hidden by the corner, peeking out for a long time after the shots from the underbrush where the intruder had taken refuge had ceased for a long time. The rest ran past cavorting and whistling among themselves like schoolboys who were going to repeat with

[273]

rifles what in their childhood streets they had learned to do with a ball, a stone, or an intention. I suddenly saw that beyond the wall he was getting up and running toward me, without any weapon, his tunic unbuttoned, with a look of joy. I even had time to think that such an expression of youth, joy, and triumph could only belong to the other side and therefore I've kept the idea of a family boy on the point of tasting in his first youth the fruits of his enthusiasm and triumph. A pair of lost shots was heard at the same instant but with an extraordinary agility he leaped over the wall and went to take refuge in the underbrush a few yards from my hiding place. His head peeped out over the stalks and a very young face, turned toward the setting sun, with a devilish expression and a couple of winks made me aware of the complicity of our mutual situation. It was a sunny and cold afternoon, quite long; a few black birds were flying over me, rehearsing their evening croaks and their timid winter acrobatics. Suddenly the house and everything around it were deserted and I felt completely alone, in the company of nothing but that half-hidden face who, not daring to give up his hiding place, kept repeating his winks. I understood then about fear and didn't want to—or couldn't—weep or tremble because I felt intoxicated, my muddled head wrapped in a pleasing and luminous chaos, accompanied by brief solitary and distant sounds, from which, as the hours drew long, I was afraid I was unable to free myself. I don't know if I slept; I raised my head again when a short whistle was repeated and, at the same time a grackle was leaving an oak tree, I saw him running again behind the bushes by the wall with only his head showing. I don't think it was an illusion brought on by the flight of the bird, although my eyes were clouded by an unknown stupor. I remembered again that immemorial infantile situation of the child who opens his eyes to find himself in a garden, abandoned by all his playmates and spied on by a thousand hidden looks that he tries to imagine behind the trembling leaves. So many times that

[274]

game, with the child in anguish because of his impotence and solitude, ends in tears and teasing, a series of heads that come out from among the branches to make fun of his cowardice and reproach him for breaking the rules. The rules . . . the rules . . . not even the precocious schoolgirl who runs off with the gym teacher one day will ever see herself in a position to elude them because she'll try, in the last instance, to govern her subversion and her foolishness by them. When I think about it, Doctor, I wonder what I'm doing here and why I came if it's impossible to reconstruct that whole youth that would incapacitate me for later maturity; I don't intend to reconstruct or disinter anything, but I do want to recover a certainty—it's required by an addicted memory, suckled by its sickly mythomania—that it's the only thing that can justify and alleviate my forty-year-old insipidity. So much time has passed and my solitude has been such that I've come to doubt that it all happened as I've said. There's something in our behavior that still doesn't obey reason and which, in secret, trusts in the power of magic. In the power of the voice, which, joined to feeling, will be capable of attracting the beloved by calling him insistently. And to the power of the look and the pure, blinded power of repetition: how many times does love think it will find the beloved again on that solitary bench where it glimpsed him for the first time on a rainy afternoon. And who, unsatisfied and annoyed, turns the blame onto a venal reason and an implacable time that only magical hope will be able to overcome. It no longer believes in the flesh nor does it wish to believe in age and refuses to become reconciled with death and only desires to be returned to the fetid limbo of an age in which all those particles go along in harmony. I don't really know what I've come for because I don't know myself, every day I know myself less. Every day I feel my authority over those particles more relaxed, the ones that before the conflict knew how to march together through mutual consent and take pride in singular order and discipline, but which since the war have made war on each other on their own in order to ridicule the command and destroy themselves in a thousand sporadic actions. I suppose I'm coming because of all that, in search of a certainty and a repetition, treading once more the sacred place where under the spell of a perfume and an exorcism the heroes who have disappeared will rise up again, the ones who injected the cancerous cells of their memory into my sterile insides, to recover their last prey. On the other hand, I've come to the conclusion that time is everything we're not, everything that's gone wrong and failed, everything mistaken, perverted, and hateful that we would have preferred leaving to one side, but which time obliges us to carry in order to impede and impose it on an emboldened will. But there was only one moment—I repeat—one single moment in which love and fear fight, where time disappeared; how many times have I returned to bed waiting for the man who, even though he couldn't give me back the taste of that moment, might at least have been capable of making me forget it, so that in the hours of shadows in a closed room through whose blinds the sounds of activity on the street came I wouldn't find only corruption, the weariness of the past, and the sloth of the future. How many times have I tried to make this trip and how many times have I stopped halfway, overcome and stupefied, befuddled by so many contradictory and critical impulses, none of which showed itself to be energetic enough to distract me once and for all from that eye-fluttering youth who took on such a false proportion with distance, like the lights of the glimmering city which, for the passenger who is saying farewell from the bay, seem to hold so many secrets that passed unperceived when he walked its streets. I've thought about recovering a part of my health in exchange for a mutilation—the only unpleasant part is aimed at a self-esteem obliged to sell its most valuable jewel in order to pay the debt of ancient blackmail. Blackmail, yes. That photograph appeared many years later among some old papers; I didn't remember ever having had it and it took a little effort on my part to recognize some traits that I knew in a less emaciated and tormented form. No, don't get up, I'm sure you know it as well as I. I'll never be able to tell by what procedure it reached my desk, one of those materializations of desire that struggled to give it back to a retina tormented by the efforts of an evocation that's impossible and is countered by a deformed, twisted, and motionless image that had been printed on a defective film, but which the mind couldn't get rid of. The rules of memory are like that too when it's a question of a matter that doesn't concern reason; they barely supply any other data than a series of atrocious gestures and exaggerated traits, repeated a thousand times and hypertrophied in a recurrent succession of deceptive contrasts. But which, on the other hand, will keep untouchable the head of that young man, fallen onto my lap on a very clear and cold January or February afternoon. I took a long time getting to him, creeping on all fours and dropping to the ground every four steps. When I got to the wall I'd almost forgotten about the head, the fighting, and the birds. I'm sure that something told me; something, with a muffled voice, and I went over to his side: he waved his hand and tried to straighten up his body, because his strength could no longer do it with his head, into a strong and unsustainable position. I tried to help him, I supported his head, and was about to put my arm around his shoulder when he raised his eyes, gave a deep belch, and his head fell onto my lap with an enormous and sudden vomiting of blood, black blood, burning, swirling, and sparkling, like molten metal in a blast furnace, in a hurry to leave that lifeless body and grope around for another more lasting lodging. I gave a shudder and remained stupefied in that peaceful end of a cold afternoon, emptied and paralyzed by that horrendous menstruation with which the adult phase of a woman exalted in the loss of fear and the mysteries of desolation was inaugurated. A hand coming from behind encircled my back, withdrew the remains from my lap, and helped me rise when

[277]

the sun had already gone down and the freeze was being announced by the twinkling of the star in the west. I woke up
again in the cab of the truck, with a taste of coagulated blood
in my mouth and the humming of the engine in my ears.
We stopped near the river so someone else could take over
the driving: 'Go slow. You can travel without lights,' he told
him. The others got into the cab and we huddled under the
blankets on the bottom of the truck. He told me to take off
those overalls daubed with the blood of the dead man and
which still gave off a thick, sour smell and which, in a certain way, worked as a barrier, a seal in wax imposed by war
and chance to our mutual urge. It was in the back of the
truck, going into the mountains on a clear and cold night
that was peeping through the holes in the canvas and the
opening in back; it was to the rhythm of a slow-motion,
hobbled engine, with the creaking of the wood and shifting
of gears; it was with the subtle and bitter aroma of the damp
blankets when the love of that man came to show me that
time can't exist, merged in its totality among all those instants that come in a troop—when in the oven that is piled
high with so many substances that have come together in
the fusion of the final product the flame is finally introduced—all the past and future instants of that long and painful process of formation of a woman that are summed up,
anticipate, are actualized, and burst forth when the man decides to introduce the flame that he stole from heaven; they
come in a troop and in the measure in which her urge has
seen itself deceived by the fraud of hope she discovers with
incomparable—and, alas, unique—lucidity which that whole
whirlwind of buried emotions and remote premonitions that
will never come to light are enjoying in a moment of sudden brilliance; a moment through which the stars of a February night and the creaking of the wood and the shadows
of the elms along the highway don't form part of a strange,
distant, and hostile world, but which make up the exceptional ornament of that present outside of time where a soul
refines the passing order of the universe.

"Now I think it lasted a short time. It lasts the time that fear takes in coming back. Another type of fear that's born inside, from an interior where ecstasy has only been of use to germinate mistrusts, insecurity, and suspicions. Then you enter the commercial terrain, as it were, because that timid and angry interior begins to suspect the hoax; woman bears within her an appetite for withdrawal—not modesty—that impedes her from giving in when she gets close. How frequent is it to get up out of the bed then with the feeling of having sacrificed oneself in vain for having tried to negotiate with a Gypsy, having paid the price agreed on to discover that all the nuts were rotten. How frequent is it to have to return to that voluntary reclusion, under the mandate of fear, where sexual love is executed as one of the terms of a contract with time that fear guarantees; and what more natural than for a woman to recur to payment in money when the exchange that she wants is, by nature, denied to her. I can see myself one morning wrapped in the blankets, my cheek stuck to the windowpane, watching how down below they were loading some boxes onto the truck; I try to understand how the man—the same hands, the same eyes, the same truck—can have gone away so quickly; how the same attention and the same intensity that took me in that cab can now turn, three or four days later, toward such a different task. Such capacity for forgetting, such strength for separating functions, such will and such order for doing everything in its turn; I can see myself then and I still see myself back in bed biting the edge of the blanket and avoiding in myself an explosion of tears that would reveal the poverty of my status to me. It's true, I'm not the one I know because the image I have of myself has been drawn in solitude, purified by abandonment, and idealized by self-esteem, but it doesn't correspond either to the image of the young girl who didn't come to the telephone but does to the German's corner, or to the woman who, in order to preserve her secret and maintain her dignity, let Juan de Tomé die in a dark basement, finally aware of the road she should take; not even

[279]

that of the poor woman who, having traveled the road, returns to the basement and to Muerte's hotel, convinced one
more time that it's necessary to make ratifications. Afterward I lost the notion of things; one spring morning, perhaps the first smiling morning after that tenacious winter,
I was at the door of the hotel, after washing the dishes, drying
my hands on an apron, when I saw the column of red berets
on the road. They were carrying blanket rolls across their
chests, rifles on their shoulders, and the second or third in
line was bowing under the weight of his burden, the two-
colored flag. They searched the house, although all their attention seemed focused on the chickens in the yard. We killed
some chickens and opened a dozen bottles of wine; when they
had finished eating they smoked cigarettes on the grass and
took up their march again. Before disappearing around a bend
in the road they waved to us. 'This story is over,' Muerte
said. 'Over? What's over?' I asked that face that understood
nothing. Still, things being what they were, what I wouldn't
have given at that time to participate in that masculine state
that almost always finds pleasure in its acts, which rarely—
and less in love—feels the suicidal desire to disappear and
become sublimated on altars of a sexed symbiosis, which always counts on a nature so integral that it doesn't need even
a carapace in which to lodge and a sex that has no reason to
annihilate itself or lower itself in order to receive what it has
always considered its due. I went out the door again after
washing the dishes to look at the few chickens that were left
and a pair of dogs who were chasing and smelling each other
among the newly washed clothes. I still spent that night almost on watch, close to the back window, scrutinizing the
mountains for the appearance of a light. There was nothing.
It was a terrible silence, much more terrible than the echo and
glow of combat, because everything it came to suggest to
me was that the woods, just like my body, had been deserted,
abandoned, and forgotten. I got my fear back, the fear that
is necessary in order to abandon a desperate illusion, but what

could I do? I knew it had been born inside me to tell me that, thanks to his betrayal, those woods and that silence and that solitude and that spite were the only joint property of a delirious marriage with the man who'd shown his intention of not coming back, who no longer existed perhaps and who—perhaps too—had never existed. That idea has tormented me to such a degree that it had come to constitute the ordeal of my femininity, the sign of the curse he left on my body in order to seal an agreement and snatch away from the invader the fruit that he had taken care to let mature.

"You didn't know I was pregnant? Of course you knew, who but you would know? Looking at the snow-covered mountain and after you left letting fantasy run behind some famished dogs, I understood that you had abandoned me precisely because I hadn't been pregnant and that the child who wasn't engendered would have obliged you to accept a solution that you would have despised later on. You couldn't have known that my father had died and you could presume, therefore, that there was a solution left for the both of us. Nor did you know that Juan de Tomé was still alive, whom you'd given up for dead in the Committee basement. And then I felt wounded, deceived, and mortified because your desertion came to show me that I wasn't even worth anything as a life preserver. And for the first time I felt ashamed of this useless body of mine that has never wanted to give what was asked of it. And I will carry the child who wasn't engendered into the future as the stigma of an imperfect and sterile nature, like the failed link that might have united us, even if my father had lived. Then I shall have no other remedy than to continue the search for that missing nucleus of my being where that unremembered one must have been engendered, the nucleus that you carried off or that you left behind, incapable of producing the necessary gland. In the future what won't I have to suffer in order to get that paralyzed organ out of its atony, to what intemperances of the body will I not have to bend and what unbearable com-

[281]

edies will I not see myself obliged to attend, like that vulgar and intrusive mother of the actress at her first performance who, incapable of appreciating the quality of her declamation from the wings, calculates the possibilities of success by the applause that surrounds her. Because it wasn't just a child: it was the past, it was you and that missing nucleus where generational virtues reside and the drive of the future is condemned, covered with a coriaceous shell that only represents a protective past. Because with the child we doubtless would have come to make up that molecular combination outside of which you and I were nothing but abstract symbols lacking physical representation in the notebook of nature and, therefore, as sterility was being shown, I was caressing with greater tenderness the debasing idea of building my vindictive survival on the adultery of that empty nucleus. But then everything was worse and I came to suppose that the forgetful one I was looking for—the one I was to have engendered, lodged, conceived, and fed as yours so that by means of a mystical transposition you would come back to life in the bosom of the trinity that would pull you out of the shadows—was obeying orders, was part of your same indifference, and refused coming to my presence. Then I desired—and supposed—that it was to be born only so that you could die and give me back a home where in the future only the father would be missing; where mother and child could have fortified themselves sufficiently so as to close the door—if one day he tried to return—desirous of not disturbing their peace with the presence of a stranger. But, on the other hand, since he wasn't being born, I had to wait for you, I couldn't aspire to much more than that, waiting, adultery, the peaceful and perverted preservation of a useless cult far beyond the limits of hope, age, reason. When I returned to Región the few people who were still there opened their doors to me; the hearth was still glowing in old Adela's kitchen and (I think it was the only thing in all Región that the war hadn't changed) in the dark hallway the boy was playing marbles with the same attention as in the year 1936. I didn't know for certain who he could be, because there is a form of weeping, muffled and restrained, that doesn't betray either age or voice or sex; but I was sure it wasn't the child: all he did was play with the marbles and from time to time he would raise a very singular look toward me, a look that came from a forgotten but unresolved fear, and which had crystallized in his eyes, behind the lenses, with that shadowy reflection of emptiness that came over his expression every time he took his attention away from the marbles and the tossing. I'd seen him a couple of days before being taken to the Committee and at the end of two years I saw him again in the same abandonment, playing in the hall or in the center of the kitchen while old Adela tried blowing to revive a very poor fire. But it gave me a start and I think I guessed it; the child was sleeping, but Adela wasn't in her bed; then I ran to the kitchen and found the trapdoor to the woodbin open; I caught a sigh and a moan enveloped in the rhythmic and buzzing throb of the shadows. A candle on the floor lighted things up and Adela had her hand on her forehead, covered with a damp cloth. I've relived and found him a thousand times, lying on a cot and covered with blankets that gave off the smell of fever, with that deep and distant rattle of the lungs by which death is announced. It was a burning, sharply etched face, the mouth open and two hollows in his cheeks, swollen lips barely moved; but he managed to see me, I'm sure, and then from that motionless mouth, with that guttural sound of a ventriloquist that can't move his lips, my name came out and, after a pause, the last sublimation of a dying breath, yours came out too. I sent Adela off: 'He's dying,' she said, but I think that was what I wanted. I don't know how long it lasted, accompanied by music and songs from the street. But I understood that it was only for me; I wanted to absorb and hide and keep it, not only as the only newly inducted member of that posthumous legacy, but— although in embryo the feeling existed that it wouldn't ever be pronounced or heard again, my pistils remained open, even when the moment of fertilization had passed, by the stratagem of a deceptive climate—so that the word would germinate in me, the blank name, mortuary and fragile, that revolved around a background of marching songs; I don't know if I killed him by hugging him against me in order to extract the last residues of your presence from him, to delve and seek in the death rattle of lifeless lips wrapped in the halo of death that last hidden nucleus from where your name had come, that last dying breath that you transubstantiated in your name in order to make your will reach me and which in the future I will never cease to seek amidst tears and damp sheets, in the amorous spasms of a desire that—in the interim—if it didn't learn to forget you, knew at least how to avenge itself on my body with the imposition of an impossible recipe: it was joined forever to that sick breath, to that deathly aroma that desire distills in the innermost in order to impede ecstasy in the uttermost where you disappeared, the breath of that angel of death who looks over all nights of love, ready to lower his hand and carry out the sentence if at some moment the rules of the game are broken and the clauses imposed in the treaty of the truck that was to regulate and maintain an unbalanced order and an unmitigated appetite, the angel who flapped his wings, heavy, sonorous, and fetid, in the basement where Juan de Tomé died, whispering your name to him and sealing my submission to a question outside of time firmly enough to guarantee my oath and ductile enough not to change into despair a condition tied to your memory, hindered by uncertainty and rendered impossible for regeneration. 'It's all over now,' Muerte said, but I didn't know how to recognize it while the embers of that fire were still lighted inside of me waiting for a new breath to come and revive them, but now that I consider this handful of ashes I've opted to return them to the spot where they should have been scattered years ago instead of coming to warm up a fictitious hope or be sheltered on a strange

[284]

hearth. I couldn't come before because I still harbored some hope and hope, standing above time, goes hand in hand with fear so as to anticipate a new disillusionment that would alter the limits of my misfortune again. I've come, then, at a time when I've reached that limit in order to know to what point I've been impure and hypocritical or to what degree I've been the victim of a fiction: to what degree love, fear, and memory, to which I tried to be faithful, are nothing but that childish fiction that you, when I became childish, induced in me and which, on breaking the virginity of the ecstasy, on placing you outside of time and death and on making me incapable of consolation and regeneration, you obliged me to embrace with all the vows of chastity, humility, poverty, renunciation, and sacrifice that I am going to break today in order to restore myself to the age of some first and perhaps last yearnings, without memory, without love, without past, without fear, and without hope."

It still wasn't daylight when the doctor awoke. He'd heard those desolate barks of "a dog who at such hours also believes in ghosts,"* wrapped in a special odor, that mixed aroma of saltpeter and organic fetidness, the first symptom of nights of vengeance. He got up, restless, but before reaching the table he stumbled over his slippers a couple of times. Then the sound of the motor reached him and a reflection of the glow of the headlights came in the window. He looked for the glass and contemplated the disorder on the table, intact for several years, the piles of papers, files, and books he hadn't cast his eyes on since he didn't know when. The photograph was still there on the edge of the table. It wasn't a card. He cleaned his glasses and with trembling hands looked at it attentively: an identification photograph with the edges wrinkled and yellowing, a sharp face and an oblique but not particularly penetrating look, digni-

*Nietzsche

[285]

fied and stupefied by a touch of anachronism. On the back was a half-erased inscription in pencil, a name of which only the first syllable was recognizable and a date that had been crossed out. "You forgot your safe-conduct pass. It wasn't going to do you any good, but you forgot it in any case. You also forgot that things are how they are and no one is capable of turning them back. If we've accepted your law it's because the one who comes to change it will impose a harsher one. Leave things as they are and don't let her come. In this land those who don't conform to their misfortune bring on catastrophe. Leave things as they are and fulfill your compromises in the same way that we respect your mandate."

The steps upstairs sounded heavier and again there was an outburst of cries. "Calm down, son, calm down." He drank a glass of castillaza; then he went to the bathroom and filled a glass with water, into which he dropped a pill. While he was stirring it he looked out the window at the night, the first glow on the horizon, and he thought that the pressure must be rising; the north wind was blowing and bringing in the smell of lavender and myrtle from the woods. Then he went about the house to see that everything was locked. He went to the office window and felt the grating. Then he stopped to listen. The steps had ceased and only a sigh could be heard from time to time. "Calm down, it won't be long now." He closed the door, threw the bar, and snapped the padlock. From a hook behind the door he took down a key the size of a pistol. On the second floor he checked the locks again. Then he turned on the light on the landing; it was a stronger door than the others, at the end of the corridor, secured by a diagonal steel bar. He knocked and waited. Not the slightest sound was heard, the room was lighted and a bluish beam came through the crack at the bottom. He knocked again and then he heard a moan.

"What's wrong? What's wrong? Why did you shout so much?"

The sobs, broken, became continuous.

"What's wrong, man? Why are you crying?"

With great care he took down the bar, putting the glass on the floor. He inserted the key and turned it, being careful not to make any sound, holding the end in both hands. Then he put his ear to the door.

"Tell me, are you in bed?"

He picked up the glass in his left hand and opened the door quickly. He was in the back of the room, huddled in a corner, his hands clasped at the back of his neck, covering his ears with his arms. He was barefoot, his open legs spattered with mud and manure. Slowly, he raised his glasses toward him, not so much to look but to be seen. His face was bathed in tears, his mouth open, and the lower lip, wet by them, was trembling convulsively; a gloomy and purple halo seemed to be born from his lenses, wrapping his face in a disorderly reverberation. Motionless, after three or four hesitations, he seemed to grow instead of rising, as if suddenly inflated by some gas he was free of his bonds all at once and filled the whole height of the corner. The doctor put the glass down on the floor.

"Wait, wait," he told him.

He didn't see; behind the thick glass of his lenses there was only a turbulent and deliquescent mixture of glow and tears, trembling and fury. He didn't say anything either, from the open mouth a kind of hollow and weak sound emerged like that of a plugged drain, which was nothing but the abortion of something else.

"No, it wasn't she. Wait. I tell you it wasn't she. Believe me. How can you believe that she would . . . ? . . . son . . ."

The door closed again under his weight. Before his sight grew cloudy he managed to see those eyes; behind the glasses there was even an amorphous, iridescent substance where the crouch before the attack glimmered, which with their calm, severity, and hardness reflected the consensus of a hidden awareness of vengeance in that substance.

When his head was smashed against the wall his glasses

fell to the floor and from his mouth came the word "son," as if fall and word were the two actions of a mechanism. He repeated it again—mechanically, the sound that was repeated with the gradual diminution of a doll's running down—three or four times to the rhythm of the blows of his head until, almost fallen, his eyes rolled in their sockets and remained looking at the floor like two captive balls, which, breaking away from the mechanism, fall to the bottom of the sphere.

The sound of his barefoot steps could be heard in the corridor until they went down the stairs.

For the rest of the night in the locked and solitary house that was almost overcome by ruin, the hurried steps could be heard, the shouts of pain, the broken glass, the furniture that hit the walls; the barriers and grating that were pounded, a sustained sob that at the end of the tears was resolved with the blow of a body against the locked doors. Until, with the light of day, between two barks of a solitary dog, the echo of a distant shot came to reestablish the habitual silence of the place.

Pantano del Porma, 1962—Madrid, 1964